STUDIES IN CHRISTIAN DOCTRINE

STUDIES
IN CHRISTIAN
DOCTRINE

BY

H. MAURICE RELTON

*Fellow of King's College, and formerly Professor
of Dogmatic Theology and Professor of Biblical
and Historical Theology in the University
of London*

LONDON
MACMILLAN & CO LTD
NEW YORK · ST MARTIN'S PRESS
1960

Copyright © H. Maurice Relton 1960

MACMILLAN AND COMPANY LIMITED
London Bombay Calcutta Madras Melbourne

THE MACMILLAN COMPANY OF CANADA LIMITED
Toronto

ST MARTIN'S PRESS INC
New York

PRINTED IN GREAT BRITAIN

CONTENTS

INTRODUCTION

THERE comes a time in a man's life when he feels that he ought to gather up the fragments that remain of his many chance contributions to the study of Christian doctrine, lest anything be lost. This book is the result of such a gathering. The contributions are dated, but reading them afresh convinces their author, if not his readers, that they are by no means out of date. In fact, in many cases they are as relevant to current doctrinal discussions and disputed issues to-day as they were in the years that are past. Much, for example, has been written since *A Study in Christology* (S.P.C.K., 1917). Yet we are not aware that anything has since appeared in print to discredit or to supersede the main thesis of that book. So also with the study of Nestorianism, under the title, in the *Church Quarterly Review*, 'Nestorius the Nestorian', that was published long before students had the benefit of the English translation of *The Bazaar of Heracleides*, by G. R. Driver and L. Hodgson (Clarendon Press, 1925), yet we still adhere to the conclusion we reached. The same comment may be made regarding the *Church Quarterly Review* article on 'Patripassianism', notwithstanding much which has been written since, and may still be maintained in favour of the 'Impassibility' of GOD. A chapter in *Some Postulates of a Christian Philosophy* on 'Christ and Metaphysics' is still the key we would maintain as essential, in any intellectual effort to solve, or even to grapple with, the Christological Problem, whether in terms of ancient or of modern thought.

We are, in fact, back at the point reached by the Church in the Chalcedonian Definition, as J. S. Lawton's penetrating study *Conflict in Christology, British and American from 1889 to 1914* (S.P.C.K., 1947) clearly shows, and J. S. MacArthur's *Chalcedon* (S.P.C.K., 1931) points in the same direction.

All this means that we to-day have to begin our thinking

afresh, and to re-study our Christian conception of GOD, and what we understand to be the meaning and value of the claim to Revelation, made by the Church in the light of the fact of the Incarnation.

Our *Church Quarterly Review* article on 'The Christian Conception of GOD' may prove helpful to students in this context.

Finally the chapters on the Church and Sacraments, and the interpretation in terms of modern thought of Gregory of Nyssa's dynamic sacramentalism, are a fresh approach, and, as we hope, a step towards Reunion.

The most generous and appreciative evaluation of such contributions to studies in Christian doctrine as we have been able to make is contained in Part I of a Thesis by Eduardo J. Soares. The whole Thesis was awarded their Degree by the Pontificia Universitas Gregoriana, but only a chapter from Part II was published. The whole of Part II was a penetrating criticism of our theory of the Incarnation, and especially of the theory of a single consciousness of Christ. This problem of the psychological unity of Christ is a *very live problem* now engaging the attention of Continental students. Dr. Kevin McNamara has drawn attention to this in his review of Mgr. Pietro Parente's book *L' Io di Cristo* (Morcelliana, Brescia, 1951) and P. Galtier's *L'Unité du Christ. Être . . . personne . . . conscience* (Paris, 1939). This review is in the Notes and Comments of the *Irish Theological Quarterly* on 'The Psychological Unity of Christ. A Problem in Christology.' Dr. Soares in his review of our work rejects the idea of a *single consciousness* of Christ, and sketches the rival conceptions of Parente and Galtier on 'Two Consciousnesses of Christ', a theory which he rightly thinks will not commend itself to us, since it points, as we feel, to a modern form of Nestorianism, and leans too heavily towards the Antiochene as opposed to the Alexandrine Christology.

None the less Fr. Galtier has undoubtedly directed Continental thinkers to a fresh study of the doctrine of the Incarnation, and in terms of a psychological approach. Since then several other writers have taken up the subject, and we have

Introduction

been privileged to read an important recent work on the psychological unity of Christ by B. Lonergan, S.I., *De Constitutione Christi, ontologica et psychologica* (Universitatis Gregorianae, 1958).

The controversy concerning the psychological unity of Christ, and the content of the 'I' as uttered by Christ, whether it was the human nature or the Divine nature or both together, obviously points us back to the time of the Christological conflict between Antioch and Alexandria, and posits the question afresh — 'Draw if thou canst the mystic line — which human, which Divine?'

This is an invitation to our younger English students to acquaint themselves with the best, and especially the French, scholarship on the Continent, and to begin again where our own Dr. Sanday left the psychological study of the Christological problem, and see whether a further step towards a solution, in terms of modern psychology, may not make it more acceptable to the modern mind.

If indeed an adequate Christology must ever elude the grasp of our finite minds, yet in religious experience the Living Lord still to our minds imparts such glimpses of His Majesty as are sufficient to stimulate us to a never-ending quest after Truth — with the promise that one day we may wake up after His likeness and be satisfied with it.

Our own obligations to thinkers and writers, Ancient and Modern, are abundantly obvious and, if not adequately, yet certainly gratefully, acknowledged.

CHAPTER I

THE CHRISTIAN CONCEPTION OF GOD[1]

I

THE purpose of this article is to elucidate a few aspects of the Christian conception of God. This conception must in the last resource stand or fall on its own intrinsic merits in rivalry with other conceptions of Deity derived from the study of comparative religions and from philosophical speculation concerning the nature of ultimate reality. There is in the world to-day a certain conception of the Being and character of God which Christians believe to be derived from a supernatural revelation, an historical Person — Jesus of Nazareth — and a Christian experience of God in Christ Jesus. I take this conception in this sense as 'given', and without discussing questions of historical criticism, or the problems which centre around the conception of Divine revelation or the objective validity of Christian religious experience, I wish simply to ask what precisely is involved in this Christian conception of God. Our treatment of the subject is thus expository rather than apologetic. We do not enquire whence the conception is derived nor whether it can be substantiated, but what it is. What do we really mean when we employ the term 'God' in Christian thought?

At the outset we must note that we are not dealing with a fixed and stationary idea, the meaning of which has not and cannot change. On the contrary, the Christian conception of God is the product of an historical and progressive revelation. The exact meaning to be attached to the term has, therefore, varied within certain limits, from age to age. It is a conception which has grown by a process of interpretation, and this still continues to-day under the

[1] This article appeared in the *Church Quarterly Review* — Part I in January 1931 and Part II in April 1931.

guidance of that Holy Spirit of promise who should lead men into all the truth. Hence it is a task imposed upon every generation and one from which no age is exempt, to interpret God to men and to review and, if need be, revise the Christian conception of God in the light of a growing human knowledge and a varying human experience.

Not that the character of God varies from age to age, but men's human insight into that character must necessarily wait upon their own spiritual progress and powers of receptivity. It is the same unchangeable God with whom men are dealing all through history; but we cannot expect from any age more of an appreciation of Divine Truth than the spiritual state of that age enables it to assimilate. There must always, therefore, be more in the revealed truth about God than any one age can appreciate, and aspects of the Divine character overlooked at one time, over-emphasised at another; lost sight of by one generation and recovered in the next. In this sense there may quite conceivably have been ages of faith in the past more sensitive than our own in apprehension of the deep things of God. There may, on the other hand, be in our own time a deeper insight into the meaning of the Christian conception of God than was possible, say, a century ago. Certainly we can find a richness of meaning in the idea of God to-day which was implicit rather than explicit in, for example, the Old Testament. No age can claim to have possessed an absolute and unclouded appreciation of the fulness of God's self-disclosure of Himself in the Person of His Son.

An historical survey, however, of the whole revelational process through the Old Testament up to the Incarnation and onwards in the history of the Christian experience of God in Christ Jesus, does enable us to grasp more fully something of the richness of the Christian revelation. The Church's task is to present as much of the whole truth of God for the benefit of our generation as can be gleaned from a broad survey of past attempts to appreciate the Christian conception. It would be too much to hope for such a co-ordination of all aspects of the truth to-day as would yield

2

us a perfectly balanced and faultless conception. That is, nevertheless, the ideal at which to aim, and in the effort to reach it by study of the whole history of the Christian doctrine of God, we are led to a very much fuller realisation of what is contained in our Christian teaching. We know what men have thought on the subject. We see where they over-emphasised or under-estimated certain aspects of the Divine character. We are warned by their mistakes and can profit by the lessons they would teach us. The Church has inherited from the past a deposit of truth and a wisdom in its interpretation which we to-day would do well to study and profit by in our attempts to enter more fully into a new understanding of God.

The Nature of God in Christian Dogma [1]

The Christian conceives of God as a Living Being possessed of all possible perfections, or attributes. He is One capable of being apprehended, though not comprehended, by the finite human mind. A full and exact analysis, therefore, of His Essence is beyond the power of our intelligence. What He is in Himself is unknown, save so far as His own self-disclosure has revealed it, generally in His relation to mankind, and specifically, in His revelation of Himself in the Person of our Lord and Saviour, Jesus Christ.

✓The Christian conception of God is that of One who is at once Eternal Activity and Eternal Repose. He has in Himself an inexhaustible fountain of possibilities, new beginnings, new revelations. We can set no limits to the wonders of His creative activity or the richness of His Divine designs. Ultimately He is to be thought of as quite independent of that particular aspect of His creative activity by which the worlds we know were made and by which they are being sustained and by which, again, life was and is being given to the sons of men.

[1] My obligations to Bishop Grafton's *Digest of Catholic Theology* in the following sections will be obvious. I have taken his work as the most convenient summary. The reader is referred for a fuller treatment to Joyce's masterly work on the *Principles of Natural Theology*.

Had this Eternal Activity not produced the world and us, God would still have remained what He is in Himself with His Perfection unimpaired, since it is not bound up with the origin and end of man. According to Aquinas, God is absolutely *self-sufficing*. Creation was no necessity of His Being. What we can say is that a dictate of His Goodness and Wisdom found expression in creation.

So far as our human minds can form any idea of God's *Oneness* or *Simplicity*, every kind of composition is excluded. He not only possesses all that is perfect but He is that which His Perfections signify. He is Truth, Wisdom, Light, Life and Love.

The simplicity of His Being makes Him invisible to all beings besides Himself except to those who attain in Christ the Beatific Vision. His Life is a Self-derived Life. As regards His *Eternity*, He is that which has always existed, having neither beginning nor ending. As touching His *Infinity*, it pertains to His understanding, will and consciousness. It signifies the possession of all perfection to which nothing better or greater can be added or conceived. It declares God's transcendence of space and time. It implies that God has every conceivable perfection, in the fulness of every conceivable form and degree. As regards His *Immutability*, God's nature is unchangeable. His decrees are immutable.

When we pass to the consideration of God, not as He is in Himself, but as He has revealed Himself, in His relation to the world, the questions of His *Omnipotence*, *Omniscience* and *Omnipresence* present problems to the finite understanding upon which men have exercised their minds in every generation and the solution of which takes us far into the field of the philosophy of the Christian religion. Our task is strictly the elucidation of these attributes and only incidentally their justification before the bar of reason. We must consider them in the light of the flood of new knowledge pouring in upon us from all sides and the problems raised by the times in which we live. Are those attributes, for example, compatible with a measure of human freedom? Is

4

God's Perfection as Truth, Wisdom, Light, Life and Love reconcilable with the imperfections of the world as we know it, the dark tragedy of human sin and the mystery of evil and suffering? These and many other questions press upon us in any attempt to appreciate the Christian conception of God and we must bear them in mind as we seek to elucidate some of the salient features in that conception.

Let us then turn to the consideration of God's attributes in relation to the world and human life, taking first the three attributes named above. It is clear that as attributes of a Personal God, whose nature is Holy Love, they must be considered not in isolation but as governed in their exercise by the character and purpose of the One whose attributes they are. God as the Absolute Energy, we say, is All-powerful. If we ask how is this Power revealed, the question is wrongly put. We have rather to ask: how does this God reveal His Power, being what He is? The quality of the power exercised will depend upon the nature of the material upon which it works. Thus, in relation to the material world, God reveals His power as the principle of all motion in the inorganic world, the principle of its vitality in the organic world, the principle of spiritual life in the spiritual world. The Omnipotence of Holy Love reveals itself as physical compulsion or as moral and spiritual suasion, according as it deals with inorganic and organic life or with the souls of men. The form of its expression is governed by the *nature* of the material. Hence God's dealings with the physical world are not the criterion by which to judge of Him in His relation to human beings whom He has made for Himself and to whom He has granted a measure of human freedom which He, being what He is, must respect and safeguard. The Omnipotence of a Being whose essence is Holy Love clearly does not imply an unrestricted power to do what God likes on the analogy of an Eastern despot wielding a compulsive power over his slaves. It is nowhere suggested, again, that Omnipotence in its exercise by Him in whom Christians believe, is power to make null and void all the laws He has set Himself by which to govern the

Created Universe. There are some things God cannot do without ceasing to be God as the Christian conceives Him in relation to the world and human life. For example, God cannot make two and two equal to five. He cannot make anything be and not be at the same moment of time. He cannot force a created human will to obey His behests, short of annihilation. He cannot contradict Himself or act in contrariety to His own Being. If we argue from the analogy of our own imperfect human lives, we see that love cannot do certain things or adopt certain attitudes without ceasing to be love. Now God is eternally, in His Essence, Holy Love and therefore His relation to us must be governed all through by this, His essential character. 'I the Lord change not; therefore ye, O sons of Jacob, are not consumed.'

The treatment of this subject by the late Mr. A. C. Turner [1] in his essay in a volume entitled *Concerning Prayer*, where he deals with the problem of Prayer and the World's Order, is one which will repay careful study, and suggests lines along which a helpful light may be found in our effort to solve some of the problems raised by the Omnipotence of God in relation to human freedom.[2] Thus, we are to-day coming to attach an increasing weight to the truth that the basis of a spiritual morality is freedom, and the morality of freedom is love.[3] Again, we can see that love is omnipotent because it can always in any circumstances give a perfect expression of itself. It has, as Mr. Turner says, no need to manipulate history, because it is always sufficient to meet any situation. The activity of love is self-giving; it can afford to give itself away, and no reception which it may meet can be either a limitation or a real defeat. If Divine Love is the author of all existence, it follows that nothing can exist

[1] With it may be compared Mr. Rolt's suggestive discussion in his book on *The World's Redemption*, and I may, perhaps, be allowed to refer also to *Some Postulates of a Christian Philosophy*, ch. vi, 'The Omnipotence of Love in relation to Human Freedom'.

[2] We hesitate to equate 'power' with 'love' even in God, or to commit ourselves to the view that there is no power except love in the last resort. Whatever 'power' God employs, it is such as is consistent with the character of Him who employs it.

[3] *Concerning Prayer*, pp. 419-20.

wherein love cannot find expression. So omnipotence and freedom, Mr. Turner contends, are complementary to one another. ✓The freedom of the creature is not a limitation of the omnipotence of God but its expression; omnipotence is not a limitation of freedom but its ground. In terms of outward relationship this is paradox for which there is no rational solution. But love is more than rationality; not contrary to it — indeed, it is its ground — but over and above it.[1] Perhaps we may look for the crowning illustration of all this to St. Paul's argument in Rom. viii, 31-3:

> 'If God is for us, who is against us? He that spared not His own Son, but delivered Him up for us all, how shall He not also with Him freely give us all things?'

There are certain things we can affirm with confidence concerning God's omnipotence. It reveals itself in the supernatural commencement of the world; by its power over all being other than itself; in the laws which regulate material things; in the manifestation of new sequences as in miracle for moral purposes; in His commencing a new work of creation in the midst of the existing order. Again, as regards its limitations, we may affirm that limitation is a condition of infinitude; self-limitation is inseparable from a perfect nature; God cannot do wrong or sin, for sin is a contradiction of His own nature; He cannot contradict His own Being, but must act in harmony with His own laws; He cannot undo the past, but He can annul the consequences of sin; He cannot produce the Infinite, because the Infinite and production are contradictory ideas.[2]

Moreover, if in our contemplation of the Omnipotence of a God whose essence is Holy Love, we allow our minds to dwell upon the qualitative rather than the quantitative aspect of this attribute, as indeed is necessary also in the consideration of His Omniscience and Omnipresence, we reach a view-point which greatly aids us in our appreciation of His dealings with us. Where shall we look for the signs of His Omnipotence? Not exclusively in those manifesta-

[1] *Op. cit.* p. 421.　　　　　[2] Grafton, *op. cit., passim.*

tions of compulsive power which we see all around us in the working of what we have come to call the laws of Nature. Rather over and above these, in those spiritual laws through which God seeks to govern our lives and which we realise to be compatible with that measure of human freedom we have seen to be the basis of a spiritual morality.

The qualitative content of Love's omnipotence is seen in its exercise. A hint or two only can be given here of the way in which we should work out this pregnant suggestion, containing as it seems to do the key to the doctrine of the Incarnation and the vexed question as to how the Omnipotent God could become Incarnate in terms of human life. If we think of His attributes of Omnipotence, Omniscience and Omnipresence in terms of quantity, the problem is wrongly set. If, on the other hand, we dwell upon these attributes in their qualitative character, then clearly they can be revealed within the limitations of a human life, whilst at the same time losing nothing of the richness of their qualitative content. Could Omnipotent Holy Love, for example, have been more fully revealed than it was in the Incarnate Life of the Son of God with its culmination in the Calvary Sacrifice? Could Love's Omniscience have been more fully shown than in our Lord's insight into the needs of human life and the sense of His own vocation and ministry as one sent to meet those needs and capable of satisfying the soul's hunger after God? Could, again, Love's Omnipresence have been more adequately demonstrated than in our Lord's power to penetrate within the inmost barriers of the human soul, knowing what was in man, discerning a Nathaniel at prayer when he thought himself least under observation? Instances could be multiplied from the Gospel narratives to show that if the qualitative rather than the quantitative content of the attributes of Omnipotence, Omniscience and Omnipresence be kept steadily in view, then their exercise within the limitations of a human life is conceivable and that they were in fact revealed in the earthly life of the Incarnate Son of God.

There are not wanting signs in current theological literature of a growing appreciation of this qualitative aspect of the Divine attributes in their revelation in terms of the Incarnate Life of God the Son. Thus one writer, speaking of our Lord's attitude towards pain and suffering, suggests that we may find that Omnipotence has a great deal more to do than we had supposed with natural sympathy and the genius for entering into the sorrows and sufferings of other people. I should be inclined myself to press the suggestion home more closely and apply it also to the exhibition by our Lord of the attributes of Omniscience and Omnipresence in the days of His flesh. Was there, for example, one single pang in human life to which His sensitive heart made no response? The wonder of His earthly life as this culminated in a Gethsemane experience, a cry of dereliction and a broken heart, is scarcely grasped until we have seen in it the life not only of a particular man but of *the* Man — of one, that is, so interwoven with our human life that the Omnipresence of His Manhood is to be sought in the direction of that mysterious union of the human and the Divine Natures in His one Person which made it possible for Him, whilst being located at a particular place, to be, nevertheless, representative of all men, bone of our bone, flesh of our flesh, and possessing such an all-inclusive Manhood that He could Himself take our infirmities and bear our sicknesses in a sense more awful and more real than perhaps we have grasped. It is along this line of thought that we should seek to penetrate more deeply into the meaning of the Calvary Sacrifice for the sin of the whole world.

His Righteousness: His Wrath

I do not think that we can dismiss lightly as mere 'anthropomorphisms' the Biblical conception of our God as a 'jealous' God or one whose 'wrath' is revealed from heaven against all iniquity. On the contrary I would attempt to maintain and to justify them as containing essential truths in the Christian conception of God. If, as we have seen, the God whom we worship is a Living God whose Essence is Holy Love, then clearly it must be a fearful thing to fall into His hands and it becomes the supreme task in human life to achieve such a measure of goodness as shall enable us to be counted worthy to be called the sons of such a God and heirs of eternal life. Our Lord's whole earthly mission would lose its significance if we failed to realise that He had come to seek and to save that which was lost. And the connotation of the word 'lost' as applied to a human soul meant something awful to Him; otherwise His atoning work has been sadly misinterpreted in its inmost significance in relation to sinners. Jesus taught the world what sin meant to a God of Holy Love. Gehenna was to the soul of Jesus 'a picture of the awful fascination death and destruction seem to have for the wicked'. I agree with Mr. J. A. Robertson when he says that if we put every conception of hell, built up by centuries of materialistic and penal theology, out of our minds, and look at Christ's picture of soul-waste with honest candour, there is nothing in the world's literature to compare with it, — nothing.[1] We do well to remember the revelation of God's Holy Love in the Person of His Son and to read in that life in its attitude towards sinners, the lesson of God's character as that reacts towards human sinfulness.

'He saw the remoteness of men from His own purity and from God, yet He felt Himself drawn close to them in love — God's love in Him. How to bridge the gulf of sin-estrangement, how to bring the Father into the emptiness of soul, in man, how to bring them back to God, how to disclose to them in His own life the infinite Holiness that knows and feels, yet stoops to bear — how to be to them, in short, the Divine Forgiveness — that was where the kernel of the problem in His vocation lay for Him. In other words, when we have penetrated to the vital nerve of Christ's consciousness of vocation, we discover it to have been an *expiatory* consciousness.' [2]

---

[1] *Spiritual Pilgrimage of Jesus*, p. 194.
[2] *Op. cit.* pp. 196-7.

There may be room for differences of opinion as to the precise emphasis we are to place upon different factors in the atoning work of our Lord, but one thing at least is clear, viz. that no conception of God is truly Christian which leaves out of sight the expiatory consciousness of Jesus in His revealing work in laying bare before the eyes of sinners the heart of mercy of our God.

It is no mere survival of a gloomy Rabbinism which makes St. Paul fix our attention in his picture of God not only upon Love and Grace but also upon Righteousness and Wrath. No picture of God's Fatherhood and Love which glosses over His severity and misses the significance of His Wrath rings true to the teaching of Jesus. If the question be pressed as to whether we have not here a series of irreconcilable attributes and a God torn by conflicting emotions utterly incompatible with that Simplicity and Spirituality which are central in our thought of Him, I should be inclined to seek a solution along the lines suggested, for example, by Dr. Stevens in his treatment of the idea of God in Pauline Theology.[1] Grace, mercy and compassion, he reminds us, are the watchwords of St. Paul's doctrine of God's nature and action. What then of His righteousness and wrath? Dr. Stevens suggests that it is

'an aspect or activity of God's Holy Love. It is', he says, 'God's Holy displeasure at sin — the reaction of His nature against it. It is the energy with which His Love, being Holy, repudiates its opposite. It is not, therefore, inconsistent with love; it does not stand in opposition to it. The opposite of love is hate, and God is not described as hating men. Wrath stands in contrast to those activities of love which are called grace or compassion. They denote the aspect of love according to which it pities the sinner and waits to forgive him. Wrath denotes the attitude of the divine love towards wilful sin. Both qualities or impulses — that of grace and that of wrath — are embraced within the divine love. The conception of

---

[1] *The Theology of the New Testament*, pp. 376 ff.

God's righteousness where it expresses His attitude towards sin, is similar. It must mean the self-respecting attribute of holiness in God, the reaction of His nature against sin which must find expression in its condemnation.'

This sets the problem of the Atonement, and brings us within sight of Calvary. The Christian need not fear to do adequate justice to the Biblical picture of the severity of God in the light of the Cross and the revelation there given of what God was prepared to do to save men. We miss the wonder of Christ's revelation of God if we fail to see in Jesus 'giving Himself away in His Love upon the Cross of His agony' the picture of 'the absolute self-forgetting, self-donating humility of God the Father'.

One may hazard the conjecture that it is because the age in which we live knows so little of real penitence and its issue in an almost irresistible impulse to make satisfaction for sin, that we fail to do justice to that value in the Christian conception of God which is represented by the terms 'wrath' and 'righteousness'.

It was Robertson Smith who strove to teach us that the Love of God is a terrible thing and that sin against Holy Love is Hell. He held that because Love's moral power is not absolute, Hell is a certainty. Sin may conquer Love. And Love lost is Hell. We need to think this out in the light of our conception of the ethical and spiritual content of Omnipotent Love. If God has willed to use no means save those of ethical and spiritual suasion in the saving of human souls and in the winning of their allegiance, then Robertson Smith is right when he tells us that God can never by His Almighty Power compel that which is the very highest gift in the life of His creatures — Love to Himself. He must receive that from us as a free gift — an act of our free will — or *not at all*. He seeks to draw us with the cords of a man and the bands of love but we are not bound to God by any unbreakable chains. In this case the final horror is not to fall into the hands of the Divine God but of our own free will to fall out of His hands and to leap into the abyss.

This, says Robertson Smith, is surely the terror of God's Love — that it can be resisted. We can baffle and in the end nullify its purpose — to save us. We can give our Saviour the anguish of rejection. This for Him is a Broken Heart and for us — Hell.

So Robertson Smith would present us with a paradox. Believe in Hell, because you believe in the Love of God! [1]

We fully appreciate the important point to which Dr. Otto directs fresh attention in his stimulating treatise on *The Idea of the Holy*, with reference to these terms 'wrath' and 'jealousy'. We must remember that they are 'ideograms' and analogical rather than conceptual. This applies in fact to all the 'attributes' of God which we adduce by analogy from our human nature. We have always to bear in mind the fact that the argument from analogy depends upon the amount of truth in the resemblance. The Scholastic theologians were most careful in this respect to point out that when we attribute to God a perfection which is found in the created world, we understand that in Him it has none of the limitations which adhere to it as it belongs to the creature; i.e. the word is employed not equivocally but analogously. A failure to observe this caution easily involves us in a crude anthropomorphism. Dr. Otto has done good service in suggesting that something supra-rational throbs and gleams, palpable and visible, in the 'wrath of God', prompting to a sense of 'terror' that no 'natural' anger can arouse. The divine ὀργή, he contends, is nothing but the 'tremendum' itself, apprehended and expressed by the aids of a naïve analogy from the domain of natural experience. He appeals in support of his case to the religious men of the Old Covenant to whom the wrath of God, so far from being a diminution of his Godhead, appears as a natural expression of it, an element of 'Holiness' itself, and a quite indispensable one. The same is true of the Divine 'jealousy'.

Commenting upon the 'numinous' in the Old Testament, Dr. Otto points out that related expressions akin to the 'Holiness' of Yahweh are His 'fury', His 'jealousy', His

[1] See *Minor Prophets*, Hosea and Amos, *passim*.

'wrath', the 'consuming fire' and the like. The import of them all, he suggests, is not only the all-requiting righteousness of God, not even merely His susceptibility to strong and living emotions, but all this ever enclosed in and permeated with the 'awefulness' and the 'majesty', the 'mystery' and the 'augustness', of His non-rational Divine nature. And this holds good, also, of the expression 'the living God'. God's 'livingness', he says, is perceptibly akin to His 'jealousy' and is manifested in and through this, as in His other 'passions' generally. It is by His 'life' that this God is differentiated from all mere 'World Reason', and becomes this ultimately non-rational essence, that eludes all philosophic treatment. This is the God that lives in the consciousness of all prophets and apostles of the Old and the New Dispensations alike. And all those who later championed against the 'God of philosophy', the 'living God' and the God of anger and love and the emotions have unwittingly been defending the non-rational core of the Biblical conception of God from all excessive rationalisation. And so far they were right. Where they were wrong and sank into 'anthropomorphism' was in defending not figurative 'anger' and 'emotion', but literal anger and emotion, misconceiving the numinous character of the attributes in question and holding them simply to be 'natural' attributes taken absolutely, instead of realising that they can only be admitted as figurative indications of something essentially non-rational by means of symbols drawn from feelings that have analogy to it.

Whether or no we agree with the main thesis of Dr. Otto's book, I think he is on firm ground in contending for the analogical reference in the use of terms like 'wrath', 'jealousy' and so on when applied to God. In this he is in line with the best scholastic thought on the subject.

The Divine Jealousy

Bearing then these cautions in mind, let us study afresh in our Christian conception of God, the truth underlying

the expression 'Jealous God'. What precisely is meant by
our saying that the Lord our God is a Jealous God, visiting
the iniquities of the fathers upon the children unto the third
and fourth generations of them that hate Him, and showing
mercy unto thousands in them that love Him and keep His
commandments? Is this also a relic of pre-Christian thought
and have we outgrown it in the fuller light of Christ's teaching? One of the best attempts to answer this question lies
buried in a little-known book on the Ten Commandments [1]
and I venture to reproduce the substance of it here in the
belief that it contains an aspect of truth too frequently overlooked in our attempts to appraise the conception of God in
both Old and New Testaments. Treating of the Second
Commandment, Mr. Senior reminds us that we have to do
with a God who is Holy Love. The word 'jealous' may be
construed unworthily, but when we question our own nature
with true reverence, jealousy stands out as one of its deepest
instincts. What is jealousy? The whole self concentrated
in the feeling of love wounded, wronged, outraged; and so
just in proportion as a man is noble will be his jealousy,
because the more he is able to love, the more he is able to
suffer through love. The purer love is the deeper it longs;
the more it gives, the more it yearns for adequate response.
Because it is a passion, a hunger of the heart, it is the very
life of life. Therefore, argues Mr. Senior, rob true love of its
due and it must ache: it burns as with a fire which many
waters cannot quench. Now God's Love is perfect, God's
nature is absolute in holiness. What then must be His
capacity of jealousy? The love of God interprets His
Jealousy. As is the love, so is the jealousy. If it be a love
that can even die, so it can burn into a consuming fire. If
the Divine Love be as deep as life itself when it blesses, so
Divine Jealousy must be as deep as life itself when it burns
against him who departs from the living God.

What is the proof? Shall we point to the evidences
of the Divine Judgment in human life? Shall we instance
the law of heredity which visits the sins of the fathers upon the

[1] *God's Ten Words*, by Rev. Walter Senior, 1880.

children? We may do so if we remind ourselves that the Bible nowhere says that God does not punish sin and if, moreover, we can see, however dimly, some moral purpose at work in the midst of human woe, remembering that much of the suffering in the world is traceable to human sin. Given a great moral end to be served, take only for granted that a Holy God desires to redeem a sinful race of beloved children and then this law of 'jealousy', working itself out in retribution, may well be a law of Holy Love. As J. B. Mozley says: [1]

'The course of things in this world is a great teacher, and the experience of life when things are looked at in their designed light is a great spiritualiser of the mind. And among the modes of teaching one is the sight of the ruinous effects of men's sins upon the condition of their families and posterity. The sin is thus held up to the world with a mark upon it; it is made to fasten on men's eyes; and it is kept up in recollection when otherwise it might be forgotten. Providence, if we may use the expression, cannot afford to dispense with the ordinary weapons of instruction, which chain the attention of mankind to the consequences of sin; thus putting the stamp of evil upon it, exhibiting it to the world in a fearful and formidable light, and converting it into a lasting spectacle of disaster and sadness before men's eyes. That the sins of one generation do issue in pain and loss to another is observed; and it makes and is designed to make a certain moral impression upon us. The fact that sin continues in its effects long after the act itself, is didactic, and creates a deep image in men's minds.'

Could we have a better comment, for example, on the World Wars of our own time than this? Certainly it elevates our conception of the moral order of Providence, and if the purpose of it all is moral, if by its means God's love is striving to win us and save us through great tribulation —

[1] *Ruling Ideas in Early Ages.*

and certainly one factor in turning men to repentance is the realisation of the consequences of their sins on the lives of others — then we need not hesitate to include 'jealousy' in our picture of a God of Holy Love. It is, as Mr. Senior says, a glorious truth to know that God's manifestations have a purifying purpose, that one action of the Divine Jealousy is to trouble the sinful conscience and make it grow, and to throw light into the darkest moral sense and make it see. We see it historically; we may, if we will, realise it individually. 'When thy judgments are abroad, the people of the world learn righteousness.' If side by side with this aspect of the truth, we set another, viz. that the same jealous God 'sheweth mercy unto thousands of them that love Him and keep His Commandments', then we have a song of hope with which the whole Bible rings. We have in our Christian conception of God the picture of One whose jealousy will not clear the guilty but it is the jealousy of a love that can die to redeem. There on the Cross is the Lamb of God taking away the sin of the world, reconciling men to God; and there along the shining track of resurrection and ascension light, the Captain of our Salvation leads many sons to glory. In this we have the assurance that Divine jealousy will work until 'He shall see of the travail of His soul and be satisfied', and God's love will be all in all.

His Transcendence and Immanence: Is God Finite?

It is along these lines that we should seek to commend the complementary aspects of God's relation to the world which in modern phraseology we seek to express by the terms Transcendence and Immanence, and avoid the implications of a 'finite God'. Men have no difficulty in accepting the belief in the Divine indwelling — the God who is closer than breathing, nearer than hands and feet. They stumble at the thought, however, of an Absentee God, remote from His world in a blissful repose in some transcendental sphere outside the range of the pain and passion of our finitude. Hence the efforts to over-emphasise His

Immanence and to miss the saving truth of His Transcendence. Yet a deeper view will show that what is really at stake is His absolute Sovereignty and in this alone is there any hope when we are confronted by the dark mysteries of pain and suffering, the enigma of evil and the seeming injustice of His ways with men.

The question in our own day is set somewhat as follows: Is God finite? Can we speak of an Omnipotent God of Love in the presence of the world's pain? Sin and suffering constitute the very crux of theism. Here again I can only hint at a line of thought which points to a possible solution and I may be permitted to refer to *Some Postulates of a Christian Philosophy* for a fuller discussion. Let us consider here a passage or two from Bishop Brent in a brief but pregnant paper under the title 'Where God Dwells'. The Bishop points out that the immanence of God in the sense of God being in His works, in the world of things and men, is not difficult for men to accept, but what *does* stagger men is the existence in a world in which God dwells, of the dark mysteries from which none can escape — the disastrous storms, the difficulties, the pains of life. If, they argue, God dwells in the world, why does He not sweep away these heavy shadows, this over-much grief?

There is only one answer and it is this:

'God does not annihilate these things because He has a high use for them; He cannot destroy that which He can inhabit; God dwells in the dark places, in the wilderness, in the storms; He has taken possession of them, and they are His just as much as the fertile land. In short, God dwells in everything short of sin, even in the fiercest, gloomiest penalty of sin. The angel of vengeance is the angel of God's blessing for all penitents who will accept Him as such.'

Now note what God's Presence in these things involves, remembering that it is the Presence of One who is not only immanent in them but transcendent above them, i.e. master, supreme Sovereign over them.

'When our Lord came in the flesh', says our author, 'He entered into every human experience to abide in it all the days. He invested temptation, so that temptation is henceforth man's highest opportunity. He seized upon difficulty, and behold, it became a revelation. He invested responsibility till it became inspiration, duty till it became privilege. He wrapped Himself in sorrow, and sorrow is turned to joy. He explored the darkest recesses of death, and death is the gate to life immortal. And these transformations are for all time.'

The Divine Presence sets in motion a process of transformation. What a revelation is this of God's Sovereignty! Could a finite God accomplish the seemingly impossible? We need the Christian conception of God Almighty because of the presence in the world of forces and factors which are quite beyond the power of anything short of Omnipotence. The Omnipotence of Love means its competence to deal with all relations and all possibilities. In that alone we have the certainty of the final triumph of good over evil.

God's Omnipotence, as we have said elsewhere, brings with it an assurance of a final consummation of Love's purpose which cannot be frustrated. The end is assured only if the Worker is absolute sovereign. Christian theism can allow for an element of contingency in the process of the working out of the Divine Plan — there is room for reverses, cataclysms, pain, and suffering in the redemptive process by which the Sovereign God leads a free creation to its final goal and secures a free ethical response to His sovereign will and purpose; but faith is bankrupt in the hands of a 'finite God' who may fail ultimately. We should have no guarantee that the whole world-process in His hands might not get so out of gear as to end in irretrievable and final disaster.

Faith's dependence, which is the very nerve of religious experience, rests ultimately upon the unshakeable assurance of God's Omnipotent Love. If we cannot depend upon a 'finite God' in the ultimate issue, we shall inevitably begin the search afresh for Someone or Something stronger and more reliable. We are driven behind the 'struggling' God to a greater 'Invisible King' or 'Veiled One', an Immutable Fate to which we do well to pay homage.

The belief in the Divine Omnipotence is the only sure ground for a sane optimism, the only sure deliverance from a hopeless pessimism as we survey the world to-day in its seeming chaotic state and its bewildering clash of interests and aims. It is only the knowledge of 'our Father which art *in Heaven*' that can steady us in the day of calamity and bid us cling in hope to the certainty of a better day.

But the really convincing story of a Transcendent God immanently active in the world and in human life, comes to us when we experience His transforming power. Let us take a telling passage from Bishop Brent's paper which sums up the thought:

'The Bible is full', he says, 'of phrases (in the Old Testament, of course they are prophetic, pointing to Messianic days) that tell of God's transforming power. Darkness shall be turned into light; the desert shall blossom as the rose; the barren shall be a mother of children; the glowing sand shall become a pool; and the thirsty ground, springs of water; the deaf shall hear, and the blind see; defeat become victory; and the instrument of shame and torture, the symbol of glory and joy. All this, which through the Incarnation has become a fact in common life, is a revelation of God's power, not to say love, which far exceeds in wonder whatever we knew before. It is appalling to think of a power so strong that it can annihilate with the force of its grinding heel; but it is inspiring to consider an Almightiness that transforms the works of evil into the hand-maidens of righteousness and converts the sinner into the saint.

'And it is this latter power which Eternal Love possesses and exhibits. He persistently dwells in the sinner until the sinner wakes up in his likeness and is satisfied with it; He enters into the shadows and holds them until they become first as the morning clouds fingered by the earliest rays of the rising sun, and eventually as the brightness of the noonday light.'

The Christian God because He is Infinite, not finite, because He is Omnipotent not limited, because He is Transcendent as well as Immanent, is One whose work in the world and in human life has in it the promise of victory, and brings with it the hope of Glory. This is a God who reveals His Almighty Power most chiefly in showing mercy and pity. This is a God therefore to whom men can pray and whose Love constrains them to worship.

So we come in the end to consider what really is involved in our Christian belief in God as *Personal*.

A Personal Living God

Fundamental to the religious consciousness is the unchangeableness of God. "Thou art the same and Thy years shall not fail." The human mind seeks for Reality in something permanent, stable, eternal, amidst the flux of life; in religious phraseology it is 'the Rock of Ages'; in philosophical speculation 'Being'. Hebrew ethical monotheism and Greek philosophy meet in the revelation of the 'I AM.' Religion and philosophy again witness to a distrust of time. To 'have a history' is a mark of finitude. Over against what human experience teaches are our creaturely vicissitudes, we set the Unchanging, the Immutable. In spite of repeated attempts in the history of philosophical speculation to interpret Reality in terms of dynamic concepts, there seems to be always sooner or later a reaction which bends the human mind back upon a static concept. Religion takes refuge in such well-known lines as these:

> Change and decay in all around I see
> O thou who changest not, abide with me.

Probably if we penetrated beneath all other secondary considerations, we should find that the principal objection to the ascription of personality to God lies in this desire to preserve *Being* as Eternal Permanence over against *Becoming*.

We are sometimes astonished at the prevalence of impersonal terms in the efforts of thinkers to describe ultimate reality. System after system culminates in the Absolute. Religion is condemned as grossly anthropomorphic and when the human soul seeks to describe as personal that with which it knows itself to be in communion in the experience of prayer, it is condemned as guilty of discolouring Reality by projecting upon it the shadow of its own imperfect finite selfhood. To postulate personality either in God or of God is to discolour Reality by 'man's giant shadow, hailed divine'. Yet the ultimate truth must do justice not only to the legitimate conclusions of the human mind and the deepest needs of the human heart but also to the plain implications of revealed religion in the quest for Reality. Our Christian conception of God meets all these demands in its thought of the Living God who is at once Being and Becoming; static and dynamic; changeless and yet Lord of change. The fact is that the deepest study of our own personalities yields us this paradox of identity in difference. It is a one-sided interpretation of the religious consciousness which gives us an Unchangeable God upon whom we may rely in the last resource. Equally fundamental to the religious consciousness is the experience in penitence of a God whose attitude towards us *does change*. We do not escape the deepest implications of true penitence when we seek to maintain that the change is to be found solely and exclusively in us. It is also a betrayal of the deepest truth about God as Perfect Personality, if we refuse to draw the obvious conclusions from that conception of His Being. We admit that there must always be an element of reverent agnosticism in all our thought about One who so transcends our finite apprehension as to be in Himself in a real sense unknown. Nevertheless our human knowledge when it interprets Him in terms of the highest we know, viz. personality, is not so utterly astray as to leave us in ignorance and confine us to the language merely of symbolism. We *do know something* of the Unknown. This is not, however, our acceptance of a purely relative knowledge of the nature of ultimate Reality. We should rather contend that what we do know is *real* knowledge and so far truth that, when we see Him even as He is, we shall not be confounded. The more we penetrate into the meaning of our own personalities, the more we find ourselves in the presence of something which ends in mystery. A merely psychological description of ourselves is no explanation. We are, in fact, forced to conclude that we are greater than we know. And certainly the persistence of identity, amidst difference, is something we can dimly conceive of by reference to our own finite experience, as persons in the time-process and within the limitations of space, and yet withal transcending both. The mystery of human personality lies in its seemingly inexhaustible powers of a higher becoming. We are never complete but always in process of becoming. We are dealing, in fact, with a dynamic concept when we allow ourselves to indulge in introspection. At the same time we know ourselves to be transcendent above the processes in which we are taking part, so much so that man's claim all through is to be in Nature yet not of it. If in one sense we are creatures of time, in another sense time is our servant. If we are in history, we are not its slaves. If it makes us, we make it. All philosophical systems which end in describing man as merely part of Nature break down in the presence of man's consciousness of moral freedom and spiritual aspiration. We rise above Nature in such experiences and know ourselves to be akin to the Eternal in a way that no mere human part of an inhuman system, however vast, could ever be.

A true philosophy of history interprets its meaning in terms which leave the historical process as ultimately the servant of *created* but none the less *creative* personalities. In a real sense events have meaning only in relation to Will and Will is inseparable from personality, human and divine.

Now the Christian conception of God does justice to this. It gives us a God who is the key to the meaning of all history and it bids us interpret all history in terms of teleology. It gives us a God transcendent above and therefore immanent in the world and human life. It gives us an

Eternal God working through time. Whilst we do not conceive of God as growing and developing in time, yet all time is in Him who is Eternal. He transcends the time-process and is immanently present in it and works out His Eternal Purpose through it. We do not fear to argue from analogy and to say that, just as a time-process and a history are essential for the revelation of the sons of God, so they are the *sine qua non* of God's own self-disclosure to a world of created moral beings. Not that He is a growing and a developing God but that in His Perfection as the All-sufficing One, the Living God chooses one amongst an infinite number of conceivable modes of Self-Revelation in the created world and in human life. The Christian conception of God forces us to take time and the historical process seriously. Were our thought confined to a purely static conception of Deity, history would have no meaning. Inasmuch, however, as we are dealing with a Personal God, then clearly for Him the whole historical process becomes real. His Omniscience, as the Omniscience of a Personal God, is His knowledge of *all that is knowable.*

Now if history is real and the time-process something more than illusion — if it is the necessary accompaniment of growth through experience, then to the extent to which God has granted man an element of real freedom and the power of creative activity, to that extent He has necessarily limited His own knowledge and left some things unknowable, because non-existent until they happen. If the time-process is something more than the unrolling of a cosmic drama, prearranged in every detail, and if in the time-process free creative human personalities are at work, then what the morrow may bring forth is clearly something which God Himself has ordained shall not be known because it does not exist. He knows the purpose of creation and the means to its fulfilment but the *actual process through history* is something He has deliberately left open both for Himself and for us as a *possibility of experience*. What the actuality will be neither He nor we know. Exactly how in every detail He will lead many sons to glory is in this sense placed by Him deliberately outside His own cognisance. Does this mean that our conception of the Godhead must allow for an element of the contingent as proper to His Being? It means that whilst God is equal to all possibilities and adequate to deal with any one, and, whilst the *total* possibilities are fixed, He nevertheless has determined to wait upon events in some real sense and to be guided in His actions by the turn things take. This does not utterly foreclose the future to Him but it does make His Incarnation in the *fulness* of time something which had to wait upon events and be determined by the facts of human sin and man's need.

Again it does mean that the Incarnation itself was an experience in the life of the Living One.

Once admit that time is real and experience something which is only possible in and through time, and we are forced to conclude that the life of God in the days of His flesh, whilst it did not add to His Perfection, or increase His Goodness, did constitute for Him an experience, otherwise unattainable.

So, again, with His attitude towards us; if He is the Living One then the relation of our individual souls to Him is in every case a unique experience for Him and for us, *which cannot be repeated or shared.* His relation to the penitent soul after confession and absolution is different, both for Him and for it, from what it was before. Nothing less than this would seem to be involved in the Christian conception and demanded by the verdict of the Christian experience of communion with God in Christ. Anything less than this, again, is short of the truth if we are to assign any real meaning to prayer and our human freedom to do His Will.

We need not fear to deduce the full implications of our Christian conception of God by any mistaken deference to objections which spring from alien conceptions of Deity reached, as we believe, by over-emphasis upon purely intellectual data and the undervaluing of the distinctively Christian religious experience with all that is involved in it.

If on purely intellectual grounds, it be urged that a God who enters into history and is capable of a growing experience is no God but the creation of a crude anthropomorphism; the answer must be that if we are to do justice to the verdict of our intellectual and spiritual experience, it can only be by a frank acceptance of the data derived from *both* sources. If these data are seemingly contradictory and paradoxical, this is evidence of their truth. The Christian conception itself of God is a paradox. He is the Changeless One who nevertheless forgives the penitent soul. He is the Abiding One who whilst inhabiting Eternity is found in Time seeking the lost. That the Absolute should become Incarnate is beyond us. That the Personal God of Holy Love should come down at Christmastide and learn as Man obedience by the things which He suffered is what may stagger the mind but be music in the heart — what in any case answers to our highest ideals and our deepest need and what consequently evokes our praises and secures our worship. If the impulse to worship is the true criterion by which we are to judge of the relative value of rival conceptions of Deity derived from various religions and philosophies and competing for men's acceptance, we do not fear to claim for the Christian conception the first place. The reminder that our thought of God is after all *finite* thought should help us when, in our endeavour to explore the Christian conception and elucidate its meaning, we come upon seeming contradictions, paradoxes, antinomies. But this is a feature of our deepest thinking about all reality. What we have to do here as in other branches of knowledge is to hold both truths as complementary and believe that ultimately they are reconcilable though to us they appear to be incompatible and like parallel lines they do not meet within the range of our vision. Nevertheless faith holds to the conviction that there is a point of convergence and our failure to see it is due not to its non-existence but to our inability to see things *sub specie aeternitatis*. The concept of a Living God implies transcendence and immanence; it necessitates our belief in One who is immutable but nevertheless personal; One who is changeless and yet as Omnipotent will be bringing things to pass which were not and things which, as created, are new to the Divine Knowledge. Will, knowledge, feeling may form no part of ultimate reality as conceived by philosophical speculation and Eastern mysticism but they are of the very texture of that Reality which we sum up under the name of the Living One and worship as the God and Father of our Lord Jesus Christ.

Were all our knowledge unclouded when we try to think out what God means, we might be certain of one thing at least, viz. that somehow we had missed our way since 'a God comprehended is no God'. If the Christian admits an element of paradox, contradiction and antinomy in his thought of God it is because the God he worships is too great for the finite mind to comprehend, and after all the Catholic faith does not as a condition of salvation bid us understand God but worship Him.

II

The thought of a Personal Living God leads us ultimately to the mystery of the Trinity. This is the final revelation of the Being and Character of God which Christianity has to offer. The approach, however, to such a doctrine lies exclusively through Christology and it is well for us in these days to face that fact. If our answer to the question — "What think ye of Christ?" — falls short of the considered judgment of the Church Catholic — no Trinitarian problem remains for our discussion. We may quite easily side-step the problem of the Trinity by an acceptance of a 'reduced' Christology. It is only when we take the Christian doctrine of the Incarnation seriously that a Trinitarian problem arises. If Jesus Christ were less than God incarnate, the question of personal distinctions within the Godhead ceases to be a live issue for Christian thought.

We cannot within the limits of an article canvass the Christological problem or discuss it even in outline. We must, however, at least define the issues at stake in order to grasp the significance of a sound Christology as our guide to a true apprehension of the Christian doctrine of the Godhead.

What then is the Christian doctrine of Christ's Person?

The Catholic doctrine maintains that He who was God, without ceasing to be what He was, became Man, i.e. entered into the conditions of our finite existence in time and space and dwelt amongst us. The opposite opinion is that He who was a man became what He was not, viz. Divine, or, if you like, that He who was a man exhibited the maximum of Divine immanence in His human life. Now the one conception is at least conceivable; the other suggests that the barrier between the Creator and the creature has been removed in such a manner as to enable that which is human to partake of the Divine essence to the extent of becoming one in nature with God.

If objection be taken to the use of the terms 'Creator' and 'creature', and we be asked to define the issue in terminology which certainly lends itself to ambiguous juggling, we do so under protest. If we use the phraseology 'Divine' and 'human', then we have this issue: Either He who was Divine became Man, or He who was a man in some sense is to be regarded as Divine. Clearly this phraseology demands definition. Is our divinity different in kind from His? If so, in what precisely does the difference consist? If it be a difference in kind, it must be the difference between the Divinity of God in His own right, and the conferred divinity we possess as creatures receiving from Him a supernatural grace. Again, His Humanity and ours differ. Ours is the creaturely humanity of the created and sinful; His is the Humanity of the Creator.

Now with these distinctions in our minds, we can consider the above two conceptions of the Person of Christ. He who was essentially Divine with a divinity consubstantial with God's, became incarnate by the Holy Ghost, of the Virgin Mary, and was made Man. Such an incarnation is conceivable, if we remember that the way had been paved for it from the first creation of man in the Divine image. This means that there is a human element in God from all eternity, and this human element had been imperfectly reflected in created form in the sons of men. The truly human is the humanity of God; the merely or purely human is the humanity of men — a created and imperfect humanity which can never become anything but human, no matter how fully indwelt it may be by the Divine. When, therefore, God became Man, the Humanity He exhibited was not a creaturely humanity, such as ours is, but the truly human such as God alone possesses, and in the likeness of which we are made. Now in the light of this, it is clear how inadequate the alternative theory of Christ's Person is. He who was a man, a creature like ourselves (for the Virgin Birth is denied), exhibited in His own person the Divine in human life. But if He were a man already, He could never have become other than merely or purely human, even if in His case the 'incarnation' be interpreted as the exhibition of the climax of the Divine immanence. Except upon the supposition (which is fundamentally subversive of Catholic teaching) that man is capable of deification, the human can never become the Divine. It may become wonderfully like it; it has affinity with it but likeness is not identity. The human at its maximum is but the likeness of the truly human which is in God alone. This means ultimately that the humanity of Jesus Christ was not the humanity we know in ourselves. It was God's humanity which differs from ours to the extent to which the Creator differs from the creature. God's humanity revealed in Christ is the unveiling before our eyes of that of which we are created copies. The original is His. Created copies may, by His fashioning, become wonderfully like unto Him; that is their goal and end. Advance in holiness will make us more truly human, not quasi-divine beings. If an approximation to the truly human reveals us as more and more like God, this likeness is never identification in essence. We may call it, if we like, the Divine in human life, but we must not identify our acquired Divinity with that of Jesus and be misled into thinking that our likeness to Him makes Him in all points identical in nature with us.

That we should see points of similarity between the Humanity of the God-Man and our humanity is to be expected, but this must not blind us to the fact of an eternal distinction between Him and us in the midst of innumerable points of contact we love to discover and dwell upon as linking the Jesus of the Gospels with our imperfect human lives. We may grant the Modernist all he asks for when he points us to the complete manhood of our Blessed Saviour, but this complete manhood, this truly human character, is only conceivable upon the supposition that it was not human as we know the human; it was the truly human as it exists not in us but in God alone, and in us only as a pale copy, a created imitation of the truly real. And surely this difference makes itself felt in a thousand ways as we study this Jesus of the Gospels, as we hear His words, and mark His attitude as He moves about amongst men. The 'man in the street' instinctively feels this subtle difference, even though he may not be able to define its content.

The merely human, even if called the revelation of the Divine in human life, cannot quite contain all that Jesus was and the 'something more' that is demanded by the evidence of the Gospel data is just this difference between the reality and its shadow in the finite human life of the creature; just the difference between the original and the copy — the Humanity of Deity and the humanity of the creature made in the image of God; like Him, indeed, at its best but not He in the ultimate analysis.

The frank recognition of these differences between His Divinity and ours, His Humanity and that we know in ourselves, is necessary if we are to make any attempt to-day to face afresh the Christological problem. Let us state quite simply, at the risk of repetition, precisely in what these differences consist:

(1) The difference between His Divinity and ours is the difference between Deity in its own right and conferred or derived divinity such as we are capable of possessing, if so be that God dwells in us.

(2) The difference between His Humanity and ours is the difference between a Humanity which is truly human because it is His Humanity, and our imperfect human nature which can approximate to the truly human to the

extent to which He dwells in it. It is thus the difference between the perfect and the imperfect — a difference, if you like, in degree, but a difference which must ever separate us from Him, inasmuch as He possesses completely what we can only come to possess as a gift from Himself when He feeds us with His Sacred Humanity. The human as we know it must ever remain imperfect apart from His gift to it of Divine Grace. The human needs the Divine in order to make it truly human. The human in Jesus Christ was truly Human only because He who was Divine dwelt in it and His Presence made the Human Nature He assumed Divinely Human.

Thus to sum up the points:

The distinction between Jesus Christ and ourselves is one that concerns both factors, the Human and the Divine. As regards the first, His is the Humanity of Deity; not a created copy such as we possess. Hence the conception of Him as the Archetypal Man. Hence also the wonder of His truly Human life which could be at once particular and limited whilst at the same time Universal and unlimited in its world-wide revelation to all races of what the truly Human really is. As regards the second, He is Divine in His own right; His Deity is not a conferred divinity such as ours is, and in the possession of which we can alone achieve our true end, viz. to become not quasi-divine beings but our truly human selves.

If, further, a theory is required to do justice to both these factors in the Christological problem and to keep us to the true perspective in our efforts to formulate the relationship between the Divine and the Human both in ourselves and in the Person of Christ, then the doctrine of the Enhypostasia reinterpreted in terms of modern thought is the only one that can cover the whole data and do justice to the reality of the Human and the Divine, and thus keep us true to the Nicene and the Chalcedonian Christology.

To make the issue plain in a sentence. We challenge the whole Modernist identification of the Divine and Human in us with the Divine and Human in the Person of Christ.

31

There is a difference in both cases, and confusion results if we persist in ignoring this difference. At the same time the differences do not preclude such a measure of affinity and likeness as to make an Incarnation possible. They do rule out identity and so preclude Pantheism.

If our conception of the Person of Christ falls short of the thought of God Himself leading a human life, we shall miss the unspeakable condescension involved in such action and so blur our insight into the character of a God who could do a thing like that. Such Majesty in meekness eludes us if we are thinking of Jesus as a man in whom God came to dwell rather than God become man. The light of the knowledge of the Glory of God in the face of Jesus Christ is dimmed for those who stumble at the terrific suggestion of Deity found in fashion as a man and learning obedience by the things which he suffered. Modern Arianism is still busily engaged in seeking some easier intellectual way out of the obvious difficulties which such a proposition suggests. Yet the mind of the Church on the question is still enshrined in its Creed. Small wonder, therefore, if a generation which prides itself upon a creedless religion and hankers after a modern version of Christianity without a Cross is preoccupied with the task of either jettisoning the Creed itself or foisting upon its phraseology a meaning which the language of its authors was deliberately chosen to exclude. More than one recent writer, starting from the basal assumption that in Jesus of Nazareth we have the man *par excellence*, has sought to use the language of the Creed to describe Him in a sense which that language itself was designedly drawn up by its authors to rule out of court. Scorn is poured upon the 'orthodox' doctrine of the Person of Christ, whilst at the same time a desperate attempt is made to regard Him as having been 'of one substance with the Father'. When the question is pressed as to what precisely we are to understand by such a phrase applied to His Person by those who deny His essential Deity, we are reminded that, after all, Perfect Humanity *is* Deity under human conditions and we are bidden to ac-quiesce in a one-natured Christ Jesus. Such an easy-going solution of the Christological problem is reached at the expense of 'confounding the substances' of the Godhead and Manhood in His Person. The Church ages ago ruled out a Monophysite solution and refused to accept the metaphysical background of Monism as a help in answering the question how Jesus Christ could be at once Perfect Man and Perfect God. The Nicene Creed and the later Chalcedonian Definition commit us, in fact, to a dualism in the sphere of Christology in the same way that any Christian Philosophy which seeks to do justice to the contrast between the natural and the supernatural, cannot rest in any equation of the two orders of reality. It must at all costs preserve the distinction between Creator and creatures, God and the world. It must refuse the easier and more enticing Pantheism which has dogged the footsteps of every thinker seeking to escape the dualism inherent in the postulates of a Christian Philosophy. Man is not Divine in the absolute sense nor dare we say with, for example, one writer (W. R. Bowie, *The Master*) that 'that which is most beautiful in men *is* God', especially as he goes on to assure us with confidence that

'if any man express the perfection of human possibilities, then in and by that fact—and not through some miraculous difference from it — he is the incarnation of the life of God'.

In a very real sense it has been left to our age to rediscover the Manhood of the Master. The revolt against the Christ of the Creeds meant a much-needed return to the Jesus of the Gospels. The result has been book after book revealing in glowing terms the newly discovered human Jesus, bone of our bone, flesh of our flesh. This Figure in all its wonderful simplicity has had a power of attraction for many whom the Two-Natured Christ of Christian dogma failed to reach. It is as though the conventional Christ of stained-glass windows has given place to a real Jesus; a dead figure with a halo was superseded by a living Saviour with a voice of gentle stillness speaking once again through the pages of the Synoptic Gospels. Back, then, behind the Creeds with their lifeless formulae to the clearer lineaments of the Gospel portrait! This has been the cry and through it Jesus for many a life has become once more real. We are not, however, wiser than our fathers, and the reaction and consequent revolt against the orthodox doctrine of the Person of Christ has brought with it dangers which the Church met and overcame in the past and must once more face in the present. Arianism is not enough. When men have exhausted language in their efforts to do justice to the truly human Jesus, there is still an over-plus which cannot be expressed in terms of the human. There is an irresistible logic of the Person of Jesus Christ which drives men beyond the human and forces them to speak of Him in terms of the Divine. Arianism, past and present, is but a half-way house and none too comfortable. Men cannot for any length of time rest contented there. A being neither fully human nor truly Divine — a demi-god — has proved to be an intellectually unsatisfactory category of thought in which to express the 'Inescapable Christ'. Once the genuine seeker after truth seeks to pass beyond the merely human in the attempt to assess the Person of Christ; once he frankly recognises the 'plus' and knows Jesus as something more than man, he is driven on to the position in which the Church finally rested, the Nicene Creed. Either Jesus Christ was a man exalted to the status of divinity or He was God become man. The Church believed the latter alternative to be the truth. There is a world of difference between the thought of a man becoming in some sense God and that of God becoming in a real sense man. The Church believes in the doctrine of 'The Incarnation' and in doing so makes it impossible for us to think in terms of the Christian Creed of any repetition of the Incarnation, such as Mr. Bowie hints at in the words already quoted. We can conceive of the climax of the Divine immanence in a person's life and go on to think of the repetition of such a manifestation in a whole series of lives of the saints all through the ages and in days which are yet to come. God dwelling in *a person's life* is something which can often happen; God leading *a personal life* only happened once when He became Man. That was twenty centuries ago and it is what the Church means when the Creed speaks of Him —

> 'who was before all time, eternal, God of God, Light of Light, very God of very God, Begotten not made, being of one substance with the Father . . . who for us men and for our salvation come down from Heaven, and was incarnate by the Holy Ghost of the virgin Mary, *and was made man*'.

That was an event in time; God led a personal life on this earth of ours. He was seen, handled, touched by men and women. He walked the streets of Jerusalem; He taught on the shores of the Lake of Galilee. He came there on a mission of redemption. He suffered on Calvary. He wrought an Atonement for the sin of the world. He was crucified, dead and buried. He rose again on the third day. He ascended into Heaven. That is what the Church all through the ages has believed and still teaches. That is what those who repeat the phraseology of the Creeds are required to believe. It commits them to a belief about the 'Jesus of the Gospels' which excludes Him from the category of the human merely and ranks Him as the Second Person of the Blessed Trinity.

It is one thing to set out to write a new life of the world's most wonderful Man. It is quite another to attempt to describe the life of God Incarnate. Here is the reason why so many recent books about Jesus are so entirely unconvincing, however attractively written. The presupposition in the minds of their authors is that the subject of their story is an ordinary person — wonderful, indeed, as such, but, in the last analysis, capable of being conformed to our human standards of measurement and entirely expressible within the limits of our human psychology. The fact is, of course, that Jesus Christ never was an *ordinary* person in this sense, however extraordinary. He cannot be confined within the picture-frames of our human devising, because we devise these to enshrine the portrait of the human. We have no framework within which the Superhuman can be compressed. He walks out of our picture-frames and eludes our detaining grasp. The psychology of the textbooks can grapple with the human and describe it. It fails us utterly when we come to apply it to one who was God and became Man — one therefore in whose consciousness time and Eternity met in some baffling synthesis. What psychology of man's devising can compass so mysterious a Person? Many books occupy space on our shelves which have been written by those who set out upon the task of describing the life of Jesus of Nazareth on the assumption that the psychology of their subject was well within the range of human analysis. Believing themselves to be undertaking to tell afresh of an historical Person, born of human parents, a man approved of God by many mighty deeds which He wrought before an untimely death cut short a promising career, they have succeeded in their measure and yet have failed us precisely at the point where we most need help. A book or a series of books yet awaits our seeking. Its title may well be borrowed and used in a profounder sense than that with which it has been recently employed as a description of the life of Jesus of Nazareth. It will depict not the life of a man raised to the status of the Divine and indwelt by God to a degree never before experienced in all the quest of human souls for commerce with the Unseen. On the contrary it will depict, as the Gospels do, the life of God the Son Incarnate. It will use all our modern knowledge and art; all our scholarship and critical insight; all our powers of spiritual discernment — in short, everything of value we possess, to write a true biography of the Master. And its title? *The Man whom Nobody Knows.* It will supersede nine-tenths of our modern biographies of Jesus because it will reveal in a flash the plain truth that most of these, because of their presuppositions about His Person, have really been engaged in depicting not the real Jesus but an imaginary *man* who has been mistaken for Him. The 'Jesus of the Gospels' in this sense never existed. He is a creation of the Liberal Criticism of last century — a figure read into the Gospel Narratives in place of the real Jesus whose life is there described. The

Gospel data supply us with the materials for bringing home to our minds and imagination an entirely new conception of what the truly human really is, in contrast to the merely human of which we have cognisance by the study of ourselves. We shall pass beyond the categories of the imperfectly human and ordinary in which the figure of Jesus cannot be expressed, and find ourselves compelled to allow a place for the mightier mysteries of personality, human and Divine, revealed in His Person for the first and last time in history. And it is the study of this figure — the real Jesus of the Gospels — which, I am convinced, will give us the key to the profounder mysteries of the Trinity in Unity and the Unity in Trinity. A sound Christology in this sense points us beyond itself to new insights into the mystery of personality. It is, I am sure, our faulty analysis of the category of personality which has caused us to miss our way when confronted by the Trinitarian problem. We have taken the merely human as our guide and applied it as our standard of reference in our analysis of the 'Person' of Christ and our analysis of the 'Persons' of the Blessed Trinity. Small wonder that we have produced as the result a figure which the Church cannot accept as an adequate portrait of the Christ of the Creeds and one which, when we try to fit it into any intelligible place in the Godhead, postulates an impossible Tritheism and drives men in despair back to Unitarianism.

Clearly, then, in our effort to commend the Christian conception of God in terms of modern thought the time is overdue for clearing the ground by the removal once for all of the fictitious creations of Liberal Protestantism. We must undertake a fresh study of the Gospel Narratives to recover the real Jesus there depicted.

It has been frequently pointed out that our whole modern conception of personality owes much to the Christian teaching, not least concerning the Person of Christ and the Trinitarian problem. Let me then borrow freely from a contribution to Christology the deep and far-reaching significance of which, I fear, has been largely overlooked or ignored precisely because so many recent writers have worked out their theories along the lines I have indicated above and so have failed to realise the relevance of this particular contribution to the solution of the problem. I refer to Bishop Knox's illuminating discussion in his work under the title — *On What Authority?* The Bishop is dealing with the question of authority in relation to personality and he shows that whoever would understand the Gospels properly must first think out what is meant by personality. We are coming more and more to appreciate personality as the essential creative factor in the making of history, and all would agree that Jesus of Nazareth was the greatest personality the world has ever seen. Moreover, we must further note that from certain happenings in Palestine twenty centuries ago has resulted a religious movement which, with whatever vicissitudes, has outlasted the rise and fall of Empires and to-day is still the most dynamic spiritual force at work in human life. We are inevitably driven back to account for this to the impact of a mighty personality whose appearance in the world drama has wrought these moment-ous changes, and the greatness of His Person cannot be assessed in lesser terms than the works which have followed His advent demand. In any case the New Testament writings, and not least the Gospels, register the impression made by the personality of Jesus upon those who directly or indirectly came under His influence.

What then is personality? A convenient starting-point is found in Kant's definition:

> 'Human personality lies in the union of the contingent and finite elements of human life with the absolute and divine reason; and implies a power of the mind to detach itself from the given fact by an act of utter spontaneity.'

Bishop Knox fixes upon this definition and draws out its implications. Human life is shown to be finite and depend-ent on forces outside itself. It cannot find within itself the freedom and independence of which it is nevertheless con-scious. That independence it reaches by union with the absolute and Divine reason.

What light is thrown by these considerations on the personality of Jesus? We find a personality which Bishop Knox shows does not fit exactly Kant's definition. Wherein lies the difference? The answer is startling and deeply suggestive. It is a personality in which the Divine, the Absolute Person or 'Logos', is united with a contingent and finite human life. The two elements are there, *but in a wholly different relation, the one to the other*. The relation of Jesus of Nazareth to the Divine was not the normal relation of one of the sons of men to the All-Father. His Sonship and theirs are of a different order. They may be sons by adoption and grace. He is the Son in His own right. They are sons in relation to the Logos which lighteth every man. He *is* the Logos and His relation to the All-Father is an onto-logical relationship. The central constituent of His Person was Divine and the Gospel picture is that of one who was Divine, becoming human — one who from Eternity was God and in time became man.

Bishop Knox takes us a step further by reference to a passage in Dr. Wallace's *Essays and Lectures* (p. 288) where the writer points out that

'A person is on the one hand an individual, or indi-vidualised being, one among many, in ordinary cases a single living human body, which, on the other hand, has a capacity of regarding itself as a universal, not bound by limits of actual achievement, but as infinite and free. This is the so-called mystery, grandeur, or contradiction of personality. In the little physical individual which is alive — in the single subject or living soul, which is a mere point excluding all others and excluded by them, there is a potential universality, a claim to absolute unconstrained existence, to complete independence of action, utter spon-taneity. Unchecked, this may degenerate into disease; the individual may see himself, in his petty individuality, as all-embracing and deserving universal Empire.'

In the little physical individual . . . there is a potential universality. Turn to the Gospels and again we are confronted by a startling difference between Jesus and the sons of men. With them we are dealing with potential sons of God. In His case we have to deal with the Son of God Himself. With them this universality is potential; with Jesus it is *actual*.

The little physical individual is there, the Bishop is careful to point out — the man of sorrows, the carpenter's son, the maniac as some deemed Him, 'beside Himself' yet claiming before Pilate to be a King of an all-embracing and deserving universal Empire. Was this a symptom of 'diseased degeneracy'? Or is it that what we have before us in the case of Jesus of Nazareth is not the union of a finite element of individual life with the Divine reason but in fact the union of the Divine Person Himself with the finite element of human life? If so, small wonder that Pilate trembled!

I pointed out long ago in my Christological study that it is precisely this revelation of the universal in the particular which confronts us in the Person of Christ. He was in this sense a man and yet the Man. Theoretically the particular cannot fully embrace its own universal. Practically in the case of one unique Person it did. Why? Because in Jesus of Nazareth we are face to face with one whose Person no human psychology can adequately analyse. And this for the simple reason that whereas in our case we are contingent finites imperfectly related to and in communion with the Absolute Infinite, in His case we are concerned with the Absolute Infinite leading a personal life within the limits of our mundane existence and yet withal transcending them at every turn. We can never afford, in other words, to overlook the fact that in the Incarnation it is the Transcendent One who is incarnate and in His Person there is achieved a synthesis between time and Eternity, finite and infinite, relative and absolute, natural and supernatural. This it is which gives us the true key to an appreciation if not an understanding of His truly human life and its revelation of powers in actuality which we, if at all, possess only potentially. Whereas it doth not yet appear what we shall be, what He

is has been once for all revealed. Given such a Person and
difficulties concerning what He is alleged to have said and
done in the days of His Flesh pale before the supreme miracle
of Himself — God Incarnate on a redemptive mission found
in fashion as a man. Again —

> 'Religion', writes Dr. Wallace, 'like everything else
> in humanity, only exists in what we may call a radical
> antithesis, a synthesis of two aspects neither of which can
> be severed from the other. It is, on the one hand, a sense
> of dependence on the Divine, of the infinite littleness of
> human nature; and on the other a sense that God is with
> man, and even now in this world God and man are recon-
> ciled into one.' [1]

Now where in the life of Jesus, Bishop Knox rightly asks,
do we find what is the ground of all human piety — the
sense of the infinite littleness of man in the presence of God?
'I and the Father are one!' not in the sense that some
'atonement', 'reconciliation' has been effected between the
Father and Himself but, as the Jews plainly recognised, in
the sense of making Himself equal with God.

Moreover, he claimed to be in an exclusive sense the
medium of the Divine revelation (St. Matt. xi, 25-8), 'he to
whomsoever the Son willeth to reveal him'.

One final passage from Dr. Wallace's illuminating essay
will point us to the key:

> 'As Fichte has hinted,' he writes, 'and as Lotze has
> enforced at some length, the finite being finds himself on
> all hands confronted by forces with which he did not in-
> vest himself, and by laws which he has to accept, as well
> as by wills different from his own: nay, even in the recesses
> of his own being he seems to meet with a dark, strange
> substance which is in him but is not he: and to which,
> as a vehicle, his personal development is attached. We
> have grown up, as it were, by piecemeal, and are never
> wholly ourselves: we identify ourselves with the particular

[1] *Essays and Lectures*, p. 276.

point of view at which we started at a particular stage of our development. The complete sanity of self-control, of self-mastery, and absolute possession of our own souls, is what we never fully attain.' [1]

Do we find in Jesus of Nazareth any such 'dark, strange substance' interfering with 'the complete sanity of His self-control, of self-mastery, and absolute possession and appropriation of all His soul'?

On the contrary, the most arresting thing to be said concerning His whole life as depicted for us in the Gospels — the verdict alike of friends and foes — is a positive relationship to God which is unclouded and perfect in communion and the complete absence of a sense of sin. In the case of every other son of man there is the sad story of thwarted aspirations in the quest after the Divine, humiliating failure to reach the ideal of purity and self-sacrifice, a long wrestle for mastery of the flesh, a life's effort to grow into sainthood. When we turn to Jesus of Nazareth He stands revealed as different alike from all sinners and from all saints. In Him, Bishop Knox would remind us, we have not a thwarted aspiration unrealised between the human and the Divine but the perfect union of the two. Here is not, as with ourselves, the contingent reaching-out in a never-ending quest for a more perfect union with the absolute and Divine reason. It is, on the contrary, the actuality of perfect union realised in an individual life. It is the human life of the Logos incarnate — God made man — God in man made manifest.

Clearly then, in the light of all this, we must revise our conception of personality, *taking the Person of Jesus as our norm and standard* and judging of ourselves relative to this. Here again Lotze helps us in his reminder that perfect personality is in God alone. We are but pale copies of a Divine original. If then the Person of Jesus of Nazareth were indeed what the Church has believed, if in Him was unveiled before the eyes of men the perfection of personality in terms of

[1] *Op. cit.* p. 275.

human life, the difference we have noted between Him and
other sons of men is just what we might expect to find.
He, and He alone, can be described as τέλειος ἄνθρωπος
because He was not merely or purely human — not the
possessor therefore of an imperfect manhood — but truly
human in that He was Divine. If man be made in the image
of God, there must be something in God to which we bear
an imperfect likeness. In what precisely in us is this likeness
to be found? We find it in that which differentiates us
from everything else in the created universe, viz. in human
personality. This is incomplete and imperfect — something
in process of becoming — an ideal towards which we are
striving. It is a faint copy of the Divine Original which God
alone possesses and in the image of which He has made us.
If then God chose to lead a human life, He could do so and
by so doing reveal in human form what a truly human
personality really is. Because He was the Son of God, we
believe that He was capable of leading a human life and
that He did so twenty centuries ago in Palestine. We have
seen that, according to the Gospel Narratives, the life He
led differed from ours in vital points. An examination of
these vital points reveals the gulf between His personality
and ours. At the same time it points us to the true meaning
of personality and shows the way in which we can avoid a
crude anthropomorphism when we come to argue from the
human to the Divine in our endeavour to conceive of a
personal God. If we argue from our own ideas of what a
person is to what therefore we conceive God to be, we end
in a crude Tritheism. Let us now take as our norm of personality not our own imperfect selves but the Person of Jesus
Christ, Divine-human. How far will it guide us in our effort
to contemplate the Godhead — the mystery of the Trinity
in Unity and the Unity in Trinity?

We may rule out at once the intellectual short-circuit
suggested in the 'economic' theory of the Trinity. No such
easy intellectual path is open to those who accept the
stupendous fact of the Incarnation. We have to face the
problem of *eternal* distinctions within the Godhead which,

43

for the want of a better term, we call 'persons'. We may not, again, fall back upon analogies derived from a study of our own personalities as in some sense triune; body, soul and spirit, or our minds as one yet psychologically tripartite; memory, understanding and will. We are not dealing with impersonal relationships and threefold distinctions in a person but with perfect personality as in some, to us inconceivable sense, triune.

We have to speak of personal distinctions in the Godhead and retain in our thought a content for the word 'personal' which covers some mode of existence more than impersonal and less than fully individual. We have as our starting-point the Unity of the Godhead. The Trinitarian personal distinctions are to be sought within this Unity and not outside it. We have to speak of personality in God rather than the personality of God. We thus move towards a higher category which we may speak of as 'perfect personality' only because it reaches beyond anything of which we have any knowledge as being ourselves imperfect persons. The word 'supra-personal' suggests itself to indicate this essential difference. We prefer, however, the term 'perfect personality' now that we are in a position to take the Person of Christ in the sense indicated above as a key. In His Person, as we have seen, in the days of His Flesh the absolute Person or Logos was united with a contingent and finite human life. We are, to borrow Pringle-Pattison's phrase, a finite-Infinite. He was Infinite-finite. The two elements were there, but in a wholly different relation, the one to the other. Clearly, then, His Person points us to a higher order of being in which the notes of limitation, dependence, circumscription, exclusiveness and particularity give place to a richer concept in which the notes of fellowship, mutual all-inclusiveness, and universality predominate.

I have drawn attention elsewhere to Canon Richmond's contribution to the discussion of personality and acknowledged our indebtedness to him for the great truth that personality is the 'capacity for fellowship'. We have moved away from the narrow individualism of last century and are coming to realise more fully the fact that if we start life as individuals with an over-emphasis upon the element of exclusiveness in our 'make up', this is only to launch us out upon a life which can claim for itself the great word 'personal' so far, and only so far, as the element of exclusiveness yields to a richer life in fellowship with others. We begin with our individuality and move towards the ideal of personality which is something in the nature of an achievement — something to be won, and only at the cost of the loss of all false selves and the treading of the path of self-sacrifice which is love on active service. As finite-Infinite our development is bound up with an ever-increasing assimilation to and acceptance of the limitless life of the Divine within and around us. We grow souls as we more and more yield ourselves to the Divine embrace and allow God to have His way with us.

The barrier of exclusiveness is gradually broken down in a Pauline experience of 'Christ *in* us', the hope of glory. In all this we experience a higher form of life, a fellowship of persons — He in me and I in Him. We thus reach a higher category of mutuality as between persons made one in love. This again points us to the Christian doctrine of the Fellowship of the Holy Ghost — and reveals Fellowship as the ideal for the Christian community.

Here we are far removed from the narrow individuality and separateness of the soul from its fellows. We are shown an ideal of growth through fellowship in an ever-increasing richness of spiritual life to be found by the breaking down of the barriers which separate us from God.

If then, as imperfect copies of a Divine Original, our whole growth is bound up with an ideal of Fellowship in which in some sense we cease to be our isolated selves and move out towards a fuller life of mutual indwelling — He in us and we in Him — does not this itself suggest the Christian doctrine of the Godhead as the Perfect Fellowship, the Three in One and One in Three?

If, as Lotze taught us in the *Microcosmus*, the ideal of personality is mutual inclusiveness rather than mutual exclusiveness, the doctrine of the Trinity is concerned to safeguard the truth that God contains within Himself the conditions of His own existence. Whilst with us the non-Ego would seem to be the essential condition of our development and the antithesis of subject-object, the particular note of our lives as individuals, all this is the mark of our imperfection. Perfect Ego-hood or selfhood can dispense with the antithesis of subject-object because it is the ground of both. If, as we have seen, the truth of our being is not an ideal of isolated imperviability but interpenetrability — an existence of self in another in whom we live and move and have our being whilst still continuing in an ever-increasing measure to be, we see that self-centredness in God is a Unitarian conception which must give place to a higher ideal of the mutual indwelling of the Three in One and One in Three.

Here we come in sight of the conception found in the final formulation of Greek Patristic theology, the doctrine of Co-inherence (περιχώρησις), a doctrine founded on Biblical data — the Son is *in* the bosom of the Father. The Spirit is *in* God.

There is an admirable treatment of this difficult but profoundly suggestive idea in Dr. Tennant's work on *Philosophical Theology* and I will avail myself thankfully of some of his paragraphs for its further elucidation. He is dealing with the question whether the world-ground is more aptly comparable with a single subject or with a society of persons, whether God is to be conceived as a society rather than as a supreme individual. Dr. Tennant's statement of the case for a pluralistic conception of Deity is all the more impressive in that he makes it abundantly clear that he himself would not advocate the views which he is concerned to expound and elucidate. It is something, however, to note that the empirical argument for theism so impressively elaborated in his valuable treatment does not require us to advance necessarily from unity of world-purpose to singularity of person. In the absence of decisive arguments in favour of this, there is nothing philosophically or even religiously shocking in the supposition that the world-ground or the

Ultimate One is a Divine society rather than a sole individual. God would then be personal but not a Person. How then are we to conceive of Him? Clearly the human associations of the term 'society' must be transcended or discarded.

'The divine society for which "God", on this supposition, will be the name,' Dr. Tennant tells us, 'is rather to be conceived as intermediate between a society and an individual, as these entities are known to us within the sphere of humanity. For the divine *hypostases*, though distinct subjects and agents, may, or rather must, be conceived as much less individual than human persons: more penetrable or less impervious than the selves which we know, or know in part. A human self presumably cannot directly know another self's experiencings; but a subject free from limitations besetting the human self may be able directly to be aware of another's states, etc. It is not necessary to suppose all subjects to be individuals or *atomoi* in the same degree as that in which we ourselves are individuals. Those forming the highest unity in the hierarchy may possess so much of mutual coinherence, in respect of cognitive and volitional experience, as enables each to be concerned in the activities of the others, and to be transparent to one another. The notion of *perichoresis* or *circumincessio*, which can only be used figuratively by Trinitarian theology such as stops short of regarding the divine *hypostases* as subjects, may be applied literally by theology such as takes the idea of the sociality of God in all seriousness. The "persons" of the Godhead, as thus conceived, would be "members one of another" in a much higher degree than are the units of a human society; and being *ex hypothesi* self-subsistent and of the same nature or substance (*unius substantiae* rather than *una res*), they would constitute a unity and one world-ground no less explanatory of all the facts that have previously been presented as suggestive of theism than is the singularity asserted by rigid monotheism. The unity comprising the

47

supreme plurality would be a unity of concurrent wills, of joint purposes, or moral harmony, and of co-operant agencies.'[1]

We have borrowed Dr. Tennant's singularly lucid exposition of the conception but the question presses whether this is in reality what he evidently regards it as being, viz. a particularly refined form of Polytheism, hinting as he does that Christian doctors have dallied with it, before recoiling from it, and that popular Christian theology sometimes implies it. Let us admit at once that to the extent to which the simple Christian allows himself to think at all concerning the doctrine of the Trinity, his thought inevitably runs along the line of a naïve Tritheism. I am not so sure, however, whether in so doing he does not reach up to a profounder truth concerning the Godhead than is attained by those who with more strict logic keep to the rigid monotheism of the pre-Christian dispensation and miss thereby something of the fuller revelation vouchsafed to us of God *in* Christ Jesus. Is it quite certain that religious experience can offer no decisive testimony because it has already *assumed* one of the alternatives in constituting itself what it has become?

I am led to press the question by a study of a particularly suggestive contribution to the subject made by Dr. Kirk in a volume of *Essays on the Trinity and the Incarnation*.

We have always to remember that the Christian doctrine of the Trinity is essentially in origin the product of the distinctive Christian experience of God in Christ Jesus. It is not a speculative construction designed to offer an elect circle the joy of intellectual gymnastics whilst incidentally causing simple folk to stumble. The history of the doctrine is the story of a desperate intellectual wrestle with a baffling problem presented to the mind from the depths of religious experience. Is it possible, then, to get behind the intellectual statement of the doctrine to the experience it is meant to embody? Will an analysis of the experience give us indications pointing to some eternal threefold distinctions in the

[1] *Philosophical Theology*, pp. 171-2.

Godhead which account for our consciousness of a threefold relationship established and experienced by the soul in its questing after communion with the Divine? In our religious experience can we differentiate between (*a*) an experience of God, (*b*) an experience of God revealed in Christ, (*c*) an experience of God the Holy Spirit?

Dr. Kirk is concerning to ask whether there is that in Christian experience which makes it necessary for us to think of Him as existing in three Persons? Is it possible to find in our traffic with God three modes of intercourse sufficiently distinct and personal, and yet sufficiently contemporaneous and continuous, for us to assert that they point to three distinguishable *termini* within the Godhead, of each of which hypostatic character must, and can, be predicated without impairing the Divine Unity? Dr. Kirk would answer the question in the affirmative and points us to the following three relationships between man and God: (1) The Κύριος-δοῦλος relationship. (2) The relationship of Communion. (3) The relationship of 'possession'.

Perhaps we shall best elucidate the content of these varied relationships if we fall back upon a somewhat novel and startling definition of religion given by one of the acutest minds of our time. 'Religion', says Professor Whitehead, 'is what the individual does with his solitariness.' If we allow ourselves to ponder upon the implications of this new definition, we may recognise in it a profound truth. We may not conclude that it is the whole truth of religion but we shall agree that it touches the nerve of all genuine religious experience and introduces us to the first of the three relationships to which Dr. Kirk has called our attention, namely the Creator-creature or King-servant relationship between God and man. We shall recognise the truth of Dr. Whitehead's contention that the great religious conceptions which haunt the imaginations of civilised mankind are scenes of solitariness: Prometheus chained to his rock, Mahomet brooding in the desert, the meditations of the Buddha, the solitary Man on the Cross. If we think it out we shall acknowledge the justice of his statement that it belongs to the depths of the religious spirit to have felt forsaken, even by God.

To be alone; to be by ourselves; to enter into the silence which can be felt; to realise the intense and awful loneliness of human existence. There are so many people who are afraid of the consciousness of themselves. They cannot bear to be alone. They must be in company. It is the herd-instinct. They are moved by an unknown fear and seek to stifle it by plunging into the crowd. What do we do with our solitariness? The answer in too many cases is simply that people side-step it and in doing so miss that awful contact with reality which is of the essence of the religious quest. Let us assume, however, that, instead of seeking to avoid our solitariness, we deal seriously with it. What is the result? We make the effort to shut out the external world. We still our faculties to an inner stillness. We hush the inner senses to a holy calm. What is the first-fruit of such a discipline? Surely the sense of the void; the feeling of utter desolation. What comes next? The sense of fear. We are afraid. And here we light at once upon what Professor Otto has termed the 'numinous'. 'How dreadful is this place!' We are in the presence of the *mysterium tremendum*; in the presence of that which he calls a mystery inexpressible and above all creatures. The sense of creatureliness; the horror of the sinful in the presence of the All-Holy; that which in religious language we call the fear of God. Here, we suggest, is the experience of the soul in the presence of the First Person of the Blessed Trinity. Many flee in terror from it and their religious life remains within the shadow of Mount Sinai with its thunders and lightnings; with its Divine pronouncements of rewards and punishments; with its awful commands and its witness to the presence of the Numinous, striking terror into guilty hearts. This is a religion of law. God is the great Taskmaster — God the All-Terrible — the Holy One of Israel. First the void; then the terror and the fear. Dare we stop there? If we persevere in the experience, there is a way through to the light. If we hold on in a Jacob's-wrestle with the darkness, in due time the soul is thrilled by the consciousness of companionship. That is the reward of successful striving in the prayer life. We win through to the discovery of One who has all the time been seeking us in the wilderness. This is the very nerve of the evangelical experience of salvation. In the region of our solitariness is a Seeker. We are the objects of a Divine pursuit. The barriers of self fall before His approach, and at long last we are safe and found in Him. We are accepted in the Beloved. We experience the second of Dr. Kirk's three relationships. This time it is Communion, the Father-Son relationship. First the void, then the fear, and then the Love grip. Fear of the All-Holy melts into joy in the presence of the All-Loving.

> May we imagine it? The sob, the tears
>   The long, sweet shuddering breath; then on his breast
> The great full flooding sense of endless years,
>   Of Heaven, and him and Rest.

He has kept His promise. 'I will not leave you comfortless. I will come to you.' It is of the essence of the experience of salvation to yield ourselves by faith to Him who reveals Himself to us as the Man of Sorrows. In Him we move through Good Friday to Easter Day — through an awful experience of crucifixion and dereliction to a joyful resurrection. A bolt is shot back of our souls, and through the door thus at last opened there floods in the sunshine of His Presence.

> Then thro' the mid complaint of my confession,
>   Then thro' the pang and passion of my prayer,
> Leaps with a start the shock of His possession,
>   Thrills me and touches, and the Lord is there!

So far all is fairly clear and I think that most of us could so distinguish between the content of the two experiences of fear and love in relationship to the Invisible One with whom we have to deal in the religious life, as to be able to say that in the first case we were in contact with the Unknown if not ultimately Unknowable God, and in the second case with the God and Father of our Lord Jesus Christ. We should put it in this way: the Atoning work of Christ made possible this second relationship and bridged the gulf of separation between man and God. We may perhaps further suggest that God expressed and revealed in terms of human life in the Second Person of the Blessed Trinity was so much more within the reach of man made in the image of God as to allow of a warmer intimacy in love with God revealed in Christ than was possible for man with the same God unrevealed and to this extent unknown. God expressed in terms of human life is clearly not all that God is in Himself. Our relationship therefore with the First Person of the Blessed Trinity must necessarily have in it that to which our creaturely reaction is expressed in terms of the 'numinous'. We can therefore the more readily react in warmer and more intimate terms to the same God when He stoops to reveal Himself within the compass of our finite understandings in an act of unspeakable condescension and a work of redemptive efficacy for us men and for our salvation.

Dare we go a step further and seek to discover yet a third relationship distinct from those already described and which will point us directly to the Third Person of the Blessed Trinity? Here I think that Dr. Kirk helps us with one of the most suggestive contributions certainly that I have ever received in my blind gropings after light in this most baffling of all our theological problems. Jewish thought, he points out, recognised a relationship of man with God to which we give the name of 'possession' — a relationship in which the human spirit is wholly controlled, if not superseded, by the Divine. In this relationship, the Spirit produces its results whether pathological or ethical by means of super-session. No summary of Dr. Kirk's arguments would do justice to the singularly persuasive manner in which he marshals his facts and warns us of the pitfalls into which we may so easily stumble when we try to allow for the truth which undoubtedly lies behind the doctrine of irresistible grace. Whilst it is easy, as he shows, to stamp this whole idea of the compulsory moralisation of man by God as a crude eschatological survival, or an intrusion into Christianity of one of the more debased characteristics of Christianity or a perverted exercise of Rabbinic logic by St. Paul, and whilst we must recognise frankly the weight of the New Testament emphasis upon moral freedom as the *sine qua non* of ethical and spiritual achievement, nevertheless Christian history bears eloquent testimony to the power of the Spirit and the catastrophic effects of his work in the conversion of human souls. No age lacks its witnesses to the experience of 'possession' by the Holy Spirit of God. Forcible conversions, apparently complete in their resultant abandonment of sin, happen and have happened continually, Dr. Kirk reminds us, in the history of religion.

'To whatever school of thought', he says, 'a Christian belongs, he looks back to a leader or reformer or poet who held this doctrine as a cardinal point in his system — to S. Paul, and S. Augustine, to Luther or Calvin or Bunyan, or Fox or Wesley, or Whitefield. The evidence is as impressive as it is unanimous, and there are few who cannot remember moments in which it has been corroborated by the evidence of the heart, moments in which their own feeble wills have been, not merely aided, but superseded by the Divine Will working in them and carrying them forward — if only for a brief space of time — to heights of which they had not dreamed themselves capable.'

Here then we are on the tracks, if indeed we have not positive proofs, of a relationship between man and God of such a distinctive content as strongly to suggest that the soul in its spiritual pilgrimage has been in contact with the Third Person of the Blessed Trinity. If the idea of moral and spiritual suasion such as is exercised by the Divine Love in wooing and winning the soul in the relationship of Father-Son in communion gives place on occasion to a more decisive action on the part of the Divine, involving a seemingly overwhelming compulsion, as, for example, when the Spirit clothed Himself with Gideon or the Holy Spirit caught away Philip and transplanted him to Azotus, those who can look back to such experiences as decisive turning-points or landmarks in the struggle against sin, the world and the devil will be the last to complain that the overriding of their human freedom has been an unwarrantable interference on the part of an unethical God. On the contrary, the reaction of the human to such movements of the Holy Spirit on its behalf is a hymn of praise and thanksgiving for mercies and blessings vouchsafed. 'He stooped in love to pull me out from the pit into which I had fallen. Praise his Holy Name.' This is our answer and we thank God that the 'Persons' of the Blessed Trinity are not two but three because of the richer fulness of spiritual experience which the third has made possible for us in the processes of redemptive grace.

Dr. Kirk would suggest to us that whilst we cannot associate this type of action exclusively with the name of the Spirit, we have nevertheless here the *differentia* of the Spirit's approach to man. The fact then of 'possession', by its very differentiation from the fact of 'Communion', points as clearly to the Divine personality of the Spirit, as the experience of Communion endorses the truth of the Divine personality of the Son.

A careful analysis, then, of the content of the Christian experience of God in Christ Jesus points us to an eternal threefold distinction in the Godhead itself corresponding to and accounting for the three relationships in which man finds himself linked to God: as a creature to his Creator; as a son to his heavenly Father; as the object of a Divine pursuit to One whose love will not let him go.

Beyond these implications from our religious experience we cannot go in our efforts to fathom the mystery of the Trinity in Unity and the Unity in Trinity. We cannot present an intellectually satisfactory formulation of the doctrine because in the last resort the doctrine eludes our finite rationalisation. It is a truth which, whilst not contrary to reason, is ultimately supra-rational. We need not then be ashamed to admit that our Christian doctrine of God ends in mystery. Clouds and darkness are round about Him.

Our intellectual framework is too circumscribed and narrow to embrace Him. Yet for our comfort we may remind ourselves that, after all, to understand Him is not the essential thing He requires of us. Rather He commands our allegiance and demands our worship. In worship we find the power to offer an allegiance of adoring hearts, and to our minds He imparts such glimpses of His Majesty as are sufficient to stimulate us to a never-ending quest after Truth with the promise that one day we shall wake up after His likeness and be satisfied with it.

IMMANENCE AND INCARNATION

Panentheism

Krause and Baader, who made use of the word, employed it to denote a synthesis of transcendence and immanence. God, they felt, was greater than all, yet all derived its entire dependence from Him. God is *over* us as well as *in* us.

Martineau: 'The Eternal is greater than all He has done'.

Panentheism maintains with Professor J. Royce that 'simple unity is a mere impossibility. God cannot be One except by being many. Nor can we various selves be many unless in Him we are One.' This, Royce says, is the deepest truth religion has been seeking to teach men.

Plotinus: 'No One is the source from which the differentiation of unity and plurality proceeds; it is the transcendence of separability rather than the negative of plurality'.

'When we call the Absolute One, we intend thereby only to exclude the notion of discerptibility.'

Lotze in the *Microcosmus* maintains that personality means mutual inclusiveness rather than mutual exclusiveness. God contains within Himself the conditions of His own existence. There is no non-Ego for Him, which is the mark of imperfect personality.

Perfect Egohood or selfhood can dispense with the antithesis of subject-object because it is the ground of both.

As regards Immanentism, the issue lies between a theocentive and an anthropocentive Christianity. *Panentheism* would, we think, maintain that Spirit is immanent, yet not *wholly* immanent in spirits, and for this reason each spirit is immanent in every other spirit. Spirit is all that Spirit is, but spirits are not all that they themselves are.

As regards Absolutism, (1) an Absolute Subject, (2) an Absolute Object, and (3) an Absolute Self-Consciousness, have all competed for the Lord of All. The most interesting, however, is the Absolute that transcends subject and object, and the duality implicit in consciousness.

Against (1) and (2) they are one-sided abstractions.

Against (3), what of creation, the problem of externality? Can there be anything external to an Absolute Self-Consciousness or an Absolute experience? Is not this *'the lion's den where all plurality disappears'*?

We have to steer between Individualism and Absolutism. Do these antitheses move within διάνοια and have they never attained synthesis of νοῦς?

The fate of the finite world and all things therein is not absorption into blank unity, it may be glorification.

Otherwise expressed, the Absolute may be the *truth*, the reality, the Alpha and Omega, of the Many.

To presuppose that the ultimate nature of the Many is *known* is the fundamental error:

The question to ask is *not*: 'Are the Many ultimate?' but 'What is the *nature* of the Many?'

Not, again, 'Is the One ultimate?' but 'What is the *nature* of the One?'

Lift the problem into the realm of *Spirit*, personal ethical relationship. Not parts in relation to a whole.

> Some little talk awhile of Me and Thee,
> There was, and then no more of Thee and Me.

Against this note (i) that the truth of spirits is not to be impervious substances but to be interpenetrable without losing identity; (ii) Uniqueness forbids identity, which incidentally is but a *logical* category, whilst it is perfected in union.

Immanence :

1. To enquire after the final cause of a thing's being, is to enquire after the mode and manner of God's immanence in that thing.

2. Immanence is not transcendence, yet it is the transcendent that is immanent.

3. Martineau thought that man transcends God because of his free will, yet we must speak of degrees of immanence.

4. A confusion may easily arise if God's relation to moral beings is misapprehended.

   'God is all man is, as well as all he is ever likely to become.' The fact of being able to violate His laws and profane His Blessedness, so far from being a mark of the possibility of transcending the Transcendent, is rather a sign of the possibility of falling short of His immanence. In what sense can a being enter a life here or hereafter, whose alpha and omega are embraced in God — in what sense can he *transcend* Him? *Some* species of immanence annul freedom, but immanence is not incompatible with moral beings. Is *ethical* immanence an impossibility, or is God less present and active when a greater likeness is manifested to Himself than when a lesser one is so? It would appear that, on the contrary, He is *more* immanent in moral beings than in nature, because He has lent them a greater portion of His nature, for this is the mark of greater immanence. Existence for self is a truer and more real existence than existence for another, because self-consciousness is a type of being more akin to God's own life than unconsciousness; but there is an existence for another within existence for self, or self-consciousness, and this is a higher mode of reality than self-centredness, because the egocentric predicament has been overcome. Again, self-consciousness spells a greater degree of Divine immanence than does unconsciousness. No doubt free-will with all its attendant risks is involved in existence-for-self, but this rather indicates a greater capacity for God than an exclusion of Him.

Never is the moral being, the finite spirit, so free as when it is under absolute necessity. Hegel was right: 'the truth of necessity is freedom'. It is only when God is completely working within, only when He is immanent to the fullest capacity of the human spirit, only when receptivity is perfect, that existence-for-self and existence-for-other mutually complement and fulfil each other.

5. The study of Nature in all her moods, as well as the study of man, convinces us that God dwells within things and persons in different degrees of intensity. The immanence of God, in a most real sense, not only alters but *constitutes* the being of everything. He is the ground, the source of all actuality, to Him in the end must everything render an account.

6. Ethical immanence involves a condition before realisation is in any way thinkable; it has to be acquired and cannot be thrust upon us. Receptivity of the good demands the primary condition of being fit for its reception. Our personality is always respected, and not overridden. God's most precious gifts, gifts that are embalmed in the spirit of the Giver, are conditional, never conditioned; grace is conditional on faith, revelation on receptivity, Love on love.

Ethical immanence is potential rather than actual, in prophecy rather than in fulfilment, a goal to be reached rather than a privilege already realised. We are not episodes in an experience greater than ourselves. God is *not* the soul's experience of *itself*.

7. God is *in* all things, not taking up a temporary abode. He is the *ground* of all the finite.

His immanence constitutes the thing being what it is. 'Created Being, of whatever status, owes its Being to God's all-present and all-powerful activity. Dependence of the finite is consequential upon this central and ontological relationship; any independence things may have — and they have it in varying degrees — is due to their participation in the Absolute Independence of the Supreme, the Unconditional One. Only through absolute dependence comes independence, only through the recognition of and reliance upon God's immanence within them, can all things, each according to its respective measure, grow up to the fulness of Him that filleth all in all.'[1]

8. Immanence admits of degrees; Incarnation admits of none.

'In the conception of Incarnation, as understood by Christian thought, we are presented with a final, supreme and absolute revelation of God to man. Henceforth the evolution of the spiritual consciousness is *within* and *up* to Christ, the Incarnate Logos; not that both He and us are subject to the same laws of evolution *up* to God.'

'The substitution of universal for particular Incarnation, so far from being a profounder and truer view of God's relation to creation, as Hegel thought that it was, is, in fact, the destruction of the significance of the Incarnation of the Logos altogether.'

Incarnation can only take place in *One* individual *once*, for it is an eternal *act* of an eternal Being. The *individual*, then, is the crown and coping-stone of Evolution.

'It is in *Spirit as such* which has concreted itself, but which is, for all that, essentially *spirit*, that is in *personality*, that divine immanence reaches its goal; for immanence is but the prophecy and promise of personality; it is personality making itself remain indirectly by way of influence, suggestion and premonition.'[2]

9. Man's recognition of transcendent reality is primarily due to his moral and spiritual nature. Revelation alone enables him to apprehend God as transcendent, while the immanence of the Divine within renders him

---

[1] H. G. Holmes, *The Presence of God*, p. 108 ff.
[2] Op. cit. pp. 112-13.

capable of receiving the revelation. Since all breach of continuity between the transcendent and immanent reality is impossible and contrary to all known laws of God's working in the world, the revelation of the transcendent shall intensify and transform the whole sphere of the immanent presence of the Divine life in creation.

'God is immanent in spirits by His creative power, for in Him by His Will and thought they physically live and move and have their being; He is transcendent in them only as they surrender themselves to the epiphany of His holiness. The human spirit has no other end than to be the home of the Divine, as the branch of the vine has no other end than to be filled with the life of the tree. Just in so far as man surrenders himself to the indwelling life of God, does the transcendent become immanent with him; just in so far as he puts on the likeness of the Divine nature is he the epiphany of His character, the agent of His service, the sufferer of His pain, and the sanctuary of His rest.[1]

10. Incarnation is the climax of immanence as God is revealed as self-imparting; by His immanent Presence He is still separated as regards *His Person* from us, but in Incarnation He perfectly assumes human nature. The difference is in reality enormous between God as immanent and as Incarnate.

In the former case He is inferentially obtained rather than experienced as such. God as Incarnate is an experience. Immanence partakes more of a philosophical theory, Incarnation of an experienced Presence.

[1] Op. cit. pp. 130-1.

CHAPTER 2

PATRIPASSIANISM [1]

WE propose in this article (1) to survey the Patripassian heresy in its origin, historical setting, and in its earlier and later forms; (2) to call attention to two great truths suggested by it to which it bears an imperfect and distorted witness, viz. (*a*) the fact that in Christ was revealed the inmost essence of God, His nature and character, (*b*) the fact of the Passibility of the Father, as revealed by the Love of God in Christ Jesus; (3) to show the significance of these two truths in the interpretation of the Incarnation and Work of Christ.

I

√The problem of the Trinity centres in the question how to reconcile the Divinity of Christ with the Unity of God. If we consider this problem from the historical standpoint, two erroneous solutions presented themselves for the Church's consideration towards the close of the second century. The one we connect with the names of Theodotus, Artemon and Paul of Samosata; the other with Praxeas, Noetus and Sabellius. In tendency the one is Unitarian, the other Pantheistic. Both will be found treated at length in the histories of Christian doctrine.[2]

Ebionitical Monarchianism (to adopt Dorner's classification) sought to solve the problem by attacking the full Divinity of Christ; Patripassian Monarchianism by seeking to obliterate the distinctions between the Three Persons of the Blessed Trinity. The strength of Monarchianism, in both its forms, lay in its insistence upon the Unity of God, which, it was felt, must be preserved at all costs. If the

---

[1] Originally published in *Church Quarterly Review*, July 1917.
[2] See, e.g., Dorner, *Person of Christ*, Div. I, ii, cc. 2 and 3.

acceptance of the full Divinity of Christ seemed to endanger this principle — and consequently to involve the Church in tritheism — then, in the interests of the 'Monarchy' thus threatened, either the Divinity of Christ must be in some sense 'reduced', or His Personality, as distinct from the Father, obliterated. Even though, on the one hand, the Divinity of Christ was not actually denied, yet it must be so interpreted as to be consistent with the fundamental tenet of Judaism, — 'Hear, O Israel, the Lord our God is one Jehovah'. If Christ were a mere man whom God raised to the Divine status, the Unity of the Godhead was not imperilled by that act. Hence it was possible to ascribe to Jesus a true humanity, even a supernatural birth and sinlessness, but, in the last resort, His was a conferred Divinity, a gift received from God, and not His own by right in virtue of His eternal identity of essence with the Father. Hence this type of Monarchianism struck at a foundation principle of Christianity. The truth that in Christ the inmost essence of God had been revealed could not be safeguarded by anything less than the uncompromising assertion of a later age that Jesus Christ was 'of one substance with the Father as touching His Godhead'. The Ebionitical Monarchians could not accept this truth because of its seeming inconsistency with their conception of the Unity of God. On the other hand, the recognition of it by the Patripassian Monarchians led them to seek a way of escape along other lines. ✓ If the Ebionites secured the Unity of God at the expense of the full Divinity of Christ, the Patripassians so pressed the identity of Christ with God as to secure the unity of the Godhead at the expense of the Personality of the Son.

Now it is this second type of Monarchianism as expounded more especially by Praxeas and Noetus on the one hand, and in a modified and more carefully safeguarded form by Zephyrinus and Callistus on the other hand, that we wish to examine somewhat more closely.

Tertullian is our chief source of information concerning Praxeas, and his treatise, *Adversus Praxean*, is the answer of the Western Church to Patripassian Monarchianism.[1]

From this source we gather that Praxeas had been imprisoned for the faith in Asia Minor and thus as a 'confessor' gained a ready hearing when he came to Rome and threw his influence into the scale against the Pope's inclination to deal leniently with the Montanists. The result of the advent of Praxeas was that the Pope, probably Victor, after having acknowledged the prophetic gifts of Montanus, Prisca and Maximilla, and after having bestowed his peace on the Churches of Asia and Phrygia, was compelled to withdraw the pacific letter he had issued and to desist from his acknowledgment of the said gifts. For this Tertullian cannot forgive him and remarks caustically that 'by this Praxeas did a twofold service for the devil at Rome; he put to flight the Paraclete, and he crucified the Father'. Praxeas then, according to Tertullian, was the first to introduce into Rome the new heresy; apparently he did not stay there for any length of time but departed for Carthage and there disseminated his views. He was denounced, however, probably by Tertullian himself, and renounced his error in a written document which Tertullian tells us was extant at the time he wrote his treatise against the heresy. Praxeas was silenced but the tares had been sown, and it was a recrudescence of the teaching in a more subtle form that led Tertullian to attack the heresy. When we read the work, we see that, although it is addressed against Praxeas, the teaching Tertullian refutes is the more developed system of Noetus and the more carefully safeguarded form of the teaching favoured by Zephyrinus and Callistus. We may therefore pass on to consider these later forms of Monarchianism.

Our knowledge of Noetus is mainly derived from the writings of Hippolytus, the bitter opponent of Callistus. Other particulars are furnished by Epiphanius and Theodoret. Of the writings of Hippolytus bearing on this question we have (*a*) an earlier extant fragment of a homily against

[1] Text in *Bibl. Pat. Eccles.* vi, pp. 247-91, ed. Leopold, Lipsiae, 1841. Translation in 'Ante-Nicene Library', xv, pp. 333-406.

the heresy of Noetus,[1] (*b*) the later treatment in Book IX of the *Refutation of All Heresies*.[2]

From these sources we gather that Noetus was by birth a native of Smyrna. He succeeded in winning over Epigonus and Cleomenes to his opinions, and by their means the heresy became disseminated in Rome at the time when Zephyrinus was administering the affairs of the Church. Hippolytus does not scruple to say that by means of bribes Zephyrinus was induced to connive at the propagation of the heresy and that he had Callistus as a fellow champion. The truth behind this statement probably lies in the fact that the Church leaders naturally welcomed at first teaching which seemed to aim at some reconciliation between orthodoxy and current philosophy, whilst at the same time vindicating so conclusively the Divinity of Christ against the Theodotians. Hippolytus, however, was emphatic in his opposition, and the active part which he apparently took in the affairs of the Roman Church at this time may account for the bad feeling between him and the bishops. If he charges them with heresy, his own orthodoxy was itself questionable. If he denounces their connivance at the teaching of Noetus and his followers, his own opposition to it laid him open to the charge of ditheism.[3] If he could not make the ignorant bishop, Zephyrinus, see the point at issue, and lost patience with his ignorance, this was no excuse for his later serious step in leaving the Church when Callistus became bishop and met his views so far as to condemn Sabellius. Undoubtedly Hippolytus was a theologian of weight; clearly also the episcopate then stood in need of learned men capable of distinguishing Catholic teaching from 'modernist' innovations put forward under the guise of a helpful reconciliation between orthodoxy and philosophy. True, too, that neither Zephyrinus nor Callistus had the requisite learning to enable them to appreciate the serious character of the new heresy by which the Church

---

[1] *C. Haeresim Noeti.* Text in Routh, *Opuscula*, i, pp. 49-80, with helpful annotations.

[2] Translations of these two are in the 'Ante-Nicene Library', ix, pp. 51-70; vi, pp. 328 ff. [3] *Ref.* ix, c. 6.

was threatened. But despair at the ignorance of bishops is no excuse for an act of schism, and if, instead of leaving the Church and abusing its leaders, Hippolytus had remained to teach them, his influence would have been far greater and his work, we may well believe, more fruitful.[1]

Turning now to a consideration of Hippolytus's treatment of the new heresy, we find that he has no hesitation in tracing back the errors of Noetus to the philosophy of Heraclitus, and chapters iii-v of Book IX of the *Refutation* are taken up with a brief survey of the Heraclitean philosophy from this point of view. We may quote the closing paragraphs of chapter v which contain the salient features of the Noetian system:

'Now it is evident to all that the silly successors of Noetus, and the champions of his heresy, even though they have not been hearers of the discourses of Heraclitus, nevertheless, at any rate when they adopt the opinions of Noetus, undisguisedly acknowledge these (Heraclitean) tenets. For they advance statements after this manner — that one and the same God is the Creator and Father of all things; and that when it pleased Him, He appeared (though, however, being invisible), to just men of old. For when He is not seen He is invisible, (but when He is seen He is visible); incomprehensible when He does not wish to be comprehended, but comprehensible when He is comprehended. Wherefore it is that, according to the same account, He is invincible and vincible, unbegotten and begotten, immortal and mortal. How shall not persons holding this description of opinions be proved to be disciples of Heraclitus? Did not (Heraclitus) the Obscure anticipate (Noetus) in framing a system of philosophy, (and conveyed, too) according to identical modes of expressions? Now, that (Noetus) affirms that the Son and Father are the same, no one is ignorant. But he makes his statement thus: "When indeed, then, the Father had not been born, He (yet) was justly styled

[1] See Duchesne, *Early History of the Church*, i, pp. 226-9.

Father; and when it pleased Him to undergo generation, having been begotten, He Himself became His own Son, not another's." For in this manner he thinks to establish the sovereignty (of God), alleging that Father and Son, (so) called, are one and the same (substance), not one individual produced from a different one, but Himself from Himself; and that He is styled by name Father and Son, according to vicissitude of times. But that He is one who has appeared (amongst us), both having submitted to generation from a virgin, and as a man having held converse among men. And, on account of the birth that had taken place, He confessed Himself to those beholding Him a Son, no doubt; yet He made no secret to those who could comprehend Him of His being a Father. That this person suffered by being fastened to the (accursed) tree, and that He commended His spirit unto (the keeping of) Himself, having died (to all appearance) and not being (in reality) dead. And He raised Himself up the third day, after having been interred in a sepulchre, and wounded with a spear, and perforated with nails. (Now) Cleomenes asserts, in common with his band (of followers), that this person is God and Father of the universe, (and thus) introduces among many (of his disciples) an obscurity (of thought) such as we find in the philosophy of Heraclitus.'

With this may be compared the summary which Hippolytus gives in Book X, chapter xxiii:

'Now (Noetus) asserts that there is one Father and God of the universe, and that He made all things, and was imperceptible to those that exist when He might (so) desire. (Noetus maintained that the Father) then appeared when He wishes; and He is invisible when He is not seen, but visible when He is seen. And (this heretic also alleges that the Father) is unbegotten when He is not generated, but begotten when He is born of a virgin; as also that He is not subject to suffering, and is immortal when He does not suffer or die. When, however, His passion came upon Him, (Noetus allows that the Father) suffers and dies. And (the Noetians) suppose that this Father Himself is called Son, (and vice versa) in reference to the events which at their own proper periods happen to them severally.'

The account given by Hippolytus in the fragment of a sermon 'against the Heresy of one Noetus' differs in no essential points from that given above in the *Refutation*, so far as the teaching of the heretic is concerned. We learn, however, of a Council of presbyters before whom Noetus was summoned and who examined him on the opinions attributed to him. When he was accused of teaching that 'Christ was the Father Himself, and that the Father Himself was born, and suffered, and died', he denied at first that he held such opinions. But later, when examined a second time, he boldly acknowledged that this represented his teaching. Accordingly he was expelled from the Church and thereupon founded a sect.[1]

We may note the following points:

(i) As regards the philosophical teaching which underlies the system of Noetus, the point of contact would seem to be the Heraclitean doctrine of the One and the Many. Thus Baur in his *Church History*[2] says:

'As Heraclitus regarded nature as the harmony of contraries, as the universal unity, in which, though in external appearance one thing ever stands opposed to another, all contraries are in fact removed, and raised into unity; as he is said to have laid down concerning the universe, that it is both subject to and exempt from destruction, that it is both originated and unoriginated, both mortal and immortal:—so Noetus is said to have

---

[1] The text of this *Concilium c. Noetum* as recorded by Hippolytus, and the corresponding account of the Verba Noeti in Epiphanius (*Haer.*, lvii), will be found conveniently in Routh, *Rel. Sac.* ii, pp. 372-5. The variations in the words attributed to Noetus before this Council are interesting. According to Hippolytus, he exclaimed in defence: τί οὖν κακὸν ποιῶ, δοξάζων τὸν Χριστόν; according to Epiphanius, his words were: τί γὰρ κακὸν πεποίηκα; ἕνα θεὸν δοξάζω, ἕνα ἐπίσταμαι, καὶ οὐκ ἄλλον πλὴν αὐτοῦ, γεννηθέντα, πεπονθότα, ἀποθανόντα.

[2] Vol. ii, pp. 94-5.

thought it not illogical to hold, that the same subject unites in itself opposite determinations, that as the Father it is invisible, unoriginated, immortal, but as the Son the opposite of all this, that God the Father and the Son is both the one and the other, when and how he will. Noetus based this assertion, apparently, on a conception of the world, according to which the one essence of God both goes forth into the ever-varying diverse multitude of phenomena, and out of it back again into himself. But the general view which underlay the teaching of Noetus, and perhaps that of Praxeas before him, is first presented plainly in the teaching of Sabellius.'

Baur works this out more in detail in a note which he concludes with the following suggestive passage:

'The distinguishing feature of the doctrine of Noetus, thus considered, would therefore be, that he predicated of the person of Jesus, regarded as a particular individual, that which was laid down by Heraclitus of the $\pi\hat{\alpha}\nu$, the whole of things, the world in general. While the doctrine thus worked out by Heraclitus, the unity of contraries, was quite defensible, Noetism only shows a phenomenon that often recurs in the history of Christology: viz. that when the universal has been substituted for the individual in the person of Jesus, this new subject is thought not to efface, but to maintain and include, his personality.'

(ii) This teaching appears at first sight to be a crude obliteration of the distinctions within the Godhead in the interests of an abstract deistic monotheism. As Hippolytus is not slow to point out, if one set of Scriptural passages clearly teaches the Divine Unity, another set of passages equally clearly indicates the number and dispositions of the Persons in the Trinity. Were the distinctions of Persons indicated by the words 'Father', 'Son' and 'Holy Spirit' to be regarded as merely nominal, as representing temporary modes or manifestations of the One God, or were they, on the other hand, to be taken as indicating eternal distinctions within the Godhead? This was the point at issue.

(iii) Moreover, if the Son were identical with the Father, it followed that the Father was born, suffered and died. Was the Logos none other than God, the Father, Himself revealed in time and space? Such seemed to be the drift of the teaching of Noetus and when challenged he did not deny it. 'I glorify the One God,' he cries, 'I know but One, it is no other than He who was born, who suffered, and who died!' Although the name 'Patripassians', therefore, was not of their own choosing, it can scarcely be said to have been unfairly applied to them by their opponents. If Patripassianism is an argument drawn from their premises by their opponents rather than a conclusion they themselves reached, it is none the less an inference from which they did not shrink, when it was brought home to them.

(iv) We can see, however, that in some sense Noetus did try to draw a distinction between the terms 'Father' and 'Son'. Adopting the Heraclitean tenets, he draws a distinction between the One God before and after the Incarnation. Noetus teaches that the 'Son' is the 'Father' revealed in time and space. The 'Father' is not in Himself the 'Son' apart from the Incarnation when He became so.

Noetus is feeling after some distinction within the one nature of God whereby it becomes possible to ascribe to Him at one and the same time impassibility and passibility; invisibility and visibility. This distinction he reaches in a roundabout way by emphasis upon the doctrine of the Divine Will. This plays an important part in the system of Noetus, and Dorner has rightly called special attention to it in his admirable summary from which we may quote the following helpful passage:

'Everything finite, all change and suffering, affects God solely through the medium of His will; which, if it continues the same and is in itself absolute (for example, as the will of love), is a sufficient guarantee of the unchangeableness of the divine being. To be invisible, ungenerated, and impassible, belongs, on the contrary, to the divine essence in itself; at the same time, however, in the

F 69

view of Noetus, this His essence cannot be a check on His will, but remains subject thereto, and on that account can be made passible, mortal, and so forth. It would be interesting to ascertain Noetus' precise doctrine of redemption, in order to see whether his conception of this will of God, on which he lays such great stress, as opposed to the divine nature, or to the physical categories of the idea of God, is an ethical one; or whether he regarded it as mere unconditioned, perfect power, which, being destitute of determinations in itself, is not raised above caprice. All that we certainly know, however, is that, in the view of Noetus, the eternal God put Himself, by His will, into the condition of passibility and visibility; such is his estimate of the significance of the appearance of Christ.' [1]

(v) But, further, if Christ were the Father manifested in and to the world, the Invisible become visible, the Impassible become temporarily clothed in a passible body, the Infinite and Omnipotent become voluntarily subject to an earthly and finite condition of life, the question had still to be faced: what relation had such a Theophany to the many which had preceded it in pre-Christian times or which might quite conceivably follow it in time to come?

Wherein lay the distinction between the Incarnation and the Old Testament revelations of God to men? Noetus does not answer this question, nor does he, on the other hand, give any security in his system for the permanence of the Personality of the God-Man.

Let us now consider the teaching of Zephyrinus and Callistus.

It would appear from the account given of the teaching of Zephyrinus by Hippolytus that the former assumed a very cautious attitude in the controversy, and whilst declining to adopt the theological point of view of the latter, contented himself with stating the problem without solving it. He would not side with Hippolytus but at the same time he refused to adopt the crude language of Noetus. Hippolytus

---

[1] *Op. cit.* Div. I, ii, p. 27.

reports him as saying on the one hand, 'I know that there is One God, Jesus Christ; nor except Him do I know any other that is begotten and amenable to suffering'. By these words Zephyrinus seeks to define his own position as clearly not accepting the Ditheism of which he suspected Hippolytus. On the other hand, his words, 'The Father did not die, but the Son', equally clearly dissociate him from the Patripassians.

Hippolytus regards this attitude as evasive and deceitful, but the truth probably is that the bishop was attempting to take the *via media* and did not wish to commit himself either way in a controversy which he did not fully understand. Callistus, however, seems to have committed himself more definitely. The following is a sketch of his teaching as given by Hippolytus,[1] who claims that the Pope derived it from the Noetians:

'Callistus', he says, 'alleges that the Logos Himself is Son, and that Himself is Father; and that though denominated by a different title, yet that in reality He is one indivisible spirit. And he maintains that the Father is not one person and the Son another, but that they are one and the same; and that all things are full of the Divine Spirit, both those above and those below. And he affirms that the Spirit, which became incarnate in the Virgin's womb, is not different from the Father, but one and the same. And he adds, that this is what has been declared by the Saviour: "Believest thou not that I am in the Father, and the Father in me?" For that which is seen, which is man, he considers to be the Son; whereas the Spirit, which was contained in the Son, to be the Father. "For", says Callistus, "I will not profess belief in two Gods, Father and Son, but in one. For the Father, who subsisted in the Son Himself, after He had taken unto Himself our flesh, raised it to the nature of Deity, by bringing it into union with Himself, and made it one; so that Father and Son must be styled one God, and that

[1] *Ref.* ix, c. 7.

71

this Person, being one, cannot be two." And in this way Callistus contends that the Father suffered along with the Son; for he does not wish to assert that the Father suffered, and is one Person, being careful to avoid blasphemy against the Father. How careful he is! — a senseless and knavish fellow, who improvises blasphemies in every direction, only that he may not seem to speak in violation of the truth, and is not abashed at being at one time betrayed into the tenet of Sabellius, whereas at another into the doctrine of Theodotus.'

Tertullian deals with this more refined and developed form of Patripassian Monarchianism, although he does not mention the name of Callistus in connection with it.[1] It is quite clearly a modified form of the teaching put forward as a compromise in order to avoid the obvious objections which Hippolytus, Tertullian and others had urged with such force against the earlier language of Praxeas and Noetus.

(1) Thus with regard to the question of the identity of the Father and the Son, an endeavour is made to avoid so crude a statement by drawing a distinction between the two natures in the Person of Christ. The term 'Son' is regarded as expressing the human nature, the flesh; the term 'Father' as expressing the Divine nature, the Spirit. The name 'Jesus' stands for the former; the name 'Christ' for the latter. The identity of 'Father' and 'Son' is found in the Divine nature as distinguished from the human nature in the one Person of Jesus Christ. Hence it becomes possible to avoid speaking of Jesus as the same as the Father. Scripture was so obviously against such a crude expression, and hence it is sought to avoid it in this way.

(2) But further, with regard to the question whether the Father may be said to have been crucified, an endeavour again is made to avoid language so open to ridicule. It is contended that in the one Person of Jesus Christ, the Divine nature did not suffer. It was the flesh, the human nature,

---

[1] *Adv. Prax.* cc. 27 and 29.

which bore pain and was crucified. The Divine can only be said to have suffered with it indirectly in virtue of the fact that it was united with that which suffered. The God-Man did not die after the Divine nature but only after the human nature. And further, therefore, just as the Divine in the Person of Jesus Christ shares indirectly in the suffering of the human, so also inasmuch as the Divine, the Spirit, was identical with the Father, He also can be said to have suffered in and with the human, the flesh, the Son. (*Si filius quidem patitur, pater vero compatitur.*) Such suffering is by way of compassion, in virtue of association. The Son, the flesh, the human nature, suffers directly; the Father, the Spirit, the Divine nature, suffers indirectly.

Tertullian will have none of this involved reasoning. 'For what is the meaning of "fellow-suffering" but the endurance of suffering along with another?' he writes. 'Now if the Father is incapable of suffering, He is incapable of suffering in company with another; otherwise, if He can suffer with another, He is of course capable of suffering.' [1]

It will not escape notice that both parties alike are agreed that the Divine nature, the Godhead, as such, whether it be 'Father' and 'Son', as distinct, or both identified as one and the same, is incapable of suffering. The doctrine of the Impassibility of God is an agreed point between Tertullian and his opponents. The question is never disputed.

Tertullian goes on to face the question: How could the Son suffer, if the Father did not suffer with Him? The answer he gives is as follows:

'The Father is separate from the Son, though not from Him as God. For even if a river be soiled with mire and mud, although it flows from the fountain identical in nature with it, and is not separated from the fountain, yet the injury which affects the stream reaches not to the fountain; and although it is the water of the fountain which suffers down the stream, still, since it is not affected

---

[1] Quid est enim compati, quam cum alio pati ? Porro si impassibilis pater, utique et incompassibilis; aut si compassibilis, utique passabilis.

at the fountain, but only in the river, the fountain suffers nothing, but only the river which issues from the fountain. So likewise the Spirit of God (i.e. the Divine nature in general), whatever suffering it might be capable of in the Son, yet inasmuch as it could not suffer in the Father (the fountain of the Godhead), but only in the Son, it evidently could not have suffered, as the Father (that which was open to it to suffer in the Son). But it is enough for me that the Spirit of God suffered nothing as the Spirit of God, since all that It suffered It suffered in the Son. It was quite another matter for the Father to suffer with the Son in the flesh.'

This passage from Tertullian is very significant. It shows us how easily an undue emphasis upon the distinction between the Two Natures in the Person of Christ may lead to Docetism. If we judged Tertullian by a passage like this, his Christology cannot be said to do full justice to the intimate union of God and Man consummated in the Incarnation. He so presses the distinction between the Impassible Logos and the passible human nature He assumes, that the former, he would have us believe, remained untouched and unchanged by the suffering and death upon the Cross which the God-Man experienced. We have only to read the twenty-seventh chapter of his treatise against Praxeas to see to what extent Tertullian was prepared to press the distinction of the Two Natures, without confusion, in the one Person of Christ. So fearful is he of any such 'transfiguration' of the Divine into the human as the result of the Incarnation, that he leaves the former quite unaltered and unaffected by the vicissitudes of the earthly life and the human experiences of Jesus. His language suggests rather the indwelling of the Logos in a human body than the advent of the Divine into the stream of human life in a manner and to a degree never before witnessed and never since consummated. Consider, for example, the following passage where he is answering the question: How the Word became flesh — whether it was by having been transfigured, as it

were in the flesh, or by having really clothed Himself in
flesh ?

'Certainly', he says, 'it was by a real clothing of
Himself in flesh. For the rest, we must needs believe God
to be unchangeable, and incapable of form, as being
eternal. But transfiguration is the destruction of that
which previously existed. For whatsoever is transfigured
into some other thing ceases to be that which it had been,
and begins to be that which it previously was not. God,
however, neither ceases to be what He was, nor can He
be any other thing than what He is. The Word is God,
and "the Word of the Lord remaineth for ever", — even
by holding on unchangeably in His own proper form.
Now, if He admits not of being transfigured, it must
follow that He be understood in this sense to have become
flesh, when He comes to be in the flesh, and is manifested,
and is seen, and is handled by means of the flesh; since
all the other points likewise require to be thus understood.
For if the Word became flesh by a transfiguration and
change of substance, it follows at once that Jesus must be a
substance compounded of two substances — of flesh and
spirit, a kind of mixture, like *electrum*, composed of gold
and silver; and it begins to be neither gold (that is to
say, spirit) nor silver (that is to say, flesh) — the one
being changed by the other, and a third substance produced. Jesus, therefore, cannot at this rate be God, for
He has ceased to be the Word, which was made flesh;
nor can He be Man incarnate, for He is not properly
flesh, and it was flesh which the Word became. Being
compounded, therefore, of both, He actually is neither;
He is rather some third substance, very different from
either.

'But the truth is, we find that He is expressly set forth
as both God and Man; the very psalm which we have
quoted intimating (of the flesh) that "God became Man
in the midst of it, He therefore established it by the will
of the Father", — certainly in all respects as the Son of

God and the Son of Man, being God and Man, differing no doubt according to each substance in its own especial property, inasmuch as the Word is nothing else but God, and the flesh nothing else but Man. . . .

'We remark here that the property of each nature is so wholly preserved, that the Spirit on the one hand did all things in Jesus suitable to Itself, such as miracles, and mighty deeds, and wonders; and the Flesh on the other hand exhibited the affections which belong to it. It was hungry under the devil's temptation, thirsty with the Samaritan woman, wept over Lazarus, was troubled even unto death, and at last actually died. If, however, it was only a *tertium quid*, some composite essence formed out of the two substances, like the *electrum*, there would be no distinct proofs apparent of either nature. But by a transfer of functions, the Spirit would have done things to be done by the Flesh, and the Flesh such as are effected by the Spirit; or else such things as are suited neither to the Flesh nor to the Spirit, but confusedly of some third character. Nay more, on this supposition, either the Word underwent death, or the flesh did not die, if so be the Word was converted into flesh; because either the flesh was immortal, or the Word was mortal. Forasmuch, however, as the two substances acted distinctly, each in its own character, there necessarily accrued to them severally their own operations, and their own issues.'

II

We have now completed our review of Patripassian Monarchianism. It is clear that the crude theology of Noetus and Praxeas never had a chance of taking permanent root in the Catholic creed. Nor, again, did the modified form of the teaching, as expressed in the carefully safe-guarded language of Zephyrinus and Callistus, commend itself to the Church. The compromise, as we have seen, struck at the root of the Monarchian principle, since the doctrine of the co-suffering of 'Father' and 'Son' admitted a distinction between them. Patripassian Monarchianism was thus rightly rejected and its adherents condemned.

But may we not learn something from it today? There are certain truths which suggest themselves as lying behind the two principles for which the Patripassians were condemned.

(1) Behind their crude identification of 'Father' and 'Son' is the Catholic teaching that in the Incarnation the essential Being and Character of God were revealed to men. Our Lord's words to St. Philip, 'He that hath seen Me hath seen the Father', express this truth, whilst safeguarding the distinction between the Father thus revealed and the Son who reveals Him. Jesus was not the Father Incarnate, but His revelation was none the less a revelation of the Father's nature and character. We do not need to seek outside Christ for a fresh revelation of God in His relationship towards mankind. Christ is the Father's revelation of Himself to this world. There may await us other and fuller revelation in other worlds, but what we have received is sufficient if only we will grasp it. This we may do under the guidance of His Spirit in fuller measure as the years go on. Do we do full justice to this truth when we endeavour to bring home to the minds and hearts of people all that is meant by the fact of the Incarnation?

(2) Behind the charge of 'Patripassianism', brought against the new teaching by its opponents, lies another great truth to which but scant justice was done. Tertullian, no doubt, scores a point when he nicknames these men 'Patripassians', but he himself fails to grasp in any sense the great truth suggested by the name, especially in that form of the teaching which we connect with the compromise offered by Callistus — the doctrine of the co-suffering of the Father in and with the Son.

In reading the history of early Christian doctrine we cannot fail to be struck with the remarkable reluctance on the part of Church teachers to ascribe anything so positive as feeling, still less sympathy and suffering, to God. They clung to the doctrine of the Impassibility of the Godhead with a tenacity which cannot but astonish us who study it in the light of the Incarnation.

For, at bottom, what is the philosophical principle which underlies this refusal to number 'Passibility' amongst the attributes of God? It is purely Platonic. It is an ante-Christian conception. It is closely and intimately bound up with that rigid deistic Monotheism which received its death-blow by the fact of the Incarnation. And yet, in spite of the new revelation of the Nature of God which the world received when He became Man, we find Church teachers still so bound by ante-Christian philosophical pre-conceptions as to the Nature of God, that they fail grievously to do justice to the fuller light upon that Nature which was shed by the revelation in time and space of God Himself in the flesh.

It will suffice to take but a single example of the kind of teaching concerning the Nature of God which was prevalent in the constructive period of Christian doctrine, when the Church's Christology was being worked out and developed in opposition to heresy. Look, for example, at Theodoret's *Demonstrations by Syllogisms*. The three theses he is concerned to prove are: (1) that God the Word is immutable; (2) that the union of the Two Natures was without confusion; (3) that the Divinity of the Saviour is impassible. Now the whole argument in Theodoret's treatment of these three points hinges upon one premiss, viz. the Immutability and Impassibility of God. We may quote the following sentences from the third thesis:

(1) 'Alike by the divine Scripture and by the holy Fathers assembled at Nicaea we have been taught to confess that the Son is of one substance with God the Father. The impassibility of the Father is also taught by the nature and proclaimed by the divine Scripture. We shall then further confess the Son to be impassible, for this definition is enforced by the identity of substance. Whenever then we hear the divine Scripture proclaiming the cross and the death of the Master Christ we attribute the

passion to the flesh, for in no wise is the Godhead, being by nature impassible, capable of suffering.'

(2) 'All things that the Father hath are Mine,' says the Master Christ, 'and one out of all is impassibility. If therefore as God He is impassible, He suffered as man. For the divine nature does not undergo suffering.'

(3) 'If Christ is both God and man, as the divine Scripture teaches and the illustrious Fathers persistently preached, then He suffered as man, but as God remained impassible.'

Fortunately the doctrine of the impassibility of God is not one by which we are bound today. It is true that the phrase did find a place in creeds, e.g. in the 'Symbolum Ecclesiae Aquileiensis' — 'Credo in Deo Patre, omnipotenti, invisibili et impassibili'; [1] and later, in a creed drawn up by the council of Sirmium in 357, it is stated that 'the Father has not a beginning, is invisible, is immortal, is impassible'. But in spite of the widespread acceptance on the part of Catholics and heretics of this doctrine, it has never found a permanent place in the Christian Creed and we are not bound to accept it today.

On the contrary, modern theology can find a large place for the teaching of its exact opposite, in the exposition of the great central facts of the Incarnation and Atonement viewed *sub specie aeternitatis*. There are many indications that the doctrine of the Suffering God is going to play a very prominent part in the theology of the age in which we live. It has much to commend it to our careful consideration. It throws a wonderful light upon the significance of the Cross and Passion of Jesus Christ as a revelation in time and space of an eternal fact.

To indicate the place which this doctrine may play in the Christian conception of God we have only to take, for example, a book like Dr. W. N. Clarke's *Christian Doctrine of God*, and to study his treatment of the question as to whether God can suffer.

[1] *Vide* Routh, *Rel. Sac.* i, 329-34.

Consider the depth of meaning suggested by the following passages:

'On abstract grounds it has been doubted whether God can suffer. Even on such grounds the doubt is needless; but when we learn of Jesus we clearly see how God suffers because of sin. From Jesus we learn, too, that redemptive suffering is the highest bliss. If the object of one's love can be redeemed from evil only by his suffering for them, there would be no bliss for him except in suffering. Jesus would not have been happy if he had withheld himself from suffering in behalf of those whom he loved; and if we think of God as living in perfect bliss while he is not bearing in love the burdens of his sinful creatures, we are not thinking of the God and Father of Jesus Christ. His eternal bliss is not destroyed by his perpetual suffering for sin, for it is redemptive suffering, and it is as a Saviour that he is bearing it. Since there is sin, Saviourhood with all that it involves is essential to the joy of God.' [1]

'As Jesus was grieved by sin, which beat upon his purity in daily contact and continually prevented the satisfaction of his love, so is God grieved and pained by the sin of the world, which daily does despite to his love and offends his holiness. In his own grief, Jesus opens for us a living vision of the heart of God, and gives us more than a glimpse of the divine sorrow over sin, which is a perpetual reality. From Jesus we learn that God is always bearing the sin of the world in the pain that it gives him, and in the constant endeavour of seeking the lost which it entails; and Jesus is our evidence that God willingly bears the sin of the world, because of his perfect and persistent grace. For the joy that was set before him Jesus endured the Cross, despising shame (Hebrews xii, 2), and so does God. If he should cease to bear the sins of the world and endure the Cross, there could be no salvation; but God has in himself the perpetual fount of mercy, and is perpetually doing the work of redemptive

[1] P. 222.

holiness. Jesus is able to save unto the uttermost because God is willing to save unto the uttermost. This revelation does not merely concern some times and seasons. The heart of it is that what is manifested in Christ goes on eternally in God.' [1]

Now it is along these lines that we think that much light of a helpful character can be thrown on the interpretation of the Incarnation and Work of Christ. Whilst avoiding the crude language and defective theology of the Patripassians, we can none the less seek to do justice to the truths suggested to our minds by their thought. And we are in a better position today for doing so than were the theologians whose thought was trammelled by the doctrine of the Impassibility of God.

For what, after all, is the significance of the Incarnation?

(1) A revelation to the world of the inmost Essence and Nature of the invisible God. (2) And what is the central thing thus revealed? ✓That God is Love. (3) And if Love is the central constituent of His Being, then He is capable of suffering, since perfect love is perfect self-sacrifice. (4) The cause of His self-sacrifice is the sin of man; the motive which prompts Him to the act for our salvation is His infinite Love. 'For God so loved the world that He gave His only-begotten Son, to the end that all that believe in Him should not perish, but have everlasting life.'

✓In view of such a revelation we may dare to say that not God's Impassibility but His Passibility is the central truth of His inmost Nature revealed in the Calvary Sacrifice.

If we view the Incarnation and earthly life and work of Christ as a revelation in time and space of the eternal reality behind and hidden from the eyes of men, then we may say that the Calvary Sacrifice was, in a sense, a sacrament, an outward and visible sign of something invisible and eternal, of which the sign was meant to be the revelation and the warning to men.

At the foot of the Cross we learn what sin costs God. We

[1] P. 218.

look through the sacrifice of Christ to the suffering God revealed in Him. We are given an insight into the very heart of Love crucified. ✓We see that Calvary is but the concrete expression in time and space of a great reality, i.e. that God suffers because of man's sin. And He will cease to suffer only when we cease to sin. Our sins hurt God. Surely this thought brings home to us individually our relationship to the Cross of Christ. In the light of this truth we can no longer dissociate ourselves from the tragedy enacted twenty centuries ago in Judaea. If the earthly sufferings of Jesus in the far-away times are the outward and visible sign of an inward, spiritual, timeless truth, then it is taken out of its historical setting and brought into relationship with us today as an eternal reality. ✓If the suffering Saviour upon the Cross is a temporal manifestation of an eternal suffering God, we must ask: When did God begin to suffer? True, we may have learned the fact of His suffering for the first time when Calvary's Cross revealed it, but how long before this was it that God began to suffer?

The answer is: When man first sinned. God was in this sense crucified in the Garden of Eden and has borne the sin of the world in His Heart from that day to this. The world first learned of it when God revealed Himself in Judaea. His prophets had foreshadowed it before He came. The picture of the Suffering Servant prepared men's minds for it, but the truth for us today lies simply here. Christ showed us twenty centuries ago that God is suffering Now. He is being wounded now for our transgressions. He is being bruised today for our iniquities. The chastisement of our peace is upon Him now, and by His stripes we are healed. The sufferings of Jesus were in time and space a three hours' agony, but none the less they bear witness to a never-ending Agony in the Heart of God which has not yet ceased. This picture of a suffering God may at first sight revolt us. A theology which can press for its acceptance may fail to gain a hearing. It would be too dreadful a conception to have to carry with us into daily life, but if it is true — what is the practical application? He is suffering now. Why? Because we *continue* in sin. He will cease to suffer if and when we cease to sin. If we repent He will smile! Love rejoices in such suffering because it has redemptive value. The Christian conception of the Suffering God is of One who for the joy that is set before Him endures the Cross, despising shame. The suffering of such an One has its origin in Love and its issue in Joy. If there is joy in the presence of the angels of God over one sinner that repenteth, how much more in the heart of the Suffering God! Does not this thought bring the Cross of Christ very near to our lives here and now? It should make the tragedy of twenty centuries ago live as a present reality in our midst. If we were not responsible for hurting Christ then, if we took no part in the tragedy then enacted, if it happened long before we were born, nevertheless our iniquities today are re-enacting the same tragedy in the Suffering God who feels our sins now just as much as He felt them on the Cross or as He felt them before that in the transgressions of the long line of sinners from Adam onwards.

In a very real sense then we may speak of a crucified God, a Father-Heart of Mercy and Compassion pouring itself forth in a never-ending Sacrifice for the sins of men. Tertullian ridiculed the Patripassians because they crucified the Father. Has there been a single age in the history of the world which has not been responsible for doing this deed? The act, in this sense, was not confined to a handful of heretics, nor even to the Jews who crucified Jesus. Every age has had its sinners and every age has crucified God afresh. We, as the sons of Adam, are not in this age behind our fore-fathers in our eagerness to re-enact the Calvary tragedy in the heart of the All-Holy and All-loving Father of Mankind.

Let us, then, in conclusion, with these thoughts in mind, approach the consideration of the stupendous fact of the Incarnation and the record of the Work of Christ which He did 'according to the Scriptures'. We shall strive to realise vividly two great truths that revelation was meant to teach us, viz.: (1) that in Christ we behold God Himself in human form; (2) that in the Work of Christ we are to see the veil lifted, and through it we are meant to behold eternal truths concerning the Being and Nature of God both in Himself and in His relationship to the world.

III

Before the advent of Christ God had revealed Himself 'by diverse portions and in diverse manners', 'in many parts and in many modes', through human messengers, Hebrew prophets, Roman statesmen and Greek sages, through law, prophecy, history. Before the coming of Christ the world had not lacked men who claimed to speak in God's name and to have a message from Him to the people. The 'messengers' spoke of God's character as a God of Love, Righteousnes, Purity. Compare Psalm ciii, especially 8-14:

'The Lord is full of compassion and mercy; long-suffering and of great goodness. He will not always be chiding; neither keepeth He His anger for ever. He hath not dealt with us after our sins; nor rewarded us according to our wickednesses. For look how high the heaven is in comparison of the earth; so great is His mercy also toward them that fear Him. Look how wide also the east is from the west; so far hath He set our sins from us. Yea, like as a father pitieth his own children; even so is the Lord merciful unto them that fear Him. For He knoweth whereof we are made; He remembereth that we are but dust.'

But what proof had people that this was so? Such witness from prophets, such guess-work and inspired speculation of Greek thinkers, such conjecture from the course of history, lacked that absolute finality of proof which could only be given by the Advent, not of messengers, but of the King Himself. The absolute convincing proof of God's Love, God's Holiness, God's Forgiving Spirit would not be the hearsay evidence of human creatures but the King's own revelation of Himself, and a demonstration in His own

Person, in the world, before the eyes of men, of the height and depth, length and breadth, of His Love and His attitude towards sin and sinful men. Hence the tremendous significance of the Incarnation from this standpoint. It was a Revelation not through messengers but through the coming of the Son Himself . . . the advent into the stream of human life of One who alone could give an authentic account of God because He was His Son. The finality and completeness of His Revelation is guaranteed by his Sonship. 'No man hath seen God at any time; the only-begotten Son, which is in the bosom of the Father, He hath declared Him' (St. John i, 18). Hence again the significance of what Christ did and said during His earthly life as giving to us a revelation and insight into the very Being and Nature of the Omnipotent and Almighty God.

The deeds and words of Jesus Christ on earth in His relationship with men were a revelation of the attitude of God Himself towards them.

Men heard the words of the Psalmist, beautiful words and full of hope for conscience-stricken sinners, but they wanted something more than an assurance in words. They wanted to see with their eyes, to hear with their ears from the lips of God Himself. So in the fulness of time 'for us men and for our salvation He came down from heaven and was incarnate by the Holy Ghost of the Virgin Mary and was made Man'.

How was He to reveal Himself to men? How was He to make His Presence known to them? He took a human body. If He had come down to earth as a disembodied Spirit, could men have seen Him? We cannot see the spirit of man. We only know our fellow-men so far as they reveal themselves to us in and through their human bodies which are the vehicles of their self-manifestation. So God's Son, that He might be seen and revealed within the limitations of time and space and under the conditions of our normal human existence, had to take a material body as His organ and the instrument of His self-revelation. He took a human body. The words are not a full statement of all that is involved in the thought of the Logos assuming flesh, but they are true so far as they go. Later heretics erred in failing to grasp that St. John's statement — 'The Word became flesh and tabernacled among us' — implied a far more intimate union of the Logos with our human nature than was suggested by His taking a human body only. The Nicene council guarded against this when they laid it down that He dwelt among men as man, i.e. He lived as man among men and assumed not merely a human body but man's whole nature, including a human soul. This was later the chief point of Gregory of Nazianzum against Apollinaris. If Christ assumed not human nature in its completeness 'what was not assumed was not redeemed'. But for simplicity's sake let us dwell upon the thought of the Pre-existent Divine Son of God issuing forth from Eternity into our little world and revealing Himself to men by means of the human body He had assumed and which had been fashioned for Him by the Holy Ghost in the womb of the Virgin Mary. He had come to seek and to save that which was lost. He had come to reveal and to redeem. How was He to reveal Himself? He took a Body as His vehicle of manifestation, as His medium of self-expression, the instrument through which He could come into touch with the multitudes, whose pitiable state as sheep without a shepherd had moved His Divine Heart to compassion as He surveyed them from the throne on high. The Incarnation was thus the result of a movement of Divine Compassion in the very Heart of God, an impulse of a boundless Love to stoop down, no matter what the cost, in order to reveal Himself to men and to save them. Thus it is that the Incarnation was 'God in man made manifest'.

Let us follow this thought out a little more in detail.

(1) How were men to learn that the Unseen God cares for the multitudes of sinful creatures whom He has created? If we read St. Matthew ix, 36, the answer is clear: 'When He saw the multitudes, He was moved with compassion for them. . . .' His human heart beat for them, His human love found expression in human emotion. Here was a

practical demonstration in the world of God's love for a particular crowd and proof positive of His universal love for all the multitudes, young and old, rich and poor, whom He beholds from Heaven and yearns over 'because they are distressed and scattered as sheep not having a shepherd'.

(2) How was He to prove that He is not indifferent to human suffering? 'And they brought unto Him all that were sick, holden with divers diseases and torments, possessed with devils, and epileptic, and palsied, and He healed them.' [1]

(3) How was He to prove that He sympathises with us in our sorrows and is not far away from the countless mourners in the hour of bereavement? [2] The angel of death had visited a home. Lazarus was dead. The heart-broken Mary and the sorrowing friends might well have wondered whether God cared. How was He to prove that in such moments, when all we hold dear is taken from us, He is no far-away, indifferent God, no unsympathetic stranger, standing afar off with eyes undimmed in the midst of all our sorrows? *Jesus wept.* And in those human tears He revealed through His human body that God weeps with us, that God cares for us in such moments. He it is who 'soothes our sorrows, heals our wounds, and drives away our fears'. 'The Jews therefore said, Behold how He loved him!'

(4) How was He to prove that God shares also our joys; that He is with us 'through all the changing scenes of life', interested in the every detail of our daily existence? Consider such passages as St. John ii, 1-11, the marriage in Cana of Galilee; St. Mark ii, 14-17, Jesus at meat in Matthew's house.

(5) How was He to prove that 'He knoweth whereof we are made; He remembereth that we are but dust'? How was He to give to us the assurance that He knows the strength of the temptations which beset us as human beings; that He can sympathise with us in all our human experiences; and that He understands our human nature through

[1] St. Matthew iv, 24.   [2] St. John xi, 35.

and through? The answer is His Incarnate Life, the fact that He has lived upon this earth; all that is involved in the Gospel narratives of His Life in the days of His flesh.

(6) How was He to prove that His prophet had spoken the truth when he said, 'To the Lord our God belong mercies and forgivenesses, though we have rebelled against Him'? and 'Though your sins be as scarlet they shall be as white as snow; though they be as red as crimson they shall be as wool'? The answer is our Lord's attitude towards sinners while He was on earth. Consider this passage: 'And there cometh to Him a leper, beseeching Him, and kneeling down to Him, and saying unto Him, If Thou wilt, Thou canst make me clean. And being moved with compassion, He stretched forth His hand, and touched him, and saith unto him, I will; be thou made clean.' [1]

That which the multitude would not touch for fear of defilement, him from whom all men shrank in horror and disgust, the Lord touched, and by His touch healed. He used His human finger as the channel through which He could reach the sinner. He, the Pure and Spotless, touched the unclean thing. So He proved God's attitude towards the sin and the sinner.[2]

(7) How was He to demonstrate conclusively to a callous world the awful character of sin? How was He to reveal what He thought about it? How was He to reveal its consequences for Him and what it costs Him? How was He to demonstrate that because of His very Love for sinners their sins hurt Him, their transgressions cut into His very Heart? How was He to convince the world that the measure of His suffering because of man's sin is the measure of His Love for sinners, and the measure of His Love is the measure of His suffering? The answer is the Calvary Sacrifice of Jesus.

That was and is the demonstration of (*a*) His infinite Love, (*b*) what He suffers when we sin, (*c*) what our sins

[1] St. Mark i, 40.
[2] Compare also St. John viii, 3-11: 'Neither do I condemn thee; go thy way; from henceforth sin no more'.

cost Him, (*d*) what He is prepared to do and to suffer in order to save us.

'For God so loved the world that He gave His only-begotten Son; to the end that all that believe in Him should not perish but have everlasting life.'

What was the proof? 'Greater love hath no man than this; that a man lay down his life for his friends.'

What men could not believe when told by prophets they are constrained to accept by the fact of the Cross and God Incarnate suffering there upon it, the innocent for the guilty, the pure for the impure, the loving One for the unloving, the unlovable and the unloved.

This was the supreme manifestation of the very Heart of God. Men beholding Jesus in His work which He did and in His Life which He lived, and in His words which He spake, beheld God Himself in act and word and deed, God in human form, God living a human life, God walking in the streets of Jerusalem or teaching on the shores of the Lake of Galilee. 'He that hath seen Me hath seen the Father.' This, and nothing less than this, is involved in the fact of the Incarnation.

Allow the mind to dwell upon it! Think what it means! If we do this we shall be at the right standpoint for a study of the efforts made to interpret the fact!

The moment we begin to reflect seriously upon what is involved in such a stupendous assertion as the Incarnation . . . 'God in man made manifest', God seen, talked to, touched, by men . . . questions of vital importance are at once raised.

The starting-point for any discussion of these questions must, however, be an endeavour to let the significance of St. John's words sink deeper into our minds.

'That which was from the beginning, that which we have heard, that which we have seen with our eyes, that which we beheld, and our hands handled, concerning the Word of Life . . . that which we have seen and heard declare we unto you also. . . .'

These are the words of one who claims to have seen, talked with and touched God Incarnate!

No better preparation therefore for a study of the interpretation of this Fact can be found than an endeavour to appreciate the Fact itself and what it implies.

> The very God! think, Abib; dost thou think?
> So the All-Great, were the All-Loving too —
> So, through the thunder comes a human voice
> Saying, 'O heart I made, a heart beats here!
> Face, my hands fashioned, see it in myself!
> Thou hast no power nor mayst conceive of mine,
> But love I gave thee, with Myself to love,
> And thou must love Me who have died for thee!'
> The madman saith He said so: it is strange!

✓ This, then, is the way in which we should propose to interpret the Incarnation and Work of Christ. We venture to suggest that by so doing we approach the study of the Gospel narratives with a key which proves wonderfully helpful in unlocking the treasures still to be won by those who will approach in simple faith and seek to interpret the acts and words and deeds of Jesus in terms of the eternal truths they are meant to teach and of which they are the signs and symbols. They show forth the Invisible God, His Being and Character, in His relationship to the world He has made, and to mankind He has redeemed. They are a sacrament, and men can look through them to the reality they disclose. In Christ Jesus the veil which conceals the Invisible God is lifted, and we behold Him. Through the Visible, the Incarnate, is revealed the Invisible, the Father. In the face of Jesus, is seen the Glory of God.

We should propose to place over these Gospel narratives of the Incarnation and Work of Christ in the days of His flesh, St. Paul's words: 'The things that are seen are temporal; the things that are not seen are eternal'. We should bid men see in and through the temporal life of Jesus, the manifestation of the eternal God thus revealed.

Men had often longed to see what God was like. Men

to-day still wonder.   St. Philip's request still finds an echo in
our hearts: 'Lord, show us the Father, and it sufficeth us!'
The Incarnation and Work of Christ are still for us to-day
the answer to this request, and we are bidden to look through
Him to the God He reveals.

We may close this study with one question: Why was
it that when God did at last reveal Himself — when He
could be seen, touched, handled, when He actually walked
this earth and wandered in the streets of Jerusalem — why
was it that He appeared as A MAN OF SORROWS?

Christian Theology would answer this question by pointing to the Sin of the World which broke the heart of the
Crucified.

CHAPTER 3

NESTORIANISM

(a) NESTORIUS THE NESTORIAN [1]

THE intolerant and uncompromising attitude towards heretics which characterised the defenders of orthodoxy in the Early Church has in our own day, whether for good or evil, given place to a large-hearted tolerance, and, indeed, we have come to recognise that any advance in our grasp of Divine Truth is only reached through the conflict of contending opinions. Thus the part which heretics played in helping to elucidate the deposit of Faith committed to the guardianship of the Church was a necessary and most important element in the growth of Dogma and the development of Christian Doctrine. The result of the recognition of this truth has led to our adopting a far more humane and generous attitude towards the advocates of heresy both past and present, and we find ourselves to-day in the midst of a reaction which has set in for some time past, in favour of those condemned from time to time by the Councils of the Church.

Nestorius especially has not lacked sympathisers from Luther onwards, and in modern times we have come to recognise that however just was the condemnation passed upon him by the Council of Ephesus in A.D. 431 because of his heretical tendencies, yet at the same time the proceedings of that Council are open to grave censure, and, moreover, a contrast between the characters of Cyril and his opponent is by no means favourable to the former.

But there have not been wanting scholars in our own day who have gone even further than this in their attempts to whitewash Nestorius, and the climax perhaps of this re-

[1] This article appeared in the *Church Quarterly Review*, January 1912.

actionary tendency in favour of the famous heretic of Eupreprius has been reached by the Lady Margaret Professor of Divinity at Cambridge in a book published in 1908 entitled *Nestorius and his Teaching*, a fresh examination of the evidence with special reference to the newly recovered 'Apology' of Nestorius. As the result of this fresh examination the startling conclusion is reached that Nestorius was not 'Nestorian'.

We propose to examine this thesis of Dr. Bethune-Baker and to put forward one or two considerations on the other side in answer to the question as to what extent we are justified in imputing 'Nestorianism' to Nestorius.

I

It may be helpful at the outset to give some account of the fresh material now available for a study of the teaching of Nestorius. We know from the statement of Gennadius that Nestorius wrote a great many treatises at the time when he was still a presbyter at Antioch and after he became Bishop of Constantinople he wrote a treatise on the Incarnation· Ebed Jesu the Nestorian (d. 1318) mentions the following works of Nestorius as extant in his day: *Liber tragoediae*; *Liber Heraclidis*; a letter to Cosman; a Liturgy; *Liber epistolarum* and *Liber homiliarum et orationum*. The Syriac translator of the *Liber Heraclidis* (to be mentioned later) in his preface mentions the following works of Nestorius — a work with the title 'Historica', and two others, the *Theopaschites* and the 'Tragedy'. The publication in 1905 of Dr. Loofs's *Nestoriana* is the first critical edition of the writings of Nestorius we have had since the days of Garnier in the seventeenth century. Dr. Loofs has brought together in a convenient form all the remains of the numerous writings to which Gennadius refers which have survived the general destruction to which the works of heretics were subject. The one very important exception which is not contained in Dr. Loofs's collection is the *Liber Heraclidis*, which came to light too late for insertion in his *Nestoriana* but with the contents of which he himself was acquainted. With the exception of the *Liber Heraclidis* we have no single work of Nestorius which has come down to us except in the form of extracts and quotations largely gathered from works and official documents drawn up by his opponents. Thus we have extracts and citations from the writings of Cyril of Alexandria, the Acts of the Council of Ephesus, the *Synodicon*, Marius Mercator and others. Dr. Loofs has discovered one very interesting sermon [1] which he attributes to Nestorius and which has been preserved in a volume of Sermons of St. Chrysostom. Extracts from other writings of Nestorius have also been recovered from Syriac MSS., and all that we have left of the works *Theopaschites* and 'Tragedy' (some few pages) will be found in Dr. Loofs's collection. We have also in a Latin translation of Marius Mercator the twelve counter-anathemas of Nestorius against Cyril and another twelve anathemas preserved in a Syriac translation. There are in all now extant fourteen letters or fragments of letters including two to Cyril, three to Celestine, Bishop of Rome, one to the Emperor Theodosius and one to John of Antioch. We have some sermons translated into Latin by Marius Mercator besides a great number of fragments of letters, etc., in Greek or Latin or Syriac. All these will be found in Loofs's *Nestoriana*,[2] and Dr. Bethune-Baker holds that these extant

[1] Dr. Haidacher made the same discovery independently of Dr. Loofs in 1905.

[2] The appendices to M. Nau's translation of the 'Book of Heracleides' contain further interesting matter, viz.: (i) A French translation of a letter written by Cosmas of Antioch dealing with the deposition and the miracles of Nestorius. This letter has already been edited and translated into German by M. Braun, who is of opinion that it ought in all probability to be identified with the 'Letter *to* Cosmas' mentioned as one of the works of Nestorius by the Nestorian Ebed Jesu, in which case it is not a letter written 'by' Nestorius but one 'about' him.

(ii) M. Nau also gives us the Greek text of three Sermons on the Temptations of our Lord which he thinks should be reckoned as genuine works of Nestorius but which have come down to us in a Syriac translation under the name of Chrysostom.

(iii) 'The Letter of Nestorius to the inhabitants of Constantinople' cited in part by Philoxenus the Jacobite bishop of Mabboug (A.D. 485–523) is extant in a Syriac translation as yet unedited, but M. Nau gives us a French translation. Readers of the 'Apology' will not be surprised to find Nestorius in this letter condemning 'Eutyches and his predecessors' and also the Nestorians (!) and Monophysites whilst he welcomes and claims as being identical with his own the teaching of Flavian and Leo. M. Bedjan adds as appendices to his writings, which are now available for a study of the teaching of Nestorius, are amply sufficient to justify the conclusion he himself has reached if investigated, as he says,

> 'without the personal *praejudicium* which is always fatal to a frank enquiry, and the unhistorical assumption that theological terms conveyed to all who used them at any given moment any more than at long intervals of time, one and the same fixed and definite sense'.

But we are not left to extant sermons and extracts from the lost writings of Nestorius for our knowledge of his teaching. Quite recently there has come to light in a Syriac MS. a work which the heretic is known to have written and which we now have edited for the first time by M. Paul Bedjan. The works of heretics were marked out for destruction, but this has survived partly no doubt to the fact that Nestorius issued it under a pseudonym, and the Syriac translator in his preface tells us why the book was published under the title of the 'Book' or 'Treatise' of Heracleides, the reason being that people might be persuaded to read it and be converted to the truth who would never look at it if they knew who was its author. A French translation based upon M. Bedjan's text has been made by M. F. Nau in collaboration with M. Bedjan and M. Brière.

The Syriac translator in his preface divides the 'Apology' of Nestorius into two books:

Book I, Part 1 deals with all the heresies against the Church and the differences with regard to the faith of the 318 Nicene Fathers.

Part 2. Nestorius's attack on Cyril. Here we have

edition of the 'Book of Heracleides' a Syriac version of the Canons of the Second Council of Constantinople on the 'Three Chapters' and also from Syriac MSS. in the British Museum the Twelve Anathemas of St. Cyril, his letter to Valerian of Iconium, a 'libellus' of Paul of Emesa to Cyril, the letter of John of Antioch to Cyril, and Cyril's letter to John, a letter of St. Athanasius to Epictetus of Corinth, 'libellus' of the bishops and presbyters of Armenia to Proclus of Constantinople, Proclus's letter to the bishops of Armenia and a fragment of Felix of Rome.

(*a*) the examination of the judges at the Council of Ephesus, (*b*) the charges of Cyril.

Part 3. Nestorius's 'Apology' and a comparison of their letters.

Book II, Part 1. An apology and refutation of the Charges for which he was excommunicated.

Part 2. The subsequent history from the time of his excommunication until the close of his life.

It will be seen, then, that we have in this 'Apology' of Nestorius an elaborate defence of his own position, and a vindication of his own orthodoxy as against his opponent Cyril, written whilst the heretic was in exile after his condemnation. In the first part of his work he reviews various heresies which have been opposed to the Church from time to time and an imaginary opponent is introduced (Sophronius), who voices the point of view and arguments in defence of the heresies which Nestorius himself combats in vigorous language. The discussion thus takes the form of a dialogue, and by this means Nestorius contrives to clear himself of any suspicion of harbouring Arian views or of agreeing with the errors of the Paulinians, Photinians and other heretical sects. He then passes on in the second part of the first book to an elaborate attack upon Cyril and the proceedings and decisions of the Council of Ephesus. Having the Acts of this Council before him, and passages from his own writings quoted against him, he comments upon these from his point of view and accuses Cyril of garbling his sayings and misrepresenting his meaning. He complains bitterly of the injustice of the whole proceedings and especially of the fact that the Council was held without the presence of John of Antioch and the Oriental bishops, and in spite of the absence of the Papal legates and the stern protests of the Emperor's representative, Count Candidian. In the opinion of Nestorius the Council was hopelessly biased against him and simply registered the opinion of Cyril and his followers. The Council was in fact Cyril. 'And so I was summoned by Cyril', he says, 'who assembled the synod, and by Cyril who was its head. Who is judge? Cyril. And who accuser? Cyril. Who is the Bishop of Rome? Cyril. Cyril was everything.'

Nestorius proceeds to elaborate his own defence and discusses the correspondence which passed between himself and Cyril. He discusses Cyril's letters at some length and challenges his appeal to the Nicene Council. He practically accuses his opponent of seeking to foist upon the Fathers his own erroneous views and of attempting to put these forward in their name when they themselves would have repudiated such teaching. Believing that Cyril taught that God the Word suffered, and that he was striving to support his Patripassian views by an unfair appeal to Scripture and the Nicene Fathers, Nestorius challenges him to substantiate if he can this teaching by any single quotation from either of these authorities. He compares his letters with Cyril's and refutes the accusations for which he was anathematised.

In the closing part of the work we have an interesting account of the course of events from the time of his excommunication until towards the close of his life. From this it appears that Nestorius lived on till possibly the opening of the Council of Chalcedon. He hailed with delight Leo's letter to Flavian (the famous 'Tome' of Leo) and regarded the latter's treatment at the 'Robber Synod' as precisely what would have happened to himself had he attended the earlier Council at Ephesus.

He examines the compromise effected between Cyril and the Easterns, the price of peace being the sacrifice of himself to the personal animosity of his rival and opponent Cyril. He claims that the opinions of Leo and Flavian are in entire accord with his own, and the fact that Leo condemned Eutyches he hails as a sign that the Church of Rome in the person of Leo has returned to that Catholic Faith which she had temporarily abandoned when in the person of Celestine she passed condemnation upon himself.[1]

The justification for his opposition to Cyril and his followers is, in his opinion, found in the fact that Eutyches,

[1] Nau, *op. cit.* p. 298.

97

a worthy disciple of Cyril, was finally condemned and thus the sole object of all his struggles was secured, namely 'that no one should call the Word of God a creature or the manhood which was assumed incomplete'.[1]

The teaching to which he was opposed all through was, in his opinion, derogatory to the Godhead, and such a confusion of the Two Natures in Christ as led to the deification of the humanity was simply 'to change the image of the incorruptible God for the image of corruptible man' and to mingle heathenism and Christianity in the false worship of an Arian demi-god.[2]

Such then in brief outline are the contents of this remarkable 'Apology' of Nestorius, and Dr. Bethune-Baker claims that it amply confirms the conclusion to which in his opinion a candid examination of the earlier writings of Nestorius as collected together by Dr. Loofs ought to lead us. Whilst we are asked to agree that the decision of the Council of Ephesus was absolutely right in the condemnation passed upon 'Nestorianism' as such, yet at the same time inasmuch as Nestorius, as judged from his own writings, was not 'Nestorian' he was unjustly condemned, and in fact in his own 'Defence' he explicitly says that if he had held the opinions attributed to him he ought justly to have been condemned. It is agreed that if Nestorius meant what the Council of Ephesus thought he meant, his condemnation

[1] Loofs, *op. cit.* p. 313: 'ne creaturam verbum deum quispiam dicat, ne humanitatem, quae suscepta est, imperfectam'.

[2] 'Ce que je dis plus haut, plus bas et toujours, c'est que je ne cherche pas à me faire aimer pas de tels hommes, mais je désire vivement que, par mon anathème, ils soient sauvés du blasphème, et que ceux qui seront sauvés confessent Dieu saint, puissant et immortel, sans changer la forme de Dieu, qui est incorruptible, contre la forme de l'homme qui se corrompt, et sans mêler le paganisme dans le christianisme, mais en confessant Dieu, tel que sa forme est, et en confessant l'homme, tel qu'il est dans sa forme, de manière que le passible et aussi l'immortel soient confessés des formes des natures; afin que le christianisme ne confesse pas un changement de Dieu ni un changement de l'homme, à la manière de l'impiété du paganisme. Qu'il soit donc en vérité oui oui et non non, sauveur et sauvé, de manière à confesser que le Christ est Dieu et homme en vérité et par nature, qu'il est par nature immortel et impassible en tant que Dieu, et mortel et passible par nature en tant qu'homme. Il n'est pas Dieu dans les deux natures ni encore homme dans les deux natures. Mon but et mon souci sont donc que Dieu soit béni et loué sur la terre comme dans le ciel.' (Nau, French translation, p. 323; cf. Bethune-Baker, pp. 197-8.)

was just, but the whole point of Dr. Bethune-Baker's argument is to prove that he did not mean what the Council thought he meant.

How far can it be said that Dr. Bethune-Baker has proved his point and to what extent are we justified still in saying, in view of all the evidence now at our disposal, that Nestorius was not 'Nestorian'?

II

That the discovery of this document — the 'Book of Heracleides' — throws a flood of new light upon the whole controversy need not be gainsaid. In some cases an entirely new complexion is put upon earlier suspicious sayings of Nestorius by his own explanations and comments in this later 'Apology'. For example, no saying perhaps of Nestorius gave greater offence to his opponents than the one recorded for us in Socrates [1] as having been used in conversation with Theodotus, Bishop of Ancyra, and quoted against him at the Council of Ephesus. When he was overheard by Theodotus to say that he 'could not call a child of two or three months old God', it was felt that he was tacitly denying the Son of Mary to be truly Divine. But in the 'Book of Heracleides' we have Nestorius's own version of the facts, and if this is accurate we are driven to assume that, in recording this saying, Socrates has reported what people believed Nestorius to have said, whereas what he himself claims to have said acquits him of any charge of seeking to deny the Godhead of Him who was born of the Virgin Mary. Nestorius's own version is too long to quote here, but the substance of it seems to be that he did not mean to say he could not call a babe God, but that he could not call God a babe. His aim apparently was, as Dr. Bethune-Baker shows, 'to safeguard the majesty on High from merely human experiences and attributes'. 'He intended to deny that God Himself could in His own being (in His essence,

[1] *H.E.* vii, 34.

99

substance, *ousia* — whatever it is that makes God, God) submit to a human birth and become a babe.'

In examining this explanation and others to be found in the 'Apology' of Nestorius, the suspicion must cross our minds as to how far he is guilty of a subtle perversion of the facts after the lapse of time following his excommunication and exile had enabled him to reflect more fully upon the true signification of words which he had allowed himself to utter rashly and hastily in a fit of temper without perhaps fully realising at the time all that he himself meant by them, or the impression they might convey to the minds of those who heard them. Dr. Bethune-Baker is of opinion that we must acquit Nestorius of any such charge, but even granting that in the particular instance we have quoted as in others the explanations put forward by Nestorius in the 'Apology' are accepted as satisfactory and lead us in consequence seriously to modify our opinion as to the justice of the treatment meted out to him by his opponents in their conduct of the case against him, yet the fact that he was ill-treated, misunderstood and misinterpreted in many points does not necessarily involve us in the acceptance of Dr. Bethune-Baker's conclusion that Nestorius was not 'Nestorian'.

In the preface to his edition of the Syriac text of the 'Book of Heracleides', M. Bedjan devotes some space to an examination of the doctrine of Nestorius as revealed in this 'Apology' where presumably we have his last word upon the controversy in which he was involved; and yet M. Bedjan is of opinion that, after reading this 'Apology' and making all allowances in view of the explanations Nestorius gives, there is still sufficient evidence in the 'Apology' to justify the condemnation of Nestorius as a heretic, and M. F. Nau, after reading M. Bedjan's examination of the doctrinal teaching of the 'Apology', agrees entirely with his conclusions. 'Out of thine own mouth will I judge thee,' says M. Bedjan in effect, and he devotes special attention to Nestorius's treatment of the 'Hypostatic Union', and 'Theotokos' and his Eucharistic teaching in its relation to the Incarnation, with a view to showing that, in spite of the precautions which Nestorius has taken and the denials he piles up, yet it is still possible to discover in a sufficiently clear manner the presence in this 'Defence' of those errors which caused him to be condemned.   As M. Nau points out, whilst welcoming the presence in the 'Apology' of passages which are in accord with Catholic teaching, we must not forget that 'the two natures' in the teaching of Nestorius 'involve two distinct hypostases and two persons (*prosôpa*) united in one by simple give and exchange', so that it is certain even with the 'Apology' as his defence that Nestorius would nevertheless have been condemned as a heretic.

But lest the conclusive character of the passages M. Bedjan selects as amply sufficient to convict Nestorius of heresy be disputed and it be urged that the 'dogmatic prejudice' of MM. Bedjan and Nau involves them in something of that 'personal prejudice' against which we are warned by Dr. Bethune-Baker, it may be well to put forward one or two considerations which appear to us sufficiently strong in their cumulative force to overthrow the conclusion that Nestorius was not 'Nestorian', even though we may take the most favourable view of selected passages from the 'Apology' and, giving Nestorius the benefit of the doubt, go as far as to admit that there is not a single passage in the whole work which *in itself* is sufficient to prove conclusively beyond question that Nestorius was a heretic.

To what extent, then, are we justified in maintaining still that Nestorius was 'Nestorian' in spite of the evidence in his favour as it appears in his 'Apology'?

III

Now in endeavouring to put forward one or two considerations in support of our contention it may help to clear the ground, and bring us at once to the main points at issue, if we readily grant at the outset that Nestorius in his protest against the use of the term 'Theotokos' as applied to the Virgin Mary did not intend by this to deny the Godhead of our Lord.   Popular clamour indeed attributed this motive to him and he was accused of being simply a follower of

Paul of Samosata, but the historian Socrates whilst noting that the general opinion attributed to Nestorius the belief that our Lord was a mere man, yet himself has no hesitation in acquitting him of this charge. Socrates claims to have read all the writings of Nestorius and he is quite convinced that the heretic was a follower neither of Paul of Samosata nor of Photinus.

'Most people thought', says Socrates, 'that Nestorius called our Lord a mere man and that he was bringing into the Church the doctrine of Paul of Samosata and of Photinus. . . . When I came to read the books put forth by Nestorius, I found that the man was ignorant — and I will speak my mind frankly. I was not actuated by hatred to him when I described his shortcomings: nor do I mean to make light of his good points, in order to please certain persons. To me it appears that Nestorius did not follow the lead of Paul of Samosata, or Photinus; nor did he assert at all that Christ was a mere man; but he shrinks only from the phrase "Theotokos" as if it were a bugbear; and this is the result of his vast ignorance. For though gifted with natural eloquence, and therefore accounted learned, yet in fact he was ill-trained, and he disdained to study the works of ancient interpreters. Puffed up with pride at his own faculty of speech he did not spend sufficient pains on the study of ancient documents.'

What then is 'Nestorianism'? The essential charges against Nestorius which we have to investigate are conveniently summarised by Dr. Bethune-Baker, and we cannot do better than quote this summary as representing the main features of 'Nestorianism' as such. The charges brought against Nestorius by the theologians were:

'that he so distinguished between the Godhead and the manhood of our Lord as to treat them as separate personal existences, as though a man and God were joined together, so that our Lord was not one Person but two Persons, and no real union of God and man was effected in Him. It was supposed that he held the Word to be a Person distinct from Jesus, and the Son of God distinct from the Son of Man, and that therefore he avoided the term which expressed the real union of both and preferred to speak of a "conjunction" between them. And so some of the old charges were raked up again and he was said, in teaching "two Sons", to introduce a fourth person into the Godhead, and to transform the Trinity into a Quaternity.'

Dr. Bethune-Baker is quite convinced that 'Two Persons' was not the teaching of Nestorius and he quotes a list of expressions and passages both from the earlier and later writings of Nestorius in support of this statement. For example, in the discussion in the earlier part of the 'Book of Heracleides' with reference to the heretical teaching of the Paulinians (followers of Paul of Samosata) Nestorius is careful to point out that he himself must in no way be taken as acquiescing in their tenets, and he does this by a vigorous denunciation of their division of Christ into two Sons.[1]

There are also various passages in his earlier sermons and letters in which he acknowledges that there are not two Sons but one. The following passage quoted by Dr. Bethune-Baker from Loofs's *Nestoriana* [2] puts this very clearly:

'The Unity of the natures is not divided; it is the *ousiae* of the natures that are united that are divided. This division consists not in the abolition of the union, but in the idea of the flesh and the Godhead. Hear this plainly stated. Christ is indivisible in His being Christ, but He is twofold in His being God and His being man. He is single in His Sonship; He is twofold in Him who has assumed and him who is assumed. In the person of

---

[1] 'Ils disent que ces choses ont été partagées entre deux Fils, en sorte que les unes conviennent à celui-ci et les autres à celui-là; afin qu'il n'y ait dans toutes les paroles qui sont (écrites dans les Évangiles) ni contradictions ni tromperies. Il y a une seule divinité, une seule domination, une seule puissance du Père et du Fils qui n'admettent pas une semblable tromperie. Ils disent ces choses et d'autres semblables et ils défendent leurs opinions, pour dire que le Christ et le Fils est double dans les *prosôpons* comme dans les hypostases. Ils disent que la forme (du Verbe) était (dans le Christ) de la même manière que les saints ont été la demeure de Dieu.' (Pp. 42-3.)

This teaching, which bears a certain resemblance to the opinions attributed to Nestorius himself, he proceeds to repudiate.

[2] P. 280.

the Son He is a single (person), but, as with two eyes, He is different in the natures of manhood and Godhead. For we know not two Christs or two Sons or Only-begottens or Lords, not one and another Son, not a first and a new Only-begotten, not a first and a second Christ, but one and the same, who was seen in the created and the uncreated nature.'

There are one or two fragments preserved only in the Syriac which are very explicit.

'the Son ought not to be called "God the Logos" inseparate wise (separately) and on the other hand "manhood" inseparate wise. For that is nothing otherwise but that we acknowledge "two sons". But the name of Sonship is a thing common to both natures. I say "the Son" and I teach two natures; I say "the Christ" and I separate neither of the natures in the sonship.' [1]

'I . . . demonstrate one and the same thing to everyone when I call Christ perfect God and perfect man — natures which are not mixed but united.' [2]

'In consequence of which He who is apprehended as one Christ in two natures, the divine and the human, the visible and the invisible, will hold the future judgment. As also there is one Judge in the two natures, because according to the decree of the Apostle, the former invisible (nature) God the Logos will hold future judgment in a visible man whom He has also raised from the dead. And He is one judge in each of the two natures as He is also a Son in both natures. For the unity of the Son is not impaired (does not suffer shame) through the difference of the natures. But in like manner as the destructible body is one thing and again the indestructible soul is another, but out of both one man comes into being so also out of the mortal and immortal, out of the destructible and indestructible, out of that which is subject to a

[1] A German translation of the Syriac fragments is given in Loofs's *Nestoriana.*
[2] *Ibid.* p. 332. Cf. p. 335, 'Ich sage: "der Sohn" und bekenne die beiden Kurzen (Worte): die geschaffene Natur und die ungeschaffene'.

beginning and out of the nature which has no beginning comes one into being. That is to say, that I acknowledge God the Logos one prosôpon of the Son.' [1]

Many other passages might be quoted from Nestorius to the same effect, and Dr. Bethune-Baker sums up the discussion by saying that

'in view of the many expressions and arguments of which these are only typical, it is impossible to doubt that Nestorius was clear in his own mind that his doctrine of the Incarnation safeguarded absolutely the unity of the subject. ✓He did not think of two distinct persons joined together, but of a single Person who combined in Himself the two distinct things (substances) Godhead and manhood with their characteristics (natures) complete and intact though united in Him.'

Now in view of the evidence afforded by these explicit statements of Nestorius it must be admitted that at any rate *verbally* he repudiates the teaching of 'Two Sons'. But the question still remains to be considered as to whether this was not the *practical* outcome of his theory of the Incarnation, though he himself would not admit this and even denies it explicitly. Even granting that the evidence Dr. Bethune-Baker produces justifies his statement that Nestorius was clear in his own mind that his doctrine of the Incarnation safeguarded absolutely the unity of the subject, we are still far from admitting that he was not therefore 'Nestorian'. We have still to consider the question as to whether he did not *so* distinguish between the 'Godhead' and 'Manhood' of our Lord as practically to treat them as

---

[1] Loofs, pp. 330-1. The following passage is worthy of note: 'God the Logos was not one and the man born therein another, for there was one person of them both, in reverence and honour distinguished neither in manner nor time by difference of decree or will.' (Loofs, p. 224. Fragment of *Acta Concilii oecum. sexti latina*, in Mansi xi, 761 E (a), οὐκ ἄλλος ἦν ὁ θεὸς λόγος καὶ ἄλλος ὁ ἐν ᾧ γέγονεν ἄνθρωπος. Ἕν γὰρ ἦν ἀμφοτέρων τὸ πρόσωπον ἀξίᾳ καὶ τιμῇ, προσκυνούμενον παρὰ πάσης τῆς κτίσεως, μηδενὶ τρόπῳ ἢ χρόνῳ ἑτερότητι βουλῆς καὶ θελήματος διαιρούμενον.) That such language should be condemned at the Sixth Ecumenical Council as Monothelite is a point in favour of Nestorius. If he could be accused of teaching 'one will after the union' it shows how closely he united the 'two Natures' together.

separate personal existences, and further, was *his* idea of the Union adequate to secure such a real union of God and Man in the Person of Christ as is secured by the Catholic teaching of the *Communicatio idiomatum* in the Hypostatic Union?

IV

It is to these two points especially that we must now address ourselves, and all through the enquiry we must bear in mind not only the personal character of Nestorius and his theological antecedents, but also the ambiguity of his language, his opposition to the employment of Catholic phraseology, and the inferences which people were drawing from his utterances.

Now with reference to the personal character of Nestorius and his theological antecedents it must be remembered that the Apollinarian controversy had resulted in the emphatic vindication of the real distinctness of the two complete natures in the Incarnate Son of God, and it is known that the error of Apollinaris had especially infected the Syrian Church. The result was that the Antiochene clergy were led in defence of the Catholic doctrine to lay especial stress on this distinction of the Divine and human natures in our Lord. But any undue emphasis upon this distinction except in the most guarded terms would inevitably lead to such an exaggeration as to divide Christ into two Persons, the man Jesus Christ and the Son of God who had united Himself to him. Nestorius was the pupil of Theodore of Mopsuestia who has generally been regarded as the 'Father of Nestorianism'. Is it not significant that Nestorius should have been charged by his opponents with precisely this exaggeration of the distinction of the two natures into a co-existence of two persons? The logical result of this tendency in the Antiochene School to exaggerate the distinction was 'Nestorianism', and in endeavouring to judge how far Nestorius himself was guilty of this undue exaggeration of the distinction of the two natures in Christ we are bound to take account of the fact that his theological training had been largely conducted in the atmosphere of the Antiochene School. We are justified in saying that his training marked him out as likely to fall into the error of Nestorianism, and when we further consider the character of the man as described for us by the historian Socrates we may say that the rashness of his utterances and his unguarded language in the heat of controversy were just the elements necessary to complete his downfall. We have no reason to doubt the accuracy of Socrates' description of the famous heretic, and we are justified in inferring from this that in the person of Nestorius we have just the kind of man who was most liable to rush headlong into an exaggeration of one side of the Truth, without pausing to grasp firmly the vital necessity of preserving an evenly balanced mind upon a subject so difficult and intricate that the least exaggeration one way or the other would result in either Nestorianism on the one side or Eutychianism on the other.

We now pass on to a consideration of the ambiguity of the language employed by Nestorius and his persistent opposition to Catholic phraseology.

Whilst allowing all due credit to Nestorius for the earnestness and sincerity of his desire to keep separate and unconfused the Godhead and Manhood in the Person of Christ, we cannot but recognise that his efforts, however well-meaning, resulted nevertheless in such an exaggeration of this distinction as to lay him open to the charge of teaching 'Two Sons' even though this result was far from his intention. The passages we have quoted may be interpreted as showing that Nestorius was anxious to avoid such a confusion of the two natures after the union as he believed Cyril to hold, and certainly when he read Cyril's letter he felt that his worst fears were confirmed. In the third anathema attached to that letter Cyril spoke of a union of natures. 'If anyone in the one Christ divides the subsistences after the union, connecting them only by a connection of dignity or authority or rule, and not rather by a union of natures,[1] let him be anathema.' It is true that Cyril's later explanation

[1] (καὶ οὐχὶ δὴ μᾶλλον συνόδῳ τῇ καθ᾽ ἕνωσιν φυσικήν.)

of this phrase clears him of the charge of Monophysitism,
because he really meant a real union into one hypostasis as
opposed to a moral or external union of two separate 'Persons', the Logos and the man Jesus. But Nestorius took
him to mean that the result of the Union was such a confusion of the Manhood and Godhead as to result in 'One
nature' after the union. Hence we find Nestorius in his
counter-anathema avoiding the word 'union'[1] and speaking
of an 'association'[2] of the 'Word' and of the Man assumed
by Him.[3]

But see what the result of Nestorius's efforts to avoid a
confusion between the 'Manhood' and the 'Godhead' leads
to. He not only persists in speaking of two hypostases after
the Union in the one Christ using the word hypostasis in
the sense of substance[4] in order to preserve intact the integrity of the two complete natures after the union, but he
also repudiates the Catholic phraseology and prefers to
speak of a 'conjunction' between the two natures rather
than to use the word 'union' lest by so doing he might ex-
tinguish that very distinction between the Godhead and the
Manhood which he was so anxious to preserve. He is led
to speak of the 'Word' and of 'the Man assumed by Him',
suggesting at once by such suspicious language the idea of a
man in whom the Logos chose to dwell, and when he further
goes on to repudiate the 'Hypostatic Union' and to speak
of an 'indwelling' of Godhead in Christ[5] this suspicion, that
his exaggeration of the distinction in his own mind is leading
him directly into Nestorianism, is considerably strengthened.
Instead of the Catholic conception of the God-Man we seem
to have here the idea of a mere God-bearing man and the
Person of Jesus is only the instrument or the temple in which
the Logos dwells.

[1] ἕνωσις.   [2] συνάφεια.

[3] 'Si quis non secundum conjunctionem unum dixerit Christum, qui est
etiam Emmanuel, sed secundum naturam, ex utraque etiam substantia tam
dei verbi quam etiam assumpti ab eo hominis unam filii connexionem, quam
etiam nunc inconfuse servant, minime confiteatur, anathema sit.' (See Loofs,
Nestoriana, pp. 211-17 for these counter-anathemas of Nestorius which we have
only preserved for us in a Latin translation of Marius Mercator.)

[4] Lat. *substantia*.   [5] ἐνοίκησις in distinction from ἐνσάρκωσις.

In his sermons at the earlier stages of the controversy
when he preached on the term 'Theotokos', in maintaining
that Mary did not bear God, but the man who is the instrument of the Godhead, whilst Nestorius was perfectly right
in his assertion that God as such could neither be born nor
suffer nor die, yet at the same time his exaggeration of the
distinction between the two natures leads him to employ
language which we cannot blame his opponents for inter-
preting in an heretical sense, and which gave great offence
at the time. Take as an example the language he employed
in his first sermon against the use of the term 'Theokotos'
as applied to the Virgin Mary: [1]

> 'You ask whether Mary may be called Theotokos?
> . . . No, my dear friend, Mary did not bear God (for
> that which is born of the flesh is flesh); the creature bore
> not the uncreated Creator . . . but the man who is the
> instrument of the Godhead.[2] The Holy Spirit did not
> create God the Word . . . but formed for God the Word
> out of the virgin a temple which He might inhabit. The
> incarnate God did not die, but quickened him in whom
> He was made flesh.' [3]

Later on in the same sermon he says:

> 'For the sake of Him also who employs the garment,
> I honour the garment, adoring what is visible on account
> of what is unseen. God is inseparable from that which is
> visible, therefore I do not separate the honour from that
> which is separated. I distinguish (separate) the natures,
> but I conjoin the reverence (or "unite the worship").[4]
> Observe what I say, He who was fashioned in the womb
> is not by Himself God — were He so, we should be man-
> worshippers . . . — but He who was assumed by God
> is called God because God is in Him.'

---

[1] The text may be found in Loofs, pp. 249 ff.
[2] θεότητος ὄργανον.
[3] 'Sed illum, in quo incarnatus est, suscitavit.'
[4] χωρίζω τὰς φύσεις, ἀλλ' ἑνῶ τὴν προσκύνησιν.

And again at the close of the same sermon he says:

> 'Let us honour as Divine with the Divine Word that form which received God. . . . Let us confess the two-fold and adore it as one. . . .' [1]

Cyril was quick to see the dangerous import of such unguarded language, however praiseworthy the object may have been which led Nestorius to use it. Thus Cyril writes to Nestorius as follows:

> 'We refuse also to say of Christ "For the sake of Him who assumes I worship Him who is assumed; for the sake of Him who is invisible I worship Him who is visible". It shocks me also to say, "He that is assumed shares the name of God with Him who assumes". For he who so speaks again makes two several Christs, one God and one man. For he confessedly denies the union, according to which there is understood one Christ Jesus — not one jointly worshipped with another, or jointly sharing the name of God with another, but one Christ Jesus, one only-begotten Son, honoured with one worship with His own flesh.' [2]

Even in the later 'Book of Heracleides' we have to complain of much the same ambiguity, and use of suspicious phraseology which creates within our minds an unpleasant feeling that, in spite of all the efforts of Nestorius to explain his earlier sayings in an orthodox sense, yet still his conception of the nature of the Union between the Manhood and Godhead in the Person of Christ is open to grave suspicion. For example, there are the passages where he speaks of 'the person of the manhood' and 'the person of the Godhead'.

> 'So it is by person that He (the Son) is distinguished. But not so as regards the union of the Godhead and the manhood — He (i.e. the Word) is not by the union in all

---

[1] ' τὴν θεοδόχον τῷ θεῷ λόγῳ συνθεολογῶμεν μορφήν . . . duplicem confiteamur et adoremus ut unum, duplum enim naturarum unum est propter unitatem.'

[2] See Heurtley, *De Fide et Symbolo*, for the letters of Cyril to Nestorius, and the English translation, p. 168, which we have followed.

those things that the person by its nature is, so that in the one person (He should become) another *ousia*. For He took him (man) into His person — not into the (Divine) ousia or nature, so that he should be either consubstantial (i.e. *homoousios*) with the Father or else another son altogether — and not one and the same Son. For the manhood is the person of the Godhead, and the Godhead is the person of the manhood, but they are distinct in nature, and distinct in the Union.' [1]

Surely the inferences Cyril draws from the language of Nestorius are justified in the light of the passages we have quoted, and we are right in saying that his fear of the *Communicatio idiomatum* which, as Hefele says, 'pursued him like a spectre', and his dread of the supposed dangers lurking behind the popular use of the term 'Theotokos', led him to the use of language which could only be interpreted in an heretical sense, and led him also to make the suspicion of his heretical tendencies still more strong by his persistent refusal on the other hand to employ explicit expressions, the use of which would have set him at once right with his opponents.

[3] *Bethune-Baker*, pp. 94-100; cf. pp. 163 ff. The following passage from F. Nau's translation (pp. 193-4) is suspicious and typical of the confused style of writing employed by Nestorius:

'Cette idée se trouvait déjà dans ce qu'il disait dans sa lettre: "les diversités des natures ne sont pas supprimées à cause de l'union"; c'est en effet par les différences naturelles qu'il sépare les choses qui sont unies, lorsqu'il sépare inséparablement, car il a séparé par le mot d'essence. Autre, en effet, est le mot et l'idée de la divinité, et autre pour l'humanité. Ceux-là qui sont séparables le sont; mais je dis deux natures, et autre est celui qui revêt et autre celui qui est revêtu; et il y a deux *prosôpons*: de celui qui revêt et de celui qui est revêtu. Mais toi aussi tu confesses "de deux natures". Ce n'est pas sans *prosôpon* et sans hypostase que chacune d'elles est connue dans les diversités des natures. On ne conçoit pas deux *prosôpons* des fils, ni encore deux *prosôpons* des hommes, mais d'un seul homme, qui est mû de la même manière même par l'autre. L'union des *prosôpons* a eu lieu en *prosôpon*, et non en essence ni en nature. On ne doit pas concevoir une essence sans hypostase, comme si l'union (des essences) avait eu lieu en une essence et qu'il y eut un *prosôpon* d'une seule essence. Mais les natures subsistent, dans leurs *prosôpons* et dans leurs natures et dans le *prosôpon* d'union. Quant au *prosôpon* naturel de l'une, l'autre se sert du même en vertu de l'union; ainsi il n'y a qu'un *prosôpon* pour les deux natures. Le *prosôpon* d'une essence se sert du *prosôpon* même de l'autre. Mais quelle essence vas-tu faire sans *prosôpon*? Celle de la divinité ou celle de l'humanité?

'Alors tu ne diras plus que Dieu le Verbe est chair, et aussi que la chair est Fils.'

The ambiguity and suspicious character of his own phrase-ology, together with his express repudiation of Catholic phraseology, laid him open to the charge of believing precisely the opposite to what presumably he did believe. Can we then wonder at his condemnation as a heretic?

Whatever he may have believed in his own mind, there is no question but that he somehow contrived to create within the minds of his accusers the impression that he did not really believe what he professed to believe. Are we to attribute the consequent misunderstanding of his position by his opponents solely to their personal animosity against the man himself and the element of jealousy due to the rivalry between the Sees of Constantinople and Alexandria? Whatever may be said of Cyril's character and conduct, it must be admitted that he was an able theologian and, like Athanasius before him, he had the supreme advantage over his opponents of having grasped from the outset the funda-mental points at issue in the Nestorian controversy.

Could anything more explicit, for example, be found than the teaching contained in his 2nd and 3rd Epistles to Nestorius?

'For we do not affirm', he says, 'that the nature of the Word underwent a change and became flesh, or that it was transformed into a whole or perfect man consisting of soul and body; but we say that the Word, having in an ineffable and inconceivable manner personally united to Himself flesh instinct with a living soul, became man and was called the Son of Man, — yet not of mere will or favour, nor again by the simple taking to Himself of a person (i.e. of a human person to His divine person), — and that while the natures which were brought together into this true unity were diverse there was of both one Christ and one Son; not as though the diverseness of the natures were done away by this union, but rather that the God-head and Manhood completed for us the one Lord and Christ and Son by their unutterable and unspeakable concurrence and unity.'

Here Cyril guards against that confusion of the two

natures which Nestorius feared so much, and later on in the same letter he warns Nestorius distinctly of the danger arising from a use of the word 'conjunction'.

'Thus we confess one Christ and Lord, not as worshipping a man conjointly with the Word, that there may not through this phrase "conjointly" be insinuated the semblance of division (as though we were dividing the one Christ into two Persons) — but as worshipping one and the same Person, because the body of the Lord is not alien from the Lord, with which body also He sits with the Father Himself; not again as though two sons do sit with the Father, but one united to His own flesh. For if we reject this hypostatic union [1] either as impossible or unmeet, we fall into the error of making two sons. For in that case we must needs distinguish and speak of the man severally (the human person) dignified with the appellation of Son, and again of the Word which is of God severally (the divine Person) possessing naturally the Sonship, both name and thing.' [2]

The answer of Nestorius to this letter of Cyril is extant,[3] and from it we see that he either cannot or will not appreciate the real points at issue. He seems to fancy that Cyril is tainted with Apollinarianism and he complains of his letter as being obscure and ill-digested. Yet a comparison of the two letters (that of Cyril to Nestorius and the reply of the latter), we venture to think, shows that at this stage of the controversy, whilst Cyril is clearly conscious of the fundamental points at issue, Nestorius simply could not or would not see the dangers arising from his own language, against which Cyril strives in vain to warn him.

If he were perfectly free from any suspicion of exaggerating in his own mind the distinction between the Divine and human natures, what was there in Cyril's letters to which he could possibly object? If the stumbling-block was in reality the supposed ambiguity of the phrase, 'Hypostatic Union',

---

[1] τὴν καθ' ὑπόστασιν ἕνωσιν. [2] Heurtley, *op. cit.* pp. 159-60.
[3] See Loofs, *op. cit.* pp. 173-80.

why did he not frankly say so at the time, and ask Cyril for an explanation? If he really thought that, by the phrase 'Hypostatic Union', Cyril meant such a unification of the two natures (hypostases) as would result in the formation of a new hypostasis compounded of both, i.e. in a confusion or compounding of the Manhood and Godhead, why did he not endeavour at once to have this point cleared up when he wrote to Cyril in answer to the latter's clear and scholarly letter? Surely Cyril in his letters makes it clear that by the Hypostatic Union he means that the 'two substances', whilst retaining their distinctive properties, found their union in one Person? That such a Union is, as Cyril says, a mystery is no objection to it, and he makes it perfectly clear that the rejection of the Hypostatic Union must result in the heretical conception of 'two Sons'. What, for example, could be clearer than those explicit statements we find in his 3rd Epistle which are in marked contrast to the very involved and tedious discussion upon which Nestorius enters in the 'Apology' when he comes to discuss at length the question of the Hypostatic Union and urges various objections against it which we cannot but think reflect his maturer judgment after he had had time in his exile to sit down and think things over quietly. Many of these objections which Nestorius urges in the 'Apology' against Cyril's 'Hypostatic Union' which he professes not to understand are already answered in Cyril's letters to him, and this confirms our opinion that Nestorius was too 'muddle-headed' to grasp at that time the dangerous import of his own language and to see, as Cyril clearly did, the consequences which his repudiation of the Hypostatic Union entailed.[1]

And yet in spite of these explicit statements of Cyril we find Nestorius in his later 'Apology' asking what in the

---

[1] The following passages from Cyril's 3rd letter to Nestorius show quite clearly in what sense he held the 'Hypostatic Union' and how its acceptance did *not* involve that confusion of the Manhood and Godhead which Nestorius so dreaded.

(i) 'Neither do we say that the flesh was converted into the divine nature, nor surely that the ineffable nature of God the Word was debased and changed into the nature of flesh, for it is unchangeable and unalterable, ever continuing altogether the same according to the Scriptures. . . .'

world Cyril means by a 'hypostatic union', and hinting that under cover of an ambiguous phrase Cyril really meant to teach not that the union of natures in the incarnate Christ is 'personal' (i.e. the result of the union is one indivisible person), but 'substantial' (i.e. the result of the union was a confusion or compounding of the two 'substances', Manhood and Godhead). Why could not Nestorius see from Cyril's letters that this was not his teaching? We cannot but feel that the real objection of Nestorius to the 'Hypostatic Union' all through was not so much its ambiguity but was due to his own mental exaggeration of the distinction between the two natures which prevented his ever accepting such a union as was signified by the Hypostatic Union, because to his mind this meant a union leading to confusion.

But before leaving these Epistles of Cyril to Nestorius there is a further point to be noted as an argument for the

(ii) 'Confessing then the personal union of the Word with the flesh ($\dot{\eta}\nu\hat{\omega}$-$\sigma\theta\alpha\iota$ $\kappa\alpha\theta$' $\dot{\upsilon}\pi\dot{o}\sigma\tau\alpha\sigma\iota\nu$) we worship one Son and Lord, Jesus Christ, neither parting and sundering man and God, as though they were connected with one another by a unity of dignity and authority. . . . Nor surely calling the Word of God one Christ, and in like manner Him who is of the woman another and several Christ; but knowing only one Christ, the Word which is of God the Father with His own flesh.'

(iii) 'But neither again do we say that the Word which is of God, dwelt in Him who was born of the Holy Virgin as in an ordinary man, lest Christ should be understood to be a man who carries God (within Him) ($\theta\epsilon o\phi\acute{o}\rho os$ $\acute{\alpha}\nu\theta\rho\omega\pi os$), for though the Word "dwelt in us", and "all the fulness of the Godhead", as it is said, "dwelt in Christ bodily", yet we understand that when He became flesh the indwelling was not such as when He is said to dwell in the saints, but that having been united by a union of natures ($\dot{\epsilon}\nu\omega\theta\epsilon\grave{\iota}s$ $\kappa\alpha\tau\grave{\alpha}$ $\phi\acute{\upsilon}\sigma\iota\nu$) (the two natures united in the one Person), and not converted into flesh, He brought to pass such an indwelling as the soul of man may be said to have with its own body.'

(iv) 'There is then one Christ and Son and Lord, not as though He were a man connected with God simply by a unity of dignity or authority, for equality of honour does not unite natures. . . . Nor certainly do we understand the mode of connection to be that of juxtaposition ($\kappa\alpha\tau\grave{\alpha}$ $\pi\alpha\rho\acute{\alpha}\theta\epsilon\sigma\iota\nu$), for this does not suffice to express a union of natures. Nor do we understand the union to be in the way of relative participation ($\kappa\alpha\tau\grave{\alpha}$ $\mu\acute{\epsilon}\theta\epsilon\xi\iota\nu$ $\sigma\chi\epsilon\tau\iota\kappa\acute{\eta}\nu$) as we, "being joined to the Lord", as it is written, "are one spirit with Him"; but rather we reject the term "connection" altogether, as insufficient to signify the union. Nor do we call the word which is of God the Father the God or Sovereign of Christ, lest we should again openly divide the one Christ, the Son and Lord, into two, and incur the charge of blasphemy, by making Him the God and Sovereign of Himself. For the word of God being personally united with flesh, as we said ($\dot{\epsilon}\nu\omega\theta\epsilon\grave{\iota}s$ $\sigma\alpha\rho\kappa\grave{\iota}$ $\kappa\alpha\theta$' $\dot{\upsilon}\pi\acute{o}\sigma\tau\alpha\sigma\iota\nu$), is God of the universe and Sovereign of the whole world.'

justice of the condemnation of Nestorius. It is quite clear from these letters of Cyril that whatever Nestorius may have believed himself, and however clear he may have been in his own mind as to the precise significance of his own ambiguous phraseology and his opposition to Catholic terms, yet the people who heard or read his sermons and listened to his teaching, understood him in a definitely heretical sense and were being led away in consequence by false doctrine. Whatever other motives may have weighed with Cyril in his decision to take action against Nestorius, this certainly in fairness ought to be reckoned as one.

'If indeed', says Cyril, 'it were only thyself whom thou wast injuring in holding and teaching such things, it would be of less consequence, but seeing that thou hast given offence to the universal Church, and hast cast the leaven of a novel and strange heresy among the lay people, and not the lay people of Constantinople only, for copies of thy sermons have been circulated everywhere, what satisfactory account can any longer be given of our silence. . . .'

Are we to assume that Nestorius was totally blind to the inferences which people were drawing from his own words? If a man of his character and theological capabilities by the use of unguarded phraseology against which he is expressly warned, the dangerous import of which apparently he is too blind to see, and in the employment of which he persists in spite of its obvious heretical tendencies, deliberately plays into the hands of the unorthodox opponents of Catholicism, is he not rightly called the founder of the heresy which results? That 'Nestorianism' as a heresy existed and still exists is unquestioned. That it appealed to many minds, was eagerly advocated as against the Catholic doctrine and led to the loss of many adherents of the Church, these are facts of history. Is not Nestorius, then, rightly condemned when his actions and language made him the central figure of the Nestorian movement? Granted that the movement would undoubtedly have taken place even though Nestorius himself had taken no part in it, yet he has only himself to blame if, in spite of warning, he makes himself the central figure and rallying point of those very tendencies in the Antiochene School which resulted in what we know as 'Nestorianism'.

V

To sum up, Nestorius became the acknowledged leader of a school of thought which undoubtedly was heretical, and it is not denied that the exponents of Nestorianism ought to have been condemned as advocates of teaching fundamentally subversive of the Incarnation. How, then, are we to-day justified in seeking to exonerate from blame the leader of the movement because he claims, in an elaborate 'Apology' written after his condemnation, to have been the victim of personal prejudice, misunderstanding and misinterpretation, when his own language is admittedly ambiguous? But we are far from thinking that he was simply the victim of the ambiguity of theological phraseology. We cannot but hold that his persistent objections to Catholic phraseology were due not so much to their supposed ambiguity as to certain presuppositions and heretical tendencies in his own mind which prevented him from grasping the Catholic truth, and frankly accepting it. We cannot help feeling that although verbally in his utterance he contrived to leave the impression that he did not teach 'Two Sons', yet at the back of his mind there was an abstract separation of the Divine and human natures, and he pressed the distinction between the two; far that it amounted (as Gieseler has pointed out), in substance, though not in expression, to 'two persons', his idea being not so much the thought of an Incarnation — God *becoming* Man — as that of a Union in the sense of an intimate and close 'conjunction' of the Logos with a perfect man. We have given reasons which in our opinion are sufficiently strong to justify our suspicion that this was the real thought at the back of his mind. Surely, then, Cyril was right in holding him responsible for the logical result of his position, even though Nestorius himself would not draw the inevitable inferences from his own mental presuppositions and reservations, but preferred to take refuge in ambiguous phraseology and to leave other people to draw the inevitable conclusions from his statements and so drift into 'Nestorianism'. Behind all the secondary causes which led to his opposition to Catholic phraseology there lay certain mental presuppositions wherein were contained the germs of Nestorianism, however carefully Nestorius himself may have consciously or unconsciously managed to conceal them in his written defence of himself. We feel convinced that if this 'Apology' had fallen into the hands of Cyril he would quickly have penetrated behind the words of the 'Defence' to those heretical mental reservations and abstract theological distinctions which lay at the root of the theology of Nestorius and are the real justification for his condemnation.

It has been pointed out that the real root of the Nestorian error was the failure to conceive of 'Nature' without 'personality'. Can it be contended that Nestorius ever grasped the Catholic position which, by its teaching of an 'impersonal manhood' in the Incarnate Son of God, secures the perfect humanity of Christ as against Apollinarianism and at the same time avoids the Monophysite error by securing the human will in perfect harmony with and complete subjection to the Divine Will? It was the failure to conceive of the possibility of such a perfect harmony and to realise that in such a union of natures there was no necessary antinomy between the human and the Divine Will that led to error, and we cannot but think that a cross-examination of Nestorius on these lines would reveal the unsoundness of this position. As Dr. Robertson, the late Bishop of Exeter, points out in a very helpful note in the Prolegomena to his edition of the works of St. Athanasius, it transcends the power of human thought to do more than state the Catholic doctrine on these points in terms which exclude the Nestorian and Monophysite alternatives.

*

'The man Jesus Christ is held to have *lacked* nothing that constitutes personality in man: the human personality which therefore belongs to it *ideally*, being *in fact* merged in the Divine personality of the Son. The "impersonality" as it is sometimes called, of Christ quâ man is therefore better spoken of as His *Divine* Personality. Personality and will are correlated, but not identical ideas.'

Whilst we are quite prepared to recognise the zeal and earnestness with which Nestorius, following the laudable tradition of the School of Antioch, strove to give due weight to the portrait of the God-Man in the Gospels and to secure that His moral development was a real and not a docetic process, and whilst he was absolutely right in his defence of the element of free choice in the humanity of Christ as against Apollinaris, yet can it be seriously contended that he solved on Catholic lines the problems raised by his endeavours to do justice to these factors in his conception of the relation of the two Natures in Christ? Did he, in his anxiety to avoid what he thought was the Monophysitism of Cyril, still himself succeed in preserving the unity of Christ's Person intact? Only by the doctrine of the Hypostatic Union and the 'impersonal' nature of the Manhood in Christ has the Church succeeded in preserving the balance of truth between Nestorianism and Monophysitism, and yet we find Nestorius far from being an ardent defender of the 'impersonal' nature of the manhood, still less an advocate of the Hypostatic Union! Is it safe to say in view of this that Nestorius was not 'Nestorian'? If, of course, the doctrine of the 'Hypostatic Union' 'dehumanises the manhood', then the fears of Nestorius were justified and no doubt he was perfectly within his rights in submitting such a phrase which admitted of an ambiguous interpretation to a carefully testing process before accepting it. But in his impatience at what is admittedly a mystery beyond human comprehension lying behind the phrase 'hypostatic union' we seem to detect just that mental reservation and presupposition as to the nature of the Union which he had settled satisfactorily to his own mind by a logical rather than an ethical solution. His idea, never perhaps explicitly stated but which we feel he held as a mental reservation in all his treatment of the problems centring round the thought of the Incarnation, seems always to be that of a moral indwelling of a perfect man by the Logos which acts as an inspiring power in the background, and this is the germ from whence 'Nestorianism' springs. In opposition to this, Catholic teaching held that the Incarnation resulted not in a perfect man *plus* the Logos united together in the closest possible conjunction, but the one indivisible Person of the God-Man united in an 'hypostatic union' which resulted in such a 'communicatio Idiomatum' as excluded the possibility either of the dehumanisation of the manhood on the one hand, or, on the other, such a 'mixture' of the Divine and human as would tend to the degradation of the Godhead.

Those who would prove that Nestorius was not Nestorian must answer the question as to how Nestorius's view of the Incarnation solves the problems which, as we have seen, only the doctrines of the 'impersonal' nature of the 'Manhood' and the 'hypostatic union' can solve, and further whether it is possible, whilst denying both these doctrines, still to avoid heresy.

The real task for those who would prove that Nestorius was not Nestorian is to show that nothing in his acts, words or deeds, and nothing in his character and theological training, is sufficient to justify the inferences we have drawn from these considerations that he was mentally if not explicitly 'Nestorian'. We do not think that Dr. Bethune-Baker has proved his case.

Loofs's *Nestoriana* (1905) was followed in 1914 by his book on *Nestorius and his Place in the History of Christian Doctrine*. The printed editions of the *Acta* of the Council of Ephesus are regarded now as superseded by the critical text of E. Schwartz in his edition of the Greek Councils, the *Acta Conciliorum Oecumenicorum* (1914–40). He wrote also an earlier paper on the so-called 'Counter-Anathemas' of Nestorius ('Die Gegenanathematismen des Nestorius', in *Sitzungsberichte der (Königlich)-bayerischen Akademie der Wissenschaften, phil.-hist. Klasse*, 1922, Heft 1). In this, Schwartz sought to prove that these 'Counter-Anathemas' were not the work of Nestorius himself, and that, in fact, the anathemas are never mentioned in the long and ardent struggle over the Cyrilline anathemas with the Orientals. The old argument that Marius Mercator incorporated the anathemas of Nestorius in his collection is seemingly destroyed by Schwartz's researches concerning the manuscript tradition. Marius Mercator is not the collector of the whole *Collectio Palatina* of the *Acta Conciliorum Oecumenicorum*, but only of a part of it, and the anathemas of Nestorius do not figure in this part, but in the later parts of the *Collectio Palatina*, and are introduced there in connection with the beginning of the 'Three Chapters' struggle, as late as the second decade of the sixth century.

All this raises an interesting and debatable historical question, and if Schwartz is correct, it only confirms the main point of our argument that Nestorius himself was not really a competent and trained theologian. He could not himself have produced so powerful an indictment of Cyril's Christology as is contained in the 'Counter-Anathemas' attributed to him, but these are really the later work of his friends, including Theodoret, and the convinced Nestorians who followed the logical conclusions of Nestorianism to the bitter end. The estimate, therefore, of Socrates, the historian, concerning Nestorius himself, is further strengthened by the research work of Schwartz. It seems to us, however, fairly certain that Nestorius with the aid of his friends, including Theodoret, did compose a set of Counter Anathemas in answer to Cyril's indictment. Otherwise it is difficult to account for the fact that the name of Nestorius is attached to these Counter-Anathemas, though the set found by Schwartz is later in origin, or has been redrafted.

(*b*) Two Ancient Christologies [1]

Under the title, *Two Ancient Christologies* (published for the Church Historical Society by S.P.C.K., 16s. net), Dr.

[1] A review of Dr. R. V. Sellers's book from *Church Quarterly Review*, 1940.

R. V. Sellers offers a fresh and stimulating study in the Christological thought of the schools of Alexandria and Antioch in the early history of Christian doctrine. This is quite the best piece of research work we have had from an English scholar since Dr. Ottley's contribution to the whole subject in his *Doctrine of the Incarnation*. Dr. Sellers in this thesis is concerned to show that the Alexandrine and the Antiochene theologians in the early history of Christian dogma were in reality both contending for the same fundamental truths, and that, in consequence, the conflict which raged between these two ancient schools of thought, and had as its outcome the break-up of the school of Antioch, is to be regarded as one of the major tragedies in the history of the Early Church. He submits the teaching of each school in turn to a searching examination; he then shows the conflict between the two and its outcome; and concludes with an attempt to assess the value of the contribution of both schools to Christology. He is fully alive to the fact that the swing-back in our own day away from immanentism means a renewed return to the standpoint of the Alexandrine theologians. Yet at the same time he would have us carefully to safeguard the truths for which the Antiochene thinkers contended, lest in our reaction against immanentism the values in Christological speculation of the school of Antioch be overlooked or even lost.

What were those values? If the contention of Dr. Sellers be accepted that the element common to both Christologies was belief in Jesus Christ as Son of God and Saviour, the distinctive thing in Antiochene Christology is their teaching on the reality of the Lord's human consciousness, and in this he maintains that they supply what is lacking in the system of the Alexandrines, as these start from the same affirmation. The claim that the Antiochene theologians, though they approach the Christological problem from another angle, and, as Dr. Sellers frankly recognises, use expressions which cannot be deemed satisfactory, are in reality at one with their opponents in maintaining the same root principles, is a bold challenge which it would need another book to canvass and possibly to refute. We must confine ourselves, therefore, in this brief notice, to one or two considerations which in our view must be borne in mind in any attempt to assess the value of the Antiochene contribution to Christological thought.

Dr. Sellers concludes his close analysis of Antiochene Christology by maintaining that the following two Christological principles of the Alexandrine theologians are those also held by the Antiochene school:

(1) In Jesus Christ, the Logos, while remaining what he was, has, for our salvation, united manhood to himself, thereby making it his own; he is not, therefore, two Persons, but one Person, the Logos himself in his incarnate state (p. 179).
(2) In Jesus Christ, the two elements of Godhead and manhood, each with its properties, are to be recognised; therefore, since these remain in their union in his Person, any idea of confusion or change in respect of these elements must be eliminated (p. 200).

Let us assume, for the sake of argument and in the terminology in which Dr. Sellers expresses them, that these two foundation principles form the backbone of the Alexandrine Christology and are at the same time common to the whole Antiochene school of thought. Let us also in fairness safeguard the position of this latter school by assuming that this is what they were meaning to say rather than what in the heat of controversy some of them actually did say or were thought by their opponents to have meant to say. We should contend, nevertheless, that whether in ancient or in modern terminology, the deepest analysis of the thought of the two schools reveals a fundamental gap which no juggling with words or charity of interpretation can successfully cover.

We can best, perhaps, indicate the nature of this fundamental difference in mentality between the two schools if we take up a point pressed by Dr. Sellers after he has proved to his own satisfaction that there is no radical difference between the two Christologies. He would have us think that at one important point the teaching of the Antiochenes is more satisfactory than is that of the exponents of the Alexandrine Christology. What is the point? We will allow Dr. Sellers to put it in his own words because it is precisely the way in which he puts it that in our judgment reveals the concealed fundamental difference to which we have referred. What does he say?

'The former (the Antiochene) most clearly affirm that in the union the manhood of Jesus Christ possesses its individuating characteristics, and functions as a free agent — though always in accordance with the will of the Logos. Indeed, it would seem that in this way the representatives of the Syrian doctrinal tradition can offer a real contribution in answer to the problem of the relation of the manhood to the Logos in the union: that manhood is, not "that of another beside the Logos", so that one must think that in Jesus Christ there are two Persons, but the "own" manhood, the *suum templum*, of the Logos, which he has so united to himself that, as a result of the union, there is one Person, at once God and man; and in this one Person, "the Man-God", the human will, which is real and free, is ever in accord with the will of the Divine. Apparently, then, it is the idea of the Man's perfect fellowship with the Logos that these theologians can put forward in answer to the problem. It is here that the Alexandrines fail: they uphold the principle that the Lord's manhood possesses freedom of choice, but do not make use of it. The Antiochenes, on the other hand, not only uphold this principle, but also seek to work it out — though in so doing they rouse a storm of opposition and for their pains are denounced as "Nestorians"' (p. 201; cf. p. 255).

Precisely! And so long as ancient or modern Antiochenes continue to clothe their thoughts in language such as Dr. Sellers here employs, so long must some of us regard them as incurably dualistic in their Christological presuppositions and therefore never able to reach the conception of the Incarnation as opposed to that of a God-indwelt Person.

Note the phraseology which in this passage Dr. Sellers uses: 'The idea of the Man's perfect fellowship with the Logos'. Surely this is incurably Nestorian. There is 'the Man' in perfect fellowship with 'the Logos'. If this is not a mental concept of 'two Persons', the Logos and the Man in whom he came to dwell, what is it? We pointed out over a quarter of a century ago (1912) in an article on 'Nestorius the Nestorian', that no matter what might be said on the ambiguity in the language of the Nestorians and the desperate attempts to acquit them of the charges brought against them of teaching 'Two Sons', the fact remains that Nestorius himself, however verbally orthodox his language at times, was all the time mentally a Nestorian. We have read nothing since which might lead us to alter that considered judgment reached after a careful study of such documentary evidence as is extant. We will conclude our notice of this latest examination of the same evidence by Dr. Sellers by putting in our own words what we conceive to be the fundamental and radical difference between these two ancient Christologies — a difference which has persisted in Christological speculations ever since and to-day to a large extent still dominates all our modern efforts to solve the same perennial problem. We desire to make the distinction between the two as sharp as possible and to show that ultimately they are incompatible. It is easy to tone down each so as to make the one apparently the equivalent of the other. This is, however, only appearance, not reality. No doubt the language of the one tends to approximate more and more closely to that of the other as the latter gradually won official status and recognition and thus classes as unorthodox by implication that of the former. Yet in the last analysis between the two is a gap which no exchange of terminology can conceal, still less remove. We will call the one the Catholic conception of the Incarnation because it became the accepted doctrine of the Church and found expression in its official dogmatic formularies. The other, by way of contrast, we may name the rational equivalent or unorthodox doctrine of the God-man. There are two possible methods of approach to the Christological problem determined by certain presuppositions regarding the contents of the Gospel narratives. Either we approach the New Testament in the belief that therein is contained the record of the life of God Himself in human form, the story of God's sojourning with men in the days of His Flesh, and how He led a human life, or we can approach these documents in the belief that therein is contained a record of the life of the most extraordinary human being that has ever lived amongst men but concerning whom one thing is certain, viz. that whatever else He may have been, indubitably He was a man, bone of our bone, flesh of our flesh, and with a consciousness of Himself as such over against God whom He called His Father. We can say either here we have the life of God incarnate depicted in these pages or we have the record of the life of a man called Jesus in whom God came to dwell. Our conclusions and the whole cast of our Christological thought will be inevitably and inexorably determined by our premises, no matter what the terminology in which we strive to express our belief. Our Alexandrian or Antiochene mentality will inevitably reveal itself as we proceed to express our thoughts on the Christian doctrine of the Incarnation. If we begin with the thought of God becoming man, our problem is how could He do so. If we begin with the thought of a man born in time with a human consciousness of Himself as such, then no matter how intimately we may succeed in relating Him to God and notwithstanding what language we may employ in our attempts to ascribe Divinity to Him in His relationship to God, we can never reach the Catholic conception of the Incarnation. At best we shall reach the conception of Jesus Christ as the maximum of the Divine Immanence in a person's life, a man called Jesus of Nazareth. The fundamental difference may be summed up in a sentence. It is the difference between the thought of God dwelling in a person's life to the *nth* degree, and God leading a personal life.

The Catholic formula is 'One Person, two natures'.

The One Person is the Pre-existent Logos who, after the Incarnation, is still the Word Incarnate. The Word ἄσαρκος is not distinct from the Word incarnate, nor is the personality of the Incarnate different from the personality of the Logos. The Incarnation does not result in a new personality. It is the same Word both before and after the Incarnation. Now Nestorius regarded the personality of the Incarnate as different from the Word ἄσαρκος. The result of the union of the two Natures was a new personality.

Whilst the Catholic regarded the unity of Christ's Person to be secured by the Word, an immutable Person, appropriating our nature which thus becomes necessarily negatively impersonal, i.e. having never existed as a separate personality in its own right and having received its personality in the Person of the Word who appropriates it, Nestorius attributes the unity of Christ's Person to a union that takes place between the respective personalities of the two natures. He cannot conceive of a nature that would exist without its connatural personality. Two Natures = Two Persons.

Catholic theology secures the unity of Christ by postulating the personality as that of the Pre-existent Divine Logos and not as the resultant personality which comes from the union of the personalities of the two Natures.

The personality of the God-man is not to be sought in a resultant personality of the union of God and a man — the human and Divine Natures with their human and Divine personalities — but in the single personality of the Divine Logos who is the subject of both Natures. The unity is found in the single personality, the difference in the two Natures united in and by the Divine personality who is the Subject of both.

According to Nestorian thought, the Word and the Man bring into the union each His own personality. This introduces an impossible dualism at the centre of the personality of the God Man. If you try to remove this dualism by postulating a single resultant personality as the issue of the union of the two personalities, you get a complex personality,

Divine-Human, and have fallen into the error of confounding the Persons.

Nestorius tried to maintain that the two Natures remain what they were: but the personalities unite so as to form but one, 'the *prosôpon* of union' which is the *prosôpon* neither of the Word nor of the Man but of the compound.

Hence in the endeavour to avoid Monophysitism — the fusion of the Natures — confounding the substances — Nestorian thought falls into the error of a fusion of the personalities, *prosôpa*.

Nestorius tried to avoid this by suggesting that the *prosôpon* of the Word and the *prosôpon* of the man remain distinct and subordinate to the *prosôpon* of union. We thus get three personalities, two subordinate to the control of the third. The *prosôpon* of the Divine Nature: that of the Human Nature: and that of the resultant *prosôpon* of their union.

> 'You (Cyril) go against (the Fathers), because you insist that in the two natures, God the Word is the *prosôpon* of Union. It is Christ, then, who is the *prosôpon* of union, God the Word is not the *prosôpon* of union, but of his Nature. It is neither the divinity (alone) nor the humanity (alone) that constitutes the common *prosôpon*, for this *prosôpon* belongs to the two natures, that both may be known in it and through it. . . .'

Thus in effect for Nestorian thought the Person of Christ resulting from the Incarnation is not entirely identical with the Person of the Word before the Incarnation.

'Where have the Fathers ever said that God the Word was born, according to the flesh, of a woman?' (Herac. 131, 132, 133.)

'Go through the whole New Testament, and you will nowhere read that death is attributed to God, but to Christ, or to the Son, or to the Lord.'

For the same reason Nestorius would not admit that Mary is θεοτόκος in the strict and natural sense of the word.

'The Logos who was begotten from all eternity had no other birth.'

Then the one who was born was not the Logos. The Word is Son truly and by nature (φύσει καὶ ἀληθῶς); the man is so only through identity of name with the Son.

So the Nestorian Christ is a 'composite personality'.

The fear of Apollinarianism with its mindless man or its impersonal manhood leads Nestorius to give personality to the man Jesus as *a* man, and then the problem how to secure a unity with two personalities — that of the Word and that of the man Jesus — leads him to a complex or composite personality — an amalgam of the two.

Catholic teaching repudiated any such association of a Divine Person with a man called Jesus, and taught in its place a real condescension of God, a unique humiliation, a real Incarnation.

(1) The Church taught that in the Incarnate Christ, it is not the humanity of an individual man but of God the Word and that this human element is subordinate to the Divine.

(2) Catholic theology conceived of a twofold generation:

(a) He was begotten of God before all worlds,
(b) He was born in time of the Virgin Mary and was made Man.

(3) He the Second Adam gives us Himself. His Flesh and Blood are not those of a holy man, however exalted, united with Himself. His Flesh and Blood are Life-giving because and only because they are His.

Because He is what He is, His work as Man is of infinite worth and efficacy in our Redemption.

(4) No Kenotic theories can be sound which deprive Him who was Incarnate of any supernatural gifts or character essential to the efficacy of His work as Redeemer.

If we stop short with Nestorian thought and hesitate to conceive of God Himself becoming Incarnate, we have no guarantee that the work of the Person called Jesus is God's work for us men and for our salvation.

(5) The essence of the thought behind the term Theo-

tokos is that Mary did truly bear the Person who is Very God. Out of her substance the Word fashioned for Himself a Nature and the flesh so assumed became the very body of the Word. All this can be studied in detail as set forth in Dr. Ottley's *Doctrine of the Incarnation* and is convincingly elaborated in Tixeront's *Histoire des dogmes*.

If Apollinarianism denied that our Lord had a human soul, Nestorianism mentally visualises Him as a man with a human consciousness of Himself as such, even though at the same time it tries to think of Him as possessing a Divine personality. It was not simply a question of the Saviour uniting His Divine Nature to a true human nature but becoming a human person. Their use of the word 'assumption' almost inevitably glides into an Adoptionist Christology, a human being to whom, at His conception, birth or baptism, the Divine Logos joins Himself and by so doing adopting this human being and endowing Him with the status of sonship in a unique sense. Even if we avoid the idea of a dual personality and of a dual consciousness and explicitly repudiate the idea of a combination of two selves in one, yet the thought of the Divine Logos entering into union with a human self or Ego inevitably suggests someone in whom the Logos came to dwell, and this 'someone' is not a pre-existent eternal Person in being prior to the Incarnation, but one already constituted in His own right as a person before the Logos united Him in a personal fellowship with Himself. Either the Divine Nature of Jesus Christ was adjectival to His human personality or His human nature was adjectival to His Divine Personality.✓ Even if, however, we can conceive of the Second Person of the Blessed Trinity becoming an earthly being with a human personality of His own or possessing a human Ego creatively produced by the very act of Incarnation, what we have in the result is a human person, a man, and not as Catholic Christology contends *a* man and yet *the* Man. There is no avoiding the fact that in the orthodox view in some undefined but none the less real sense, the manhood assumed into union with the Deity was impersonal and such personality as it came to possess by virtue of the Incarnation was the personality of Very God of Very God. It never had a personality of its own before the Second Adam made the human nature He took His own. That is the significance of the Virgin Conception. The offspring of two human parents would result in a man with a personality of his own. The offspring of the Virgin Mary was the Divine Son of God. We need not deny the reality and completeness of His Manhood when we deny to that Manhood a human Ego of its own, since the Logos in becoming Himself incarnate conferred upon the Manhood He took His own selfhood.

And this because Divine Personality contained within It all that goes to the making up of a truly human and not a merely human self. If the Archetypal Man from Heaven is the Logos, then the Incarnate Lord was Perfect Man as well as Perfect God, not merely a man but the Man. Let us then compare and contrast two views of the Incarnation so as to define the issues involved in as clear a way as our modern language permits:

(*a*) The rational unorthodox view. A man indwelt by God.
(*b*) The Catholic conception of the Incarnation. God becoming Man.

A MAN, INDWELT BY GOD

Begin from empirical standpoint; history contains the record of a Life lived which, whatever else it may have been, was human.

A man Jesus lived in Palestine twenty centuries ago. Talked, ate, walked, revealed all the essential characteristics which justify our placing Him in the category 'Man'. All the evidence goes to show that He was conscious of His own distinct individuality as a man among men. He was a Jew of Palestine with an intellectual horizon limited by the conditions of His time and influenced by the circumstances of His Jewish upbringing and the Nazareth life. In these conditions and within these limitations He revealed a life which subsequent study shows us to have been a Divine Life. The verdict of a few at the time, of more after His Resurrection, and of thousands in the course of subsequent history has been that more must be said of Him if justice is to be done to His extraordinary character and the influence He exercised and still exercises upon men.

The subject of His Birth is of secondary importance, so it is argued. Some hold that He was miraculously born; others that this is a mere legend quite in accord with similar stories which become associated with the births of great men. More probably, so it is contended, He was born of two earthly parents — Joseph and Mary — in the ordinary course of nature. In any case no decision one way or the other need detain us, since it has no real bearing upon the question who He was and this last question must be decided on other grounds.

After a full and presumably exhaustive study of His life and its subsequent influence upon the world, it is felt that the best formula to cover the whole phenomenon would be the Pauline phrase 'God was in Christ (Jesus), reconciling the world unto Himself'. We have then God and Christ Jesus — two distinct entities. God in Heaven, the man Jesus Christ on earth. There is an intimate connection and relationship between the two. Jesus Christ was the maximum revelation of the Divine in human life. God dwelt in Christ ὡς ἐν οὐδένι ἄλλῳ as Paul of Samosata said, and was condemned for saying it. The man Jesus was a real person with a real human consciousness capable of revealing to Himself at once His distinction from God and His intimate communion with Him. He in his earthly life 'responded to the Divine advances with exquisite sensitiveness and with entire completeness'. In this He was at one with the saints and godly men of the past, yet He differed from them in the degree of the Divine inspiration and Divine indwelling. God dwells in the hearts of the humble and meek, yet their sinfulness constitutes a barrier which in the case of Jesus did not exist in so far as He was morally pure. Without pronouncing a verdict one way or the other upon the question of His sinlessness — since it is impossible to prove a universal negative

— yet it is almost generally agreed that the character of Christ Jesus stands out as a moral and spiritual mountain peak — approached in height indeed by others before and since, yet so far not equalled, still less excelled. Hence the Divine in Him has reached its hitherto maximum expression and revelation, though there is no reason on *a priori* grounds for excluding the possibility of its being surpassed in the future moral progress of the race.

Such in brief outline seems to us to be the rational or unorthodox view of Christ's Person. We refrain from associating any particular names of individual persons with the view outlined because of the notorious difficulty of expressing, even by the use of their own phraseology, what exactly and precisely any particular individual means. There is always the danger of being accused of misrepresentations. But apart from any question of individuals, we think that the views we have outlined do represent a fairly widespread cycle of thought and conclusions on the Person of Christ.

Now such a Christology is poles asunder from Catholic teaching in vital points. The utmost it can ever yield us as regards His Person is that Jesus of Nazareth was a man approved by God: it can never reach the Catholic verdict: He was God incarnate. We want to make the antithesis as clear-cut and sharply defined as possible.

The Catholic Christology : God Incarnate

If we begin our thought of the Incarnation with the picture before our minds of a man, Jesus, with a distinct consciousness of Himself as such, we can never reach the heart of the mystery of the Word made Flesh. The whole point of the Catholic Christology is a distinct and emphatic repudiation of this line of approach. It says in effect: you cannot start with the thought of Jesus as a man distinct from God. If you do so, your Christology ultimately reduces itself to some form of Adoptionism. If you persist in thinking of Jesus as a man indwelt by God, then no matter what the

degree of indwelling may have been, it never gives you anything beyond a man, the chief of the saints, a demi-god if
you like, higher than the angels, but in the last analysis not
God Himself in human form — God manifesting Himself in
a human person to the fullest possible extent, if you like, but
this is not what is meant by the Incarnation.

How, then, are we to approach the problem from the
Catholic standpoint?

The Church has held that the only way is to begin with
the thought not of a man in whom God comes to dwell but
of God Himself becoming Man, and between the Antiochene
and Alexandrine methods of approach to the problem there
is a great gulf fixed.

✓ Therefore the question of the Virgin Birth is not a side-
issue: it is a vital factor in the whole problem.

Why?

Because if you think of His Birth as the normal product
of two human parents, you have the existence in the physical
world of a man, distinct and distinguishable from God,
having an existence in His own right in relationship to God.
Then no matter how intimate that relationship may have
been — and you can exhaust the language of human thought
in attempting to describe it — nevertheless it falls short of
the real truth, viz. that ultimately the central constituent of
His Person was Divine — He was God Himself Incarnate.

Catholic theology is concerned with the problem: how
could God Himself lead a human life? Its answer is the
mystery of the Virgin Birth. Who for us men and for our
salvation came down from Heaven: and was Incarnate by
the Holy Ghost of the Virgin Mary and was made Man.
Not that a man became in some sense God but that God in
some sense became Man.

If, then, the central constituent of His Person was
Divine, it means that there never existed a human man
Jesus with a consciousness of His own apart from God. But
you may say, 'Surely He was Perfect Man as well as Perfect
God, and if so Perfect Manhood is meaningless unless it
contains the central constituent of Manhood, viz. a human

personality?' This the Church admitted in rejecting Apollinarianism. If then He was Perfect God and Perfect Man
— does not this involve two personalities co-existing side by
side in the One Christ Jesus? Here we meet with the problem raised by Nestorianism and the criticism urged against
Chalcedonian Christology which, it is said, never solves the
problem but states the premises and leaves us with an in-
curable dualism.

Two Natures involve two Persons. Could two Persons,
God and the man Christ Jesus, exist side by side and live a
common life in the Person of Jesus of Nazareth?

Yes, certainly, some would say; Jesus was indwelt by
God. The mode of the Divine indwelling is known to us in
some degree by the experience of the saints and godly men
who can say, 'I live yet no longer I but God liveth in me'.
Just as St. Paul could say of his own personality, 'I live, yet
no longer I, but Christ liveth in me', so Jesus Himself could
say, 'I live, — I, Jesus of Nazareth, born of Mary, live, yet
My life is in God who dwells in Me as in no other and of
whom I am so conscious as penetrating into and abiding in
the deepest recesses of My human being that I cannot say
if I am I, and He is He — all I know is that We were two,
He entered into Me and now We are one'.

Such a picture of the Incarnation, elaborate it as you will
— and to any extent — still remains ultimately *Nestorianism*
and is not the Catholic Faith. So many modern 'Lives of
Jesus' ultimately, if regard be taken not only to what they
say but what they leave unsaid, stop short of the Catholic
teaching and in fact can never reach it, simply because their
starting-point is the wrong one. They commence with the
'Jesus of History', whom they conceive of as a man, and
they go on to try to show how conceivably He was more than
a man. The task is hopeless. The plain fact is that the
'Jesus of History' in this sense never existed. It is a fictitious
character conceived of as portrayed in the Gospels, but we
submit that the Gospels rightly interpreted contain no such
figure. The Jesus of the Gospels — the Jesus of true History
— is from first to last a Divine Figure — not a man clothed

with Divine attributes but the Two-Natured Christ Jesus from first to last.

It may be contended that, after all, the Christological problem is an intellectual challenge which the Chalcedonian definition merely states but fails to solve. If, then, we reject the whole Antiochene standpoint as doomed from the outset never to reach the proper conception of the Incarnation as the Church came to think of it, still less to present us with an adequate Christological theory, what can we offer in its place as a more satisfactory contribution? Are we to rest satisfied with a Christological formula such as that of the Council of Chalcedon which admittedly fails to solve the problem and is a stumbling-block to the intelligence, and a formula which has been severely criticised both at the hands of Liberal and Conservative theologians? Dr. Sellers does not pursue his studies beyond the point reached by the two ancient schools of thought and so fails to assess the contribution of Leontius of Byzantium. This was the last word of the Ancient Church in the effort to penetrate deeper into the mystery, and the doctrine of the Enhypostasia, whether as Leontius presented it or as we have tried to reinterpret it in modern terms in *A Study in Christology*, remains as marking the limits to which human ratiocinative activity can reach so long as we are held within the circle of the categories of thought employed by the ancient Christologists. It is possible, of course, to jettison those categories and to start afresh with an entirely new set of terms more in accord with our modern outlook and current modes of thought, and the resultant Christology still awaits our eager and expectant hopes. But so far what has been offered by more recent thinkers has not impressed us. May we hope that the thesis of Dr. Sellers, marked as it is by prolonged research, careful exegesis, exact scholarship and a firm appreciation of the issues at stake, may prove to be the stimulus to a younger generation to take up the study afresh at the point where the Ancient Church halted and give us a modern Christology, enshrining primarily and essentially all those spiritual values in a true doctrine of the Incarnation for which the Alexandrine theologians contended, whilst at the same time trying to do justice to the contribution which we believe with Dr. Sellers the Antiochene school may still offer ?

It is a pity that considerations of space and cost of printing should have forced Dr. Sellers to relegate to footnotes in small type some of his best work, including a courteous but effective handling of the shortcomings of an ill-balanced production of Dr. Raven's on *Apollinarianism*. There is ample material, however, in what he has managed to compress into these pages to kindle afresh the enthusiasm of us older men and to inspire the younger students in the never-ending quest after an adequate Christology.

CHAPTER 4

THE PERSON OF CHRIST AND RECENT DISCUSSION

The Person of Christ and some Modernist attempts
at reconstruction in terms of Modern thought

THE problems of philosophy are ever new and yet old. A perusal of the history of philosophy shows us that each succeeding age has to think out the answers to the same questions which perplexed previous generations. The same problems reappear with varying emphasis but with a certain uniformity of sequence. The terms employed may vary from age to age but the substance of the thought remains the same. The problems which beset the modern mind are at bottom the same problems as those which perplexed the ancient Greek thinkers. In philosophy nothing is fixed and settled finally. No one theory of Reality has ever succeeded in gaining such universal acceptance as to secure for itself the status of a dogma or the label of infallible certitude. The struggle between the Realist and the Idealist is never ended. Rival philosophies can never call a truce. If this is true in philosophy, it is equally true in theology. The task of a philosophy of religion is to relate the truths of natural and revealed religion to the wider fields of human thought. Hence each age needs its philosophy of religion adapted to the growth in thought and progress in discovery reached by succeeding generations.

There cannot be anything static about a philosophy of religion. It must from time to time adapt itself to varying thought-forms and express itself in the prevalent concepts of the age. From the intellectual standpoint the great need of our time is a Christian Philosophy. It must adequately relate Christian truth to the rest of human knowledge gained in other departments of thought and research. The lack of such a Christian philosophy is revealed in the conflict between Science and Religion and between modern philosophy and Christian revelation.

Now 'Modernism' is an attempt to relate Christian truth to the modern mind; to explain the Christian Creed in terms of modern thought; to re-think out the theological concepts of the past (as found in the history of dogma) and to present them afresh in the thought-forms of the present. No age can expect to escape such a task. If the Church refuses to undertake it, men outside the Church will not fail to do so. The rationalists, outside the fold, are the real explanation of the Modernists inside. In this sense we are all 'Modernists', or rather, we all ought to be. None of us can escape the task of the intellect and the discipline of clear thinking, if we consider our Christian belief and try to express it in the thought-forms of our own day and generation. The trouble is that, whilst the task and the discipline are an obligation upon all, so few are found either capable or willing to undertake it. We have to be reminded, in these days, that there is a mental sleep begotten of familiarity with revealed truth. There is a real danger lest we should be content to rest in the false security of 'fixed opinions' and thus lose the capacity to think at all. In one of J. S. Mill's essays he says that 'the fatal tendency of mankind to leave off thinking about a thing when it is no longer doubtful, is the cause of half their errors'.

There is a certain type of Churchmanship whose formula is 'the Faith once for all delivered to the saints'. This apparently is an excuse for a prolonged mental sleep, in which there is gradually formed in a man a kind of opaqueness of mind which makes it practically impossible for him to take in new truth. If perchance a modernist movement wake such a one from his dogmatic slumbers, his only weapon of defence is abuse of a scholarship he himself too often lacks and an appeal to authority in defence of a truth he himself is incapable of understanding, still less of maintaining in the face of opposition. The decay of scholarship

in the English Church to-day, and the lack of mental alert-
ness, are a source of great weakness. As we read the history
of the great Christological campaign which culminated in
the fifth century, with such notable triumphs for the Church
in the sphere of intellectual achievement, we remind ourselves that there were giants in those days on the side of
orthodoxy, equal, if not superior, to their opponents in intellectual grip and capacity for sustained thought. If in
our day the rationalism of the secularists without, and the
questionings of the Modernists within the Church, do seriously threaten to undermine the foundations of our Christian
Faith, the defence of it lies not in the direction of mental
inertia. We must be prepared to say not simply that the
Modernists are wrong but why they are so. We must be
prepared to give a reason for the faith that is in us. If the
Christological problem is ultimately a metaphysical one, we
need not be surprised to find in these days a repetition of
ancient speculation; a reappearance of imperfect and inadequate thought on the subject; the emergence once again
of half-truths, over-emphasis, lack of balance in the presentation of the truth.

Dr. Luce has reminded us that heretical tendencies will
be found in the Christian community in every generation,
and the religious thought of individual Christians will pass
through heretical phases. Such heresy is rather an intellectual than a moral fault; but the possibility of being the
heirs, without knowing it, of the opinions of Nestorius and
Eutyches throws on thinkers to-day the responsibility of
examining their Christological beliefs and of testing them
by the canon of orthodoxy.[1]

This being so, no age is exempt from the task of reconstruction. If we are always to have Christological heresies
with us, we must ever be ready to study afresh the great
Christological constructions of the Church of the fourth and
fifth centuries. We must find out exactly what conclusions
the Church reached; what errors it rejected: what pitfalls
it sought to safeguard thinkers from; what positive truths it

[1] *Monophysitism Past and Present*, pp. 117, 118.

fought to preserve. We must be prepared and fully equipped to do for the Church of the twentieth century what was done by great minds in ages past, viz. to present in terms of the best thought of to-day the truth of the Person of Jesus Christ as we know it in Christian experience.

If Christology is an attempt to explain in terms of personality the relation between God and the world, then it is clear that a metaphysical problem lies behind the Christological construction of ancient times and the attempted reconstruction of modern times. According to Dr. Luce, the Nestorian, Monophysite and Catholic Christological systems are really three phases of the cosmic problem — the attempt to conceive and find expression for the relation between God and the world.

Dualism postulates the co-existence of God and the World. God is and the world is; the relation between them is expressed by an 'and'. God *and* the World. The counterpart of dualism and deism is Nestorianism. The dualist, content to couple God and the world by an 'and', so couples the Logos and Jesus in his Christological theory.

Monism postulates the identity of God and the world. God *is* the world and the world *is* God. The counterpart of this Monism and Pantheism in terms of personality, Dr. Luce contends, is Monophysitism — the assertion of the absolute numerical unity of the Person of Christ.

Theism would take as its starting-point neither God nor the world, nor the two as co-existing, but the relation between the two. Not 'God and the World' in an irreconcilable dualism nor 'the World and God' as ultimately identical in a Pantheistic sense, but 'God of the World' in a relationship and the relation such that the terms related are preserved in the relation. Neither identity nor difference is the full truth, but identity in and through difference. The cosmic relation is then expressed not by an 'and' nor by an 'is' but by an 'of': so in Christology in the Person of Christ we have not 'God and Man' co-existing side by side in an irreconcilable dualism, nor have we any Pantheistic identification of Deity and Humanity such as Monophysitism suggests, but we have the two-Natured Christ in whom the difference between the Human and the Divine is preserved in their union inasmuch as the Two Natures or Substances are not confounded: in whom the Unity of Person is preserved, inasmuch as in the Christ there is One Person in Two Natures: in whom finally there is preserved a relationship between the Human and the Divine which is of such a character that its existence proves the affinity between the two, whilst its preservation in the midst of this difference proves that the relationship is not merged in an identity of one with the other. The very fact that Divinity is not Humanity, whilst Humanity is at the same time akin to Divinity, makes a relationship between the two possible. Such a relationship could not exist if one term were identical with the other.

The Chalcedonian Christology which makes Jesus Christ consubstantial with God and Man, and thus reveals Him as the Mediator between the Two, the GOD-MAN is a Christology which has as its background such a solution of the Cosmic problem as excludes a Monism of identity; and a dualism of difference; a Christology which steers a middle course between Monophysitism and Nestorianism, refusing to confound the substances or divide the persons: rejecting alike any confusion between the Human, the Divine and the idea of the Incarnation as that of a man in whom the Logos dwelt. The Church rejects the thought of the Incarnation as a theophany — God in the semblance of a man called Jesus; the Church equally rejects the idea of a man called Jesus, who in some sense can be called God, a Divine being because, and only because, He was a Perfect Man. The Church has rejected both Docetism and Adoptionism in all their varied forms, and has maintained, and still teaches, a true Incarnation of the Son of GOD, who though He was rich yet for our sakes became poor that we through His poverty might be made rich.

(a) THE DOCTRINE OF THE ENHYPOSTASIA

The Catholic doctrine maintains that He who was GOD without ceasing to be what He was, became man — i.e. entered into the conditions of our finite existence in time and space — and dwelt amongst us. The opposite opinion is that He who was a man became what He was not — viz. Divine — or, if you like, that He who was a man exhibited the maximum of Divine immanence in His human life. Now the one conception is at least conceivable; the other suggests that the barrier between the Creator and the creature has been removed in such a manner as to enable that which is human to partake of the Divine essence to the extent of becoming one in nature with God.

If objection be taken to the use of the terms 'Creator' and 'creature', and we be asked to define the issue in terminology which certainly lends itself to ambiguous juggling, we do so under protest. If we use the phraseology, 'Divine' and 'human', then we have this issue: Either He who was Divine became man, or He who was a man in some sense is to be regarded as Divine. Clearly this phraseology demands definition. Is our divinity different in kind from His? If so, in what precisely does the difference consist? If it be a difference in kind, it must be the difference between the Divinity of God in His own right and the conferred divinity we possess as creatures receiving from Him a supernatural Grace. Again, His Humanity and ours differ. Ours is the creaturely humanity of the created and sinful; His is the Humanity of the Creator.

Now, with these distinctions in our minds, we can consider the above two conceptions of the Person of Christ. He who was essentially Divine with a Divinity consubstantial with God's became incarnate by the Holy Ghost, of the Virgin Mary, and was made man. Such an Incarnation is conceivable, if we remember that the way had been paved for it from the first creation of man in the Divine image. This means that there is a human element in God from all eternity, and this human element had been imperfectly reflected in created form in the sons of men. The truly human is the humanity of God; the merely or purely human is the humanity of man — a created and imperfect humanity which can never become anything but human, no matter how fully indwelt it may be by the Divine. When, therefore, God became Man, the Humanity He exhibited was not a created humanity, such as ours is, but the truly human such as God alone possesses, and in the likeness of which we are made. Now in the light of this it is clear how inadequate the alternative theory of Christ's Person is. He who was a man, a creature like ourselves (for the Virgin Birth is denied), exhibited in His own person the Divine in human life. But if He were a man already, He could never have become other than merely or purely human, even if in His case the 'incarnation' be interpreted as the exhibition of the climax of the Divine immanence. Except upon the supposition (which is fundamentally subversive of Catholic teaching) that man is capable of deification, the human can never become the Divine. It may become wonderfully like it; it has affinity with it, but likeness is not identity. The human at its maximum is but the likeness of the truly human which is in God alone. This means ultimately that the humanity of Jesus Christ was not the humanity we know in ourselves. It was God's humanity, which differs from ours to the extent to which the Creator differs from the creature. God's humanity revealed in Christ is the unveiling before our eyes of that of which we are created copies. The original is His. Created copies may, by His fashioning, become wonderfully like unto Him; that is their goal and end. Advance in holiness will make us more truly human, not quasi-divine beings. If an approximation to the truly human reveals us as more and more like God, this likeness is never identification in essence. We may call it, if we like, the Divine in human life, but we must not identify our acquired divinity with that of Jesus, and be misled into thinking that our likeness to Him makes Him in all points identical in nature with us.

That we should see points of similarity between the Humanity of the God-Man and our humanity is to be expected, but this must not blind us to the fact of an eternal distinction between Him and us in the midst of innumerable points of contact we love to discover and dwell upon as linking the Jesus of the Gospels with our imperfect human lives. We may grant the Modernist all he asks for when he points us to the complete manhood of our Blessed Saviour, but this complete Manhood, this truly human character, is only conceivable upon the supposition that it was not human as we know the human; it was the truly human as it exists not in us but in God alone, and in us only as a pale copy, a created imitation of the truly real. And surely this difference makes itself felt in a thousand ways as we study this Jesus of the Gospels, as we hear His words and mark His attitude as He moves about amongst men. The 'man in the street' instinctively feels this subtle difference, even though he may not be able to define its content. It suggests to his mind that modern Churchmen in conference, in spite of their obvious sincerity, their appeal to reason and common sense, and their helpful attempt to do justice to the personality of the wonderful figure of the Gospels, have somehow missed their way and fallen short of the true solution in their efforts to describe the indescribable solely in terms of the best we know in human life.

The merely human, even if called the revelation of the Divine in human life, cannot quite contain all that Jesus was, and the 'something more' that is demanded by the evidence of the Gospel data is just this difference between the reality and its shadow in the finite human life of the creature; just the difference between the original and the copy — the Humanity of Deity and the humanity of the creature made in the image of God; like Him, indeed, at its best, but not He in the ultimate analysis.

The frank recognition of these differences between His Divinity and ours, His humanity and that we know in ourselves, is necessary, if we are to make any attempt today to face afresh the Christological problem. Let us state quite simply, at the risk of repetition, precisely in what these differences consist:

(1) The difference between His Divinity and ours is the difference between Deity in its own right and conferred or derived divinity such as we are capable of possessing, if so be that God dwells in us.

(2) The difference between His Humanity and ours is the difference between a Humanity which is truly Human because it is His Humanity, and our imperfect human nature which can approximate to the truly Human to the extent to which He dwells in it. It is thus the difference between the perfect and the imperfect — a difference, if you like, in degree, but a difference which must ever separate us from Him, inasmuch as He possesses completely what we can only come to possess as a gift from Himself when He feeds us with His Sacred Humanity. The human as we know it must ever remain imperfect apart from His gift to it of Divine Grace. The human needs the Divine in order to make it truly human. The Human in Jesus Christ was truly human only because He who was Divine dwelt in It, and His Presence made the Human Nature He assumed Divinely Human. Thus to sum up the points:

The distinction between Jesus Christ and ourselves is one that concerns both factors, the Human and the Divine. As regards the first, His is the Humanity of Deity, not a created copy such as we possess. Hence the conception of Him as the Archetypal Man. Hence also the wonder of His truly Human life, which could be at once particular and limited, whilst at the same time Universal and unlimited in its world-wide revelation to all races of what the truly Human really is.

As regards the second, He is Divine in His own right; His Deity is not a conferred divinity such as ours is, and in the possession of which we can alone achieve our true end — viz. to become not quasi-divine beings, but our truly human selves.

If, further, a theory is required to do justice to both these factors in the Christological problem and to keep us to the true perspective in our efforts to formulate the relationship between the Divine and the Human both in ourselves and in the Person of Christ, then the doctrine of the Enhypostasia, reinterpreted in terms of modern thought, is the only one that can cover the whole data, and do justice to the reality of the Human and the Divine, and thus keep us true to the Nicene and the Chalcedonian Christology.

To make the issue plain in a sentence. We challenge the whole Modernist identification of the Divine and Human in us with the Divine and Human in the Person of Christ. There is a difference in both cases, and confusion results if we persist in ignoring this difference. At the same time the differences do not preclude such a measure of affinity and likeness as to make an Incarnation possible. They do rule out identity and so preclude Pantheism.

The conception of the Incarnation as the climax of Divine Immanence in human life falls short of the Catholic teaching in this, that ultimately it comes to the thought of God dwelling in a man, a particular person, Jesus of Nazareth, in whom He dwelt ὡς ἐν οὐδενὶ ἄλλῳ. This gives us two persons — a particular person, Jesus, and God, who dwelt in Him. We thus reach Nestorianism. This is inevitable if we regard the central constituent of the Person of Christ as human. The problem, then, is to say whether any degree of Divine indwelling in a human person can make that person other than human. And, if we argue from our experience of the Divine in human life, the answer must be that it would not. No amount of inpouring into the human can make it other than human. The more fully we are endowed by Divine Grace, the more truly ourselves we become; the more intimately the Holy Spirit of God pervades us through and through, the more truly human we find ourselves becoming. St. Paul's experience of a life hid with Christ in God did not make him other than human. He was never more truly himself than when he had surrendered himself wholeheartedly to the Divine embrace. And with this deep truth is bound up the whole question of our future destiny as the sons of God. In it we have the guarantee, as against all forms of Eastern Pantheism, that God will preserve and respect our individuality and save us from such an absorption into Himself as shall involve the loss of our own created and distinctive personality. The maximum, then, of the Divine Immanence in human life leaves that human life truly human, not Divine. The human remains itself and is not transmuted into the quasi-divine. We may speak of the man as human with the Divine in him, but we cannot call him a Divine Person in the sense in which the Church regards Jesus Christ as such.

We must then postulate that in His case the central constituent of His Person was Divine. A pre-existent Divine Person, One with God in Essence, at a certain point in the world's history was born into the conditions of our finite life. The problem, then, is to conceive of the possibility of such an event, and to define so far as possible what are the conditions under which such an event could have taken place. How could God live a human life? How could that which is immortal and infinite be at the same time mortal and finite? How, again, can we speak of His having been a real human person when the human ego in His case was *ex hypothesi* not there. Does not this inevitably suggest an Impersonal Manhood? Have we not drifted into Apollinarianism? Are we not thinking of a Divine Person clothing Himself with the attributes of humanity — taking a human body and dwelling in it? The contention of the Modernists is that this is precisely what is implied in the Christology of the Chalcedonian Fathers, and that it is fundamentally subversive of the reality and completeness of the Manhood of Jesus Christ as that is revealed to us in all its truly human naturalness in the Gospel portrait.

Now in the first place the Chalcedonian formula was not meant as an explanation of the mystery, but as a clear statement of the problem involved, with a warning that in the attempt to solve it we must be careful above all else not to neglect or overlook any of the data. If we do so, the formula tells us we shall inevitably fall into certain clearly defined errors, such as Apollinarianism, Nestorianism or Eutychianism. We may fail to do justice to the reality and completeness of Christ's Manhood. We may fail to realise the truth of His Essential Consubstantiality with God. We may think of His Person as in some sense an amalgam of the Divine and the Human, thus confounding the Persons. We may be led to think that there were really two Persons: a man, Jesus by name, and God who dwelt in Him as in no other. All these solutions had been put forward by thinkers in the endeavour to solve the Christological problem, and the Chalcedonian Fathers warn us that these solutions failed because of some one-sided exaggeration of one or other factor in the data. We are told what to avoid. We are instructed what to bear in mind as essential to a right faith. We are not bound, however, by any theory. Certain erroneous theories are ruled out, it is true; but the Church does not bind us to any positive theory in so many words. We are still free within these limits to construct a theory for ourselves if we can. Now the significance of the Modernist movement lies in the fact that they are attempting to construct a theory in the light of what they consider to be the better opportunities opened before us to-day as the result of the advance in knowledge since the days of Chalcedon.

It comes, then, to this, that no true solution of the Christological problem is adequate if our starting point is a human Jesus, the central constituent of whose person is a human ego. We must begin with the Alexandrian conception of a Divine Personality, and then face the real crux of orthodox Christology — viz. the charge of Apollinarianism.

Can this charge be met? We think it can to an adequate extent by the doctrine of the Enhypostasia.

Leontius of Byzantium was perfectly aware of the fact that the Chalcedonian formula must be interpreted either in an Antiochene or in an Alexandrian sense. He saw clearly that this latter sense was the only sound one to secure a real Incarnation. He was well aware of the Apollinarian danger, and he set himself to combat this on the basis of Aristotelianism.

The modern reinterpretation of this doctrine has these points in view:

(1) An analysis of human personality reveals it as ever incomplete and in process of becoming. An investigation of religious experience in general and the specifically Christian experience of communion with God in Christ in particular suggests that the incompleteness of human personality is met by, and its growth depends upon, the Divine Grace; the impartation of the Divine Life to the human in communion and fellowship. The result of such Divine Self-donation is an ever-increasing approximation of the merely human to the truly human. The greater the fulness of the Divine Grace, the more truly, not purely, human, a man becomes. The lives of the saints testify to this. The Ideal is seen in the Person of Christ, who alone can be spoken of as τέλειος ἄνθρωπος because He was not merely or purely human — not the possessor, therefore, of an imperfect manhood — but truly human in that He was Divine. His Divinity therefore gave to His Humanity just that element which was needed for its completeness and perfection.

(2) God is perfect Personality, and our human personalities are mere approximations to this — pale copies, as Lotze taught us long ago.

(3) There is a human element in God, and this alone makes an Incarnation possible, inasmuch as it secures such an affinity between the human and the Divine as is essential to any true union of them both. Affinity, however, is never identity.

(4) From this it follows that God already possessed in Himself, prior to the Incarnation, everything needful to enable Him to live a truly human life. In the Incarnation, therefore, the pre-existent Divine Logos brought to the human nature He assumed just that element which we have seen above (under our first point) to be essential, if the merely human is to become truly and completely human. The Divine Logos was capable, therefore, of being the Ego, not only of the Divine, but also of the Human nature. Because His Personality, in virtue of its Divinity, already possessed

all that is most distinctive of a truly human personality, it follows that if the Divine Ego were the central constituent in His Person, the Manhood was not impersonal. Why? Because this same Divine Ego possessed all that was needful to impart a truly human personality to that which otherwise would have remained impersonal and merely a series of detached human attributes, lacking a central focus such as our human ego gives to our human nature. His Ego was Divine — it was also, therefore, in His case human. Had it lacked the human element in God, it could not have had a Manhood other than impersonal, but the whole point of the doctrine of the Enhypostasia is that the greater contains the less — the Divine Ego, because it is God's Personality, must contain the human ego in the image of which we are made.

If man be made in the image of God, there must be something in God to which we bear an imperfect likeness. Now in what precisely in us is this likeness to be found? Not in our bodily shape, surely, but in that which differentiates us from the animal creation, that which we call human personality. In our case, as we have seen, this human personality is incomplete and imperfect, a faint copy of the Original which God alone possesses, and in which He has made us. Therefore, if He chooses to live a human life, He can do so, and reveal in human form what a truly human personality really is. Because He was the Son of God, He was capable of living a human life, not as a merely human person, one of ourselves, would live it, but as it should be lived and as He alone has lived it. He was perfect Man because He was perfect God. He alone could live a truly human life, because at every moment of His earthly career He was also the Divine Son of God.

What was wanted was a revelation of One who was Divine, and therefore perfectly human, even if infinitely more than this. The human ego in man is incomplete. The Manhood of Christ, if it had possessed a human ego only, would have been incomplete.

Now the Modernists are demanding that we recognise the completeness, the reality and the perfection of Christ's

Manhood. They think that this is secured if the central
constituent of His Person is a human ego. According to our
view, this is precisely the condition of securing that His Manhood would be incomplete. If the central constituent were
a human ego only, He would be *ipso facto* imperfect. They
think that if His Personality were Divine His manhood
would be impersonal. Precisely the opposite would be the
case, according to the doctrine of the Enhypostasia.

We grant with Leontius that a φύσις ἀνυπόστατος is a
mere philosophical abstraction. Manhood as an attribute
or series of attributes has no meaning, if meant as a substitute
for a truly personal life such as we know Jesus lived in the
days of His flesh. We contend, however, that the Manhood
of Jesus Christ was not without hypostasis — it was not impersonal even though His personality was a Divine Personality. The human nature became hypostatic in the Person
of the Logos. As against Nestorians we deny that the
human personality ever had an existence in its own right
as a distinct entity before the Incarnation. Jesus Christ,
the merely human man, never existed. Although the manhood had no independent personality of its own, and had, in
fact, no existence at all before the Incarnation, nevertheless
it became hypostatic in the Person of the Logos, and received
its subsistence from Him. The human nature of the God-
Man was from the first inseparably united with the Divine
Nature, and in virtue of that union received from the Logos-
Personality its personality, and thus its completeness.

If Divine Personality already contains in Itself all that
goes to make up what is distinctively human personality,
then the doctrine of Enhypostasia escapes the charge of
Apollinarianism whilst doing justice to the truth contained
in that error — viz. that there is a human element in God —
and this is the basis of the Incarnation.

We are well aware that in thus attempting to state in
popular language a theory of this kind we lay ourselves open
to misinterpretation, and are exposed to the charge of
misuse of phrases. What is here written is no philosophical
treatise, but an effort to state in untechnical language, so

far as possible, a theory which can in reality be substantiated in the light of the profoundest analysis of personality, human and Divine, of which modern philosophical speculation and psychological investigation is capable.

For a much more exhaustive treatment we may perhaps be allowed to refer to *A Study in Christology*, (S.P.C.K., 1917). All we ask is that the Modernists will study the doctrine of the Enhypostasia in all its bearings, and then ask themselves whether it does not do justice to all for which they are contending when they plead for the reality and completeness of Christ's truly human life, and whether the doctrine does not at the same time acquit the received Church Christology of the charge of Apollinarianism whilst enabling us to do full justice to the Deity of Christ.

We have still, in our modern thought on the Problem of Christ's Person, to make up our minds in the choice between two rival Christologies. Was it a man called Jesus leading a Divine life, or GOD the Son leading a human life — which? It is in effect to-day the point at issue in the ancient rival schools of Antioch and Alexandria. If we begin with the full humanity of the GOD-Man as personal, then the Divinity appears to be adjectival. If we begin with the Divinity as personal, then the humanity appears to be adjectival.

The Church in the Monothelite controversy decided in favour of the Two Wills and therefore presumably in the 'Two Consciousnesses' of the One Christ. We can still include all this in our modern reinterpretation of the doctrine of the Enhypostasia. We can think of the One Christ with His dual consciousness as God leading a human life in the days of His flesh.

As such He would know Himself as God the Son in relation to God the Father, and fulfilling the rôle of the Messiah, the Son of Man, the Suffering Servant, in obedience to the Divine Will, whilst at the same time fully conscious of Himself as of One Substance with the Father as touching His Godhead, yet for our sakes leading His human life, and winning our salvation. The doctrine of the Enhypostasia suggests that the Divine Ego was capable of being the human ego, the subject of the human nature He had assumed in order to lead a human life. The Church at the Second General Council decided upon the full Manhood of the Master, the τέλειος ἄνθρωπος, the completely human, that is to say a Manhood of the God-Man which meant Two Wills and Two Consciousnesses, but not necessarily, therefore, an impossible dualism, since it was the One Christ who functioned in the two natures, the Divine and the human.

The late Dr. Wm. Temple once asked us whether by 'Enhypostasia' we really meant what Kant meant in his distinction between the transcendental and the empirical ego? This certainly would throw some further light upon the subject now being debated on the Continent concerning the Two Consciousnesses of the One Christ.

For English students it would be best to start where Sanday left off with his attempt to define the *locus* of the Divine in the subliminal consciousness. What is needed is a reassessment of the whole problem in the light of an up-to-date psychology. The choice would still lie between the Alexandrine and Antiochene approach. Either the Chalcedonian Definition and its defence in a reinterpretation of the doctrine of the Enhypostasia as Leontius of Byzantium outlined it, or a fresh attempt to penetrate what Nestorius had in his mind in his fumbling efforts to do justice to the Antiochene standpoint. Dr. Vine, in his book, *An Approach to Christology* (Independent Press, 1948), has tried to show us what the metaphysic of Nestorius was, and how he was groping towards a better Christology than that of Cyril of Alexandria, and one which could do full justice to the Antiochene standpoint. We think that Dr. Vine's book has not received the attention of students which it deserves. Certainly it is now highly relevant to the debate now going on amongst Continental thinkers concerning the Two Consciousnesses of the One Christ Jesus.

Meantime we can include in our doctrine of the Enhypostasia this fresh emphasis upon a psychological approach to the Christological problem. We can call to our aid, for example, the line of thought suggested by the late Dr. G. L. Prestige in his Bampton Lectures on *Fathers and Heretics*, and especially what he says on pages 160-1:

'Apollinarius defined man as "consciousness in flesh" (Frag. 72), but refused to admit the need for that consciousness to be subjected to human limitations; a fully Divine and unreduced consciousness, unconditioned by its association with the flesh, and operating the flesh like a mechanical instrument, satisfied both his definition of human nature and his theory of the Incarnation.

'Cyril did not fall into that mistake. He saw that a human consciousness is subject to special conditions and limitations with its physical organism, and he improved the definition accordingly. "What else", he asked, "is the nature of Manhood except flesh consciously ensouled, in which we assert that the Lord suffered in the flesh?" (*Ad Succens*, 2, 145D). To deny the human soul is to eliminate the conditions which make the consciousness genuinely human.

'Christ, then, had a human soul. Or more strictly, just as deity is something that God is, rather than something which He has, so a soul or finite consciousness is really something that a person is, rather than a possession that he owns; and as Christ became a man, rather than took possession of a man, so it would be truer to say that He subjected His divine consciousness, within the incarnate sphere, to the limitations involved in a physical existence. He adapted Himself to "flesh consciously ensouled", voluntarily limiting the range and action of his divine mind to physical conditions, and Himself, thus limited, became the soul of his "ensouled flesh". This view, which is what Cyril's teaching really amounts to, involves a number of corollaries.

'It implies the real continuity of the human soul of Christ with His divine consciousness, on which Cyril laid great stress. It further involves the conception that man is not a combination of two disjunct elements of soul and body, regarded as almost independent and unrelated factors, so much as a mind physically conditioned — psychologically a far more satisfactory definition. It requires the assumption that Christ's human life was a real addition to His eternal life, yet an addition characterised rather by a new mode of action than by fresh content: what was always within His range as God, He now experienced over again as man. It argues that in His earthly life He made Himself less than He eternally was, reducing and contracting His infinite, eternal compass. And it assumes that human nature has certain definite constitutive principles, to the scale and limits of which He confined His human action.'

And again on pages 162-3:

'. . . there is a long succession of Christian thinkers who picture the relation between these two elements (soul and body) not as that subsisting between two equal and parallel components, but as that of a finite consciousness, which is the true self, to the physical conditions that permanently determine its character.

'Cyril is simply building on that tradition when he puts forward the self of God the Son, appropriately limited and conditioned, as the personal subject of the Manhood of Christ. . . .

'The relation between Christ's divine and human consciousness was not, as the strict two-nature school was bound to say, if pressed, that He took to Himself a second mind, but that within the sphere of His Incarnation He caused His own mind to be physically conditioned and limited.

'That is the point of Cyril's ruthless war upon Nestorius.'

On page 168 Prestige continues:

'Cyril is implying exactly what Theodore and Nestorius had attempted to express: the deity has its personality and the manhood also has its personality, but the two personalities are identically one and the same. The Antiochene leaders left the matter there as a mere assertion, unsupported by any attempt at explanation. Cyril adds the vitally important link: the reason why the two are identical is because the human personality is simply that of the divine subject under submission to physical condition.

'Cyril understood by the "nature" of God the Word, the divine Word in person, i.e. "nature" meant personality. It made no difference to the sense of the phrase whether he said that God the Son, or His personality, or His objective reality, was incarnate: the three expressions were exactly equivalent — that which exhibited in terms of deity is God the Son, is also when exhibited in terms of manhood, Jesus Christ.

'If His "nature" be regarded from the abstract point of view, as illustrating the terms which constitute or condition Him, then it must be admitted to be twofold; the terms of deity are quite distinct from those of manhood, and so remain. But if it be regarded from the concrete point of view, as the person, being or subject embodied and expressed in the terms, then He is One Christ, both God and Man.

'The manner of the Incarnation, however, is entirely beyond human understanding. The Incarnation depends on a continuous act of the Divine Will. It is fundamentally a condescension, a moral and personal dispensation of the loving-kindness of God.'

We can further call to our aid what the late Bishop Gore wrote in his one-volume *Reconstruction of Belief* in the appended note on Mackintosh's *The Doctrine of the Person of Christ* (*vide* especially pp. 848 ff., 858 ff. and 861-2), where he says:

'The human faculty of willing in Jesus came into existence when He became man. But there was another will-power, older than the human being of Christ, the divine will of the eternal Son — the will of Him who, not yet incarnate, emptied Himself, impoverished Himself, to be made man, and to "learn obedience" under conditions of human nature.

'. . . the will of Jesus is still the will of the eternal Son, though acting in and through a human will.

'Again, the consciousness of Jesus in His human life is the consciousness of the Man; but behind it is an older consciousness — that of the Eternal Son who has temporarily condescended to act under conditions of a human mind . . . the willing, and knowing and acting of the Man was not merely human, but had for its substratum the willing, and knowing and acting of the Eternal Son.' (Quoting pp. 861-2.)

In all our discussions, in our modern terminology, as to who is the 'I' in the Person of Jesus Christ, we must always keep clearly in our minds the distinction between *human nature* and *human personality*. If we ask, What is human nature? the answer is that it is what we share in common with the whole human race. If we ask, *What is human personality?* the answer is that it is what we share with no one else. It is that which separates me off from the race, and thus constitutes the meaning and value of finite individuality. From Adam, or the first human man, is transmitted to all his descendants human nature. The human individuality of each of us, however, is something that has not been transmitted to us, but constitutes in each of us a distinct and distinguishable self or 'Ego'. Human nature, then, is transmissible, but human personality is not. So human nature unites us all as members of the human race. Human personality separates us one from another, and is something all my own, and no human being can part with his human personality. Canon MacColl, in his book *Christianity in relation to Science and Morals*, insisted that whilst we are all one through our unity of race, that unity which we have in common as children of Adam, yet we are all separate individuals through our possession of that sovereign principle of action in the soul to which we give the name of personality. By natural descent from Adam each of us possesses the integral essence of humanity; but this humanity is organised in every individual on a new personality not derived from Adam.[1]

This distinction, then, between human nature and human personality, is all-important when we face the Christological problem and ask the question, *What was it our Lord took when He became Incarnate?* Did He assume human nature or a human personality? Had He a single consciousness or two consciousnesses? If we say that He took a human personality, we fall at once into the Nestorian heresy. As Canon Bright put it in his *Notes on the Canons of the First Four General Councils* (p. 65), the Nestorian conclusion was not 'God really Incarnate, it was a man morally deified'. We must also remember that 'consciousness' and 'will' may both be regarded as functions or attributes of a person, and need not be equated with the whole personality. If, how-

---

[1] G. W. Allport (*Personality: A Psychological Interpretation*), whilst listing fifty possible definitions of Personality, admits that the Person, ontologically considered, is more of a unity than he is from the empirical point of view, and every personality develops continually from the stage of infancy until death, and throughout this span it persists even though it changes. As he says, there are many ways to study man psychologically, yet to study him most fully is to take him as an individual.

For a more profound study of the root of personality, reference may be made to the French Thomist philosopher, Jacques Maritain, and especially to his treatment in *The Degrees of Knowledge* (Geoffrey Bles, 1959), pp. 231 ff. and Appendix IV.

In defining the name of Person, he says that a person is a centre of liberty; a person confronts things, the universe, GOD; talks with another person, communicates with him by understanding and affection. The notion of personality, however complex it may be, belongs primarily to the ontological order. It is, he says, a metaphysical and substantial perfection which unfolds in the operative order in psychological and moral values. The first metaphysical root of personality is what is called subsistence. Subsistence presupposes a (substantial) nature that is individual or singular (i.e. having the ultimate of actuation and determination in the very line of nature or essence). What it properly signifies, in so far as it gives the final completion to the order of created things, is that this nature, from the fact that it is endowed with subsistence, cannot communicate with any other substantial nature in the very act of existing, it is, so to speak, absolutely enclosed in itself with regard to existence.

My person exists before acting; and it possesses its existence, as it possesses its nature, in a way absolutely proper to it and incommunicable. Not only is its nature singular, it owns so completely the existence which actuates it that it desires to keep it to itself alone; it can share this existence with no other. . . . Subsistence is for the nature an ontological seal, as it were, of its unity. When this nature is complete (a separated soul is not a person), and above all when it is capable of possessing itself, of taking itself in hand by the intellect and the will, in short, when it belongs to the spiritual order, then the subsistence of such a nature is called personality.

ever, it is so equated, then the God-Man had a single consciousness. But if He be the God-Man, this *one* person may possess 'two consciousnesses' or 'two wills'. Of these two consciousnesses, the one would be that of the Eternal Son, the other begins in time with the Virgin conception. There is a pre-existent Divine Humanity of the Eternal Son, with a Divine consciousness, and this enables Him to lead a human life with a finite 'centre of consciousness'. This comes into being in His Incarnation when He became Man, the Second Adam, to re-create our fallen humanity again into the Divine Image.

What the Church taught was that, when our Lord took human nature, it was not like ours centred in a new personality, but was taken up into the Personality of the Eternal Word, the Second Person of the Blessed Trinity. The Two Natures, the Godhead and the Manhood, were united in the One Self or Person, the Divine Person of the Eternal Son, 'God's Presence and His Very Self; an Essence all Divine', and in that *One* Person the Two Natures were united, never to be divided. Christ, then, is all humanity, as He is all Deity. He is distinct from God in the content of His two consciousnesses. His Logos 'consciousness', that of His Divine Humanity, pre-exists, whereas the finite 'centre of consciousness' in His Incarnation had a beginning in time.

Whether the Incarnate Lord as the God-Man had one or two consciousnesses turns upon the question as to what we understand by personality. What do we mean by a person? If we equate personality with consciousness, then our Lord had a single consciousness. If, however, we regard consciousness as an attribute or function of personality, then the God-Man had two consciousnesses.

Defining personality in terms of consciousness does not contravene physiological psychology, or deny the body, but, as, for example, Dr. E. S. Brightman shows, only insists on the most fundamental fact of experience, namely, its consciousness. Whatever more may be the content of the experient and his Ego or Self, at the very least, he experiences, and can differentiate between what Dr. Brightman calls 'situations experienced' and 'situations believed in'. The only situation experienced by anyone is his own consciousness. Thus a situation experienced is a self, or person, or an experient, because it is a self-experimenting whole, which includes thinking, choosing, remembering, anticipating and purposing, as well as feeling and sensing. A whole self includes all these 'situations experienced', which are related by self-identifying memories and anticipations. I am what I experience myself as being — a conscious self. The 'situation experienced' is what Dr. Brightman called the *datum self* (or the empirical situation) as the source of all evidence for belief in society, the world or God. The point of view that takes my personality to be my consciousness is also a religious point of view, for religion, as Dr. Brightman reminds us, is concerned with man's conscious experience of values, with man's spirit, and with religious experience. The goal of religion is the development of worthy consciousness.

Moreover, the unity and identity of personality are of special importance to religion. If a person is not a true identical unity through all the changes in his experience, then spiritual development is impossible. Every *datum self* contains signs of a larger self to which it belongs; memory and anticipation assert the identity of the present person with a person that has been, and a person that will be. Thus the whole self, or person, is a total conscious process which is never present to itself in one single experience, but which is aware of its identity and wholeness by means of its backward-looking memories and its forward-looking purposes. The whole self, or person, then, consists of all the conscious experience that is or has been or will be present in all the empirical situations that constitute the history of the person. The unity of personality, therefore, is the unity of consciousness; personality includes consciousness only, and does not include any of its environment — physiological, subconscious or social — as part of it. (*Vide* Brightman, *A Philosophy of Religion*, chap. xi, pp. 192 ff.) If we are made in the image of God, then there will be likenesses and differences between Human and Divine Personalities. The Divine

Person alone is completely and perfectly personal. Man is only fragmentarily conscious. We are in fact pale copies of a Divine original.

With this may be compared the Kantian distinction between the transcendental and empirical Ego. Kant's transcendental apperception was consciousness in general, or the 'I', or 'self' or 'Ego', whereas 'apperception' was distinguished from perception by Leibniz.

According to the Kantian analysis, the production of the object does not go on in the individual consciousness, but lies already at the basis of this consciousness; for its production, a higher common consciousness must therefore be assumed, which comes into the empirical consciousness of the individual, not with its functions, but only with its result. This Kant termed in the *Prolegomena*, 'consciousness in general', and in the *Critique*, 'transcendental apperception', or the 'I' (or 'self' or 'Ego').

All this cuts across empiricism as such, in the origin of human ideas, and how we come to know objects: the mind in relation to the external world, or the Ego in relation to the Non-Ego.

Applying all this to the doctrine of the *Enhypostasia*, we might interpret the doctrine in terms of the transcendental and the empirical Ego, and say that in the One Person of the God-Man with His Two Natures, the Godhead and the Manhood, the Godhead was eternal, pre-existent Divine 'consciousness in general', whereas the Manhood had a beginning in time in the Virgin conception, when the empirical Ego comes into being by the assumption of the Divine Person beginning to lead a human life on earth. The One Person, therefore, would have Two Consciousnesses, the Divine pre-existent 'transcendental Ego', and the Human 'empirical Ego', by which He grew in wisdom and stature and in favour with God and Man, whilst able still to say 'I and the Father are One', or 'Before Abraham was, I am'.

If finally we ask, *Which Human Nature did the Eternal Son assume?* — was it a perfect human nature before the Fall, or a human nature distorted and disfigured by the sin which we from Adam onwards have added to it? — we should answer the question as St. Leo does (in his Epistle xxviii, 3, of *The Tome*): 'He assumed the form of a servant without the defilement of sin, enriching what was human, not impairing what was divine'.

The first Adam fell: the second Adam came to the rescue by the assumption of a perfect human nature, the original *Imago Dei*, and by His work started a new race of mankind, 'ransomed, healed, restored, forgiven' and ever more His praise to sing. Thus the vital connection between Christology and Soteriology is kept firm, as the Church has always insisted must be done.

(b) CHRIST AND METAPHYSICS [1]

The Gospel portrait of Jesus of Nazareth, in its consistency, naturalness and absence of incongruities, impresses us as a rescript from life, a first-hand impression, ultimately derived from eye-witnesses, of One whom they had seen, talked with and observed — a real Person, not a literary creation or the product of poetic imagination. Had the writers set out to describe from their own imagination a Person combining in Himself Divine and Human attributes: had they wished to give their own version of the life of the God-Man, apart from any available knowledge or evidence of any such life having been lived in actual fact, how different the result would have been! The biography of Jesus was never constructed by tabulating Divine and Human characteristics and then seeking to combine them together into an impossible amalgam — the result would have been a monstrosity. There is no trace of any such thing in the Gospels. From first to last the Person of Christ is a unity, and never once does the problem of the Two-Natures obtrude itself upon our notice by any seeming incongruity in the narratives themselves. The Gospel portrait derives from an aesthetic activity which gives a first-hand impression of the Reality as a whole.

[1] This article appeared in *The Interpreter*.

But now apply the logical criterion of judgment to the elucidation of the same Reality. Approach it, i.e. from the intellectual standpoint. Instead of knowing the Life of Jesus by sympathetic acquaintance and intimate personal contact, try to know about it by intellectual analysis. What a contrast! Instead of the simplicity of life, we have the complexity of incompatibilities and antinomies.

What a change when we pass from Gospel language to the Athanasian Creed or the Chalcedonian Definition!

'The child grew and waxed strong; increased in wisdom and stature.' All this we can grasp. A normal human growth; advance in knowledge through experience — what more natural.

Yet the intellect must go on to criticise this experience; to analyse it and to tabulate the Life so lived in a series of propositions; to translate history into Creed.

And the Church was forced to do it in self-defence, because men could not be content to leave the intellectual problem unsolved. Hence the Nicene and Chalcedonian terminology as a clear intellectual analysis of the Problem of the Two-Natured Christ: 'One and the same Christ, Son, Lord, Only-Begotten, to be acknowledged of two natures; without confusion, without conversion, without division, never to be separated; the distinction of natures being in no wise done away because of the union, but rather the characteristic property of each nature being preserved, and concurring into one Person and one subsistence, not as if Christ were parted or divided into two Persons, but one and the same Son and Only-Begotten God, Word, Lord, Jesus Christ'.

Thus does the Church express in metaphysical terminology the truth hidden in the simplicity of the Gospel language.

Being Very Man of the substance of the Virgin Mary, His Mother, He must needs grow in wisdom and stature and in favour with God and man. Being Very God of Very God, Begotten not made, how can He pray for a Divine Grace of which He Himself is the Fountain Source, or plead in an agony for the execution of a Divine Will, not His own and yet His very possession? If we say that He functions in two Natures, and that we must attribute the human feelings, tears, sorrow and finitude to the one source, and the glory, the miraculous power, the profound spiritual insight, to the other source, then how can we conceive of a unity of Person in One who possesses two Natures, two Wills, two Souls? Is not this the very quintessence of abnormality?

Given the Church's belief in His true Deity; given the Incarnation; given the fact that these Gospel narratives reveal to us God leading a truly human life; given the God-Man as the true key to the interpretation of the Gospel story — then how can One who is All-Wise grow in wisdom — One who is Omniscient advance in knowledge — One whose dwelling is the supra-mundane and whose Being is transcendental, move about on the shores of the Lake of Galilee, feel hungry and go to sleep in a boat, live in short the restricted life of our terrestrial existence and taste of its finitude and necessary limitations? So does the intellect, grappling with the problem, raise for itself a host of insuperable difficulties, and create a dense fog of its own making to obscure the Gospel Figure from the eyes of simple faith. And the Church, in self-defence, is forced to draw up Creeds and Conciliar Definitions to safeguard the truth in the terminology of the speculative schools in reply to the hard questions the intellectuals insist upon propounding.

The Church is blamed for expressing its belief in terms of metaphysics. Yet it must needs do so, since its claim for Christ is that He is the clue to the nature of Ultimate Reality. This is a claim in the sphere of philosophy. From the intellectual standpoint the Christological problem is a metaphysical problem. The attempt to express it purely in terms of ethical and spiritual categories is doomed thus to failure. The Church's belief in the true Deity and perfect Humanity of its Master means a claim that the Ultimate Reality for the Christian cannot be expressed in concepts which are less than truly personal, and that the key to the whole problem of the relation between the Divine and Human is to be found in the Person of Christ; nay, that the final end and meaning of the whole evolutionary process and the true interpretation of all human life is to be stated in terms of Him who was, and is, and is to come. Christ for the Christian is of *Cosmic* significance, and this claim means the invasion by Christianity of the realm of philosophy and a claim to a voice in the philosophical disputes as to the nature of the Ultimate Reality.

Does the Church offer any solution of the Christological problem? It is content in its dogmatic formularies to state the problem, tabulate the essential data and warn men, as the result of centuries of intellectual speculation and effort, that there are certain solutions which are defective, and must be avoided — solutions which have reached a logical consistency at the expense of truth — which have satisfied reason only by a failure to do justice to one or other factor in the problem. Within the limits thus laid down of what to avoid, the Church leaves men free to pursue the intellectual quest and to solve the problem if they can.

Ultimately, however, it will be found that the problem is insoluble.

To-day modern Churchmen tell us that the great advances in human knowledge since the days of the Council of Chalcedon (A.D. 451) enable us to approach the problem of Christ's Person with better hopes of success. Hence the fresh effort to restate the question in terms of modern thought, and the demand, not for the abolition of all creeds, but the substitution of new ones for the old. Now, whilst fresh investigation and discussion may help many to grasp more fully the essential difficulties of the problem, it is well for us to recognise that no intellectual solution will solve it.

The plain fact is (as I said many years ago) that the Person of Christ is the bankruptcy of human logic, and that it is better for us to acquiesce in this rather than to seek for intellectual consistency at the expense of ignoring or explaining away essential data in the problem. True, we can gain intellectual consistency by calling the Divine Human or the Human Divine; we can, if we like, seek to obliterate the distinction between Creator and Creature; we can rule out the supernatural or miraculous. We can, again, eliminate from our Christianity all that leaves room for wonder and that in our belief which confronts human reason with a flaming sword. In this way we can present a religion eminently adapted to supply the needs of the rationalists, BUT it will not be Christianity.

Ultimately we are driven back to Tertullian's famous dictum, and must believe, because of the very *absurdity* of our faith, if judged by the human criterion of the logical faculty. Moreover, we can never have *infallible* certitude. The assaults of reason must ever be with us, attacking and criticising our belief. Had we infallible certitude there would be no room left for faith's activity. There is no way of proving rationally the Deity of Christ. On the contrary, there are many lines of thought which suggest the incredibility and impossibility of His ever having appeared as the God-Man. The Church, however, bids us see that whilst His Person cannot be confined within the limits of rationality, yet *beyond these limits* lies the irrational or the supra-rational, and since the supreme triumph of reason is to cast doubt upon its own validity (as a great Spanish writer has been trying to teach us in *The Tragic Sense of Life*), we are left to seek to gain a nearer approach to the truth than is open to us by mere intellectual contemplation of the mystery, as it were, *ab extra.*

Is there any other way of approach?

The suggestion we make is that the aesthetic activity which, according to the Italian philosopher Croce, is prior to the logical, gives us the Gospel portrait and the intellectual abstraction which comes later is revealed in the Athanasian Creed and the Nicene and Chalcedonian terminologies. The one is a rescript from life; the other the product of intellectual analysis.

Which gives us a deeper insight into Reality? Which is nearer to the truth? The question is answered for some of us by considering our own approach to the Christ. Do we find Him by intellectual activity, pondering over the historical records, and analysing the implications involved in the concept of the Two Natures? Can any such process of abstraction and formularisation ever bring us within measurable distance of the Gospel Figure? On the other hand, we know that, through experience in prayer, communion and self-sacrificing devotion to His ideals, we do find God in Christ Jesus. His Presence is a felt reality in the Christian life. Striving to live at the level of His ideals, following in His steps, we taste of Eternal Life in time and space, and so live His Life — we in Him, and He in us. Thus, by an activity of the whole personality at its deepest levels, we discover Him in whom we live and move and have our being. Through life then, rather than through intellectual processes, we get a deeper knowledge of the truth. Not that the intellect has not its part to play, but that it has not the last nor the only word to say in the quest after Reality. Not by process of logical reasoning, but by dutiful practice of the Presence of God, do we attain to an intuitive apprehension of the Living One. Thus we gain a fuller knowledge of His Reality in the intenser activity of a lived experience than was open to us in the comparatively barren zone of abstract thought.

And this is justified in our own day by the growing appreciation of the limitations of the intellectual approach to Reality. Bergson's attack upon the intellect and his exaltation of direct intuition as a surer way to the discovery of the Real is significant in this connection, as also the emphasis upon the 'reign of relativity' in every department of human knowledge. If we realise that by intellectual abstraction we are confining ourselves in a 'strait-jacket of static and spatial moulds', we shall the more readily grasp the fact that our 'Dogmas' and Credal Forms have, after all, given us simply 'frozen thought', and that what we are really searching for is His Life: His Personality in its living content, not our elaborated logical propositions concerning Him.

'Metaphysics', says Mr. Bradley, 'is the finding of bad reasons for what we believe upon instinct, but to find these reasons is no less an instinct.' And Lord Haldane, in quoting this sentence, reminds us that Bradley is really warning us against pedantry, the undue exaltation of the abstract mind. 'His warning', says Lord Haldane, 'is one which those who are disposed to regard lightly the faith of simple minds would do well to bear in remembrance. For that faith is, in itself, a correction of abstractions. It is the sense of the fuller significance of experience.'[1]

We have in many striking ways a parallel to the Christological problem in the efforts made to solve the difficulty of the relation between soul and body, mind and brain.

Living our everyday life we know soul and body, mind and brain in indissoluble union. But let intellect approach the problem, and at once we are confronted by endless perplexities. If we start with an analysis of either factor we are left wondering how two such diverse entities can ever come together. Dr. Wildon Carr has dwelt upon the antithesis which arises from such a process of mental abstraction and logical analysis. 'The constituent elements of the mind and the constituent elements of the body', he tells us, 'are absolutely heterogeneous, and there is no common factor in physical and physiological process.' Physiologists and psychologists have elaborated these differences, and have sought a solution of the problem either in terms of pure materialistic mechanism or in terms of pure idealistic subjectivism. Destroy the brain and the mind goes too. Consciousness is an epiphenomenon of cerebral activity, an accompaniment of the physical and chemical changes which occur in the brain. So the Materialist argues that consciousness is a by-product of physiological processes. On the other hand, the Idealist would contend that all our knowledge of physiological processes is perceptive and that cerebral activity has no meaning apart from a perceiving subject. Hence the theory of Psycho-Physical Parallelism, and the possibility of its interpretation in terms either of materialistic 'psychology without a soul' or in terms of an idealistic philosophy which see the physiological accompaniment of consciousness as simply the reality of consciousness itself as this is perceived by another mind.

[1] *Reign of Relativity*, p. 417.

Again, there is the theory of interaction with its perplexing dualism of mind and matter and the grave philosophical problem of any real relation existing between what is pure immateriality and what is pure extension. Dr. Wildon Carr would point us to Bergson's more subtle psychological treatment of the problem in *Matter and Memory*. This makes a clean sweep of all theories which arise from the intellectualist approach to the problem and an effort to know the reality at the deeper level of intuitive apprehension. At this level we do not start with two diverse abstractions, a mind without a body or a body without a mind. On the contrary, it is pointed out that 'mind and body are not an original diversity'. This being so, the separation of the two is due to an intellectual activity which, for purposes of analysis and for the convenience of scientific investigation, abstracts subject from object, perceives from perceived and so leaves us with the two in an isolation never found in the reality itself. The intellect is thus responsible for 'the dichotomising of an original unity' of which real life knows nothing. Quite simply, we can see how true this is if we reflect upon our own experience. Living our life gives us a knowledge of Mind and Brain, Body and Soul, in indissoluble union. We have no intuitive knowledge of either in separation. Intuition in this problem is nearer to the reality which living experience enables us to grasp in a way no logical analysis of the problem could do.

So in Christology. The problem how the Human and the Divine — seemingly so diverse — could possibly be united and function as indissolubly one baffles the intellect. Read the Gospels, however, as a description from life of how it was actually done in the earthly career of Jesus Christ and the picture is simplicity itself, much the same, in fact, as any description of our own life as we live it would baffle the mind of a thinker who was puzzled over the problem of the possibility of the union of immateriality with material substance, and convinced on intellectual grounds of its incredibility. Yet the simplest peasant could inform him, not why it could be done or how, but that actually it is done.

We know from actual experience that mind and body do exist in a wonderful harmony in life, in spite of all the objections against its possibility from the physiological or psychological standpoint. So experience taught the followers of Jesus that a Divine-Human Life could be lived, and be seen to be, not a monstrosity, but to all appearance a perfectly natural phenomenon. If intellect creates difficulties of its own making in physiology and psychology, we must not be surprised if it seeks to dichotomise an original unity in the Person of Christ and presents us with an apparently unbridgeable gulf between the 'Jesus of the Gospels' and the Christ of the Creeds, the Human and the Divine as two irreconcilable incompatibilities — the one within our experience as terrestrial, the other beyond our apprehension as transcendental. Intellect may well halt in perplexity before the problems it thus raises and seek logical consistency as Idealism and Materialism, in the denial of one or other factor in the problem. Mutilate the Human and we get Apollinarianism: dichotomise the two and we get Nestorianism with its impossible dualism; absorb the one into the other and we reach Monophysitism. All these heresies are the result of intellectual efforts at consistency in the elucidation of a mystery which refuses to yield its secret to the wise and understanding, but which is known as a living reality to the foolish and revealed to babes in Christ and Galilean peasants in communion and fellowship with their Risen Lord.

The parallel we have sought to draw is at least significant in the insight it affords us into the difficulties created by the intellectual approach to Reality and the comparative ease with which intuition apprehends quite simply the 'mysteries' which the logical faculty brings to the surface and spatialises for our contemplation. Consider in this connection, further, another suggestive line of thought in the difference between structure and function. What could be more simple than the functioning of the human eye! Yet what, on the other hand, could be more marvellously complex than an analysis of its structure. Pages of a textbook go to the elucidation of its intricacies and the delicacy of its mechanism. Yet when it functions, how simple is it in operation. Wherein lies the difference? Our knowledge of its structure is derived from an intellectual analysis of its component parts — it is the result of scientific investigation. Whereas our knowledge of its function is a direct intuitive apprehension of a living whole. A description of the mechanism in terms of physiology will never give us the key to knowledge of what it really is. We learn this by *seeing*. Life, as an activity, in other words, is the key to the reality we are seeking.

And Biology is gradually coming to realise this. The mechanistic interpretation of life is now being realised as a palpable absurdity. We are now being told that philosophy is putting a question-mark against the validity of the scientific inductive method as the sole guide to a true solution of the nature of Reality. Life is a greater Reality than our short-sighted interpretations of it. We are coming at long last to realise that 'the phenomena of life are of such a nature that no physical or chemical explanation of them is remotely conceivable'.[1]

'Life (so we are told) manifests itself in two ways — as structure and as activity. But we also recognise — a biologist feels it in his very bones — that this is *living* structure and *living* activity. . . . But the more closely living activity in general is examined, the more clear does it become that all living activity is structural or metabolic activity, either directly or indirectly.' [2]

If, then, the structure itself is to be conceived of as active — as alive, then in Biological investigation of living organisms we are dealing, as Dr. Haldane has shown, with a conception radically different from any physical concept. And if this be so, then 'sooner or later . . . it will be realised that the materialism of the nineteenth century has been nothing but an insignificant eddy in the stream of human progress'.

[1] J. S. Haldane, *Mechanism, Life and Personality*, p. 64.
[2] *Op. cit.* pp. 77-8.

But how shall we have learned thus to emancipate ourselves from the trammels of materialism? It will have been
due to our growing apprehension of the essential limitations
of the intellectual approach to the study of Reality. It will
have been by a more direct apprehension of that Reality in
its manifestation in life that we shall have gained a deeper
intuitive grasp of what it really is.

Now just as the living organism is or should be the
fundamental conception of Biology, so the Living Christ and
not dead and mental and intellectual abstract concepts of
His Person, is or should be the fundamental conception of
Christology. Christian experience must give us the truth
concerning Him. Our method of approach must not be by
analytical mental gymnastics 'confounding the Natures' or
'dividing the Persons', but by living the Life.

If we strive to live His Life in the world, reaching up to
the ethical and spiritual level He has revealed to us as of the
very essence of Eternal Life in time and space — we shall at
that level find Him in a lived experience of personal union
and communion. Living true to the deepest in us we shall
touch Him in whom we live and move and have our being.
In life and not by intellect only do we make the great discovery. Where intellect bids us halt, faith makes its leap,
and thus by a living activity of the whole human personality
Godwards, do we take hold of Reality Himself, and dis-
covering thus the Divine in Human life, living in Him
and He in us, all questions concerning the possibility of a
union between the Divine and Human are answered — not
theoretically, but practically. And Faith can claim a closer
knowledge of the Truth than was ever possible by means of
speculative conjecture and the conclusions of logic.

> The rest may reason and welcome,
> 'Tis we musicians *know*.

Need we be surprised, then, if we discover that the
Portrait of Jesus Christ in the Gospels given to us by those
who knew Him in the days of His Flesh differs profoundly
from the whole series of mental abstractions which have

appeared since in numerous 'Lives of Christ', issued from the study rooms of learned professors. The attempt has been made to confine His Figure and Personality within the limits of intellectual categories, but without success. We have had the Humanitarian Christ, the 'Jesus of the Gospels'; the Ethical Teacher; the ideal Labour leader; the Aesthetic Jesus; the religious enthusiast; the eschatological Wonder-worker — all these pictures are but mental abstractions. The 'Jesus of the Gospels' so dear to the heart of modern Liberalism never existed — it is a fiction resulting from a one-sided and narrow view of the Reality, its consistency is only secured by the elimination of one whole side of His Personality and the attempt to express Him within the limitations of the finite human. Schweitzer's exposure of the bankruptcy of modern Liberalism in its attempts to re-write the life of Jesus ought to have warned him that his own effort to state the problem purely in terms of 'other-worldliness' and eschatological categories must equally fatally suffer from the infection of relativity. All these attempts at reproduction of the Divine Reality in photographic form from different angles do but emphasise the point we wish to make, viz. that the Reality Himself is too big to be confined within the limitations of our logical categories of thought and our spatialised imagery cannot hold Him. He walks out of our picture-frames in which we seek to confine Him, and we must find another way of approach if we are to apprehend something of His immensity and transcendence. Like Life itself, defying the mechanistic biologists and demanding an explanation in terms not less real than itself, so does the Living Christ demand of us that we know Him not primarily or exclusively by intellectual speculation, but by and in and through a living activity of our deepest life — a sympathetic contact and intimate personal touch — the activity of a living faith in a living relationship to a Living Person — this is the way to knowledge — this the approach to a deeper and more intimate apprehension of Him. It is only in that intimacy of communion when His Spirit touches ours in living union that the human can awaken to a true consciousness of itself; it is when His Spirit beareth witness with our spirit that we are the Sons of God, then it is that we have the spirit of adoption, whereby we cry: 'Abba, Father !'

The case of St. Thomas is in point. Left to intellectual contemplation, the crude reality of the Cross, the gross realism of the nails was too much for faith. But a living personal contact with the Risen Lord evoked faith's activity once again and the Apostle, held back by intellectual hesitation and logical incredulity, swept all aside in one supreme intuitive affirmation: 'My Lord, and My God !'

So it must be with us. The intellectual quest is not the pursuit of the many, and its fascination must not blind us to the fact that when all is said and done our intellectual knowledge of Jesus of Nazareth and our deep insight into the perplexing problem of His Person give us probably less real apprehension of Him than is open to the simplest Christian who smiles at our Trinitarian profundities and says quite simply: 'By faith, I know that my Redeemer liveth'.

> Then thro' the mid complaint of my confession,
>   Then thro' the pang and passion of my prayer,
> Leaps with a start the shock of His possession,
>   Thrills me and touches, and the Lord is there !
>
> Whoso has felt the Spirit of the Highest
>   Cannot confound nor doubt Him nor deny.
> Yea, with one voice, O world, though thou deniest,
>   Stand thou on that side, for on this am I.

If our readers will pardon some repetition, we may sum up this problem of The Person of Christ and recent discussion somewhat along these lines.

The Logos decides to lead a human life. In order to do so, He does not select someone else's Life, that of a man already existing, in whom He comes to dwell to the nth degree, but chooses to lead His own personal life, and so becomes Man. 'The Word was made flesh and dwelt among us, and we beheld His Glory, the Glory as of the Only-Begotten of the Father, full of grace and truth.' The Gospels

tell us how He did this. They do not say how He came to
dwell in another man's life, but how He led His own personal
life, growing from babyhood to manhood in the days of His
flesh. His Ego therefore was that of the Logos, submitting
His Godhead to the limitations inherent in leading the life of
a man, and yet as such revealing Himself to be the Man, the
perfect embodiment of what Man is capable of being and
becoming, when the central constituent of His Person is
Divine.

This incarnation necessitated His coming to possess Two
Natures, Divine and Human. The one He already possessed: the other He assumed. It was not a case of a Man
becoming in some sense Divine, but of God Himself becoming
a Man and the Man.

He remained the Divine Logos all through His assumption of Manhood, and He came into this world by means of
a Virgin conception. This was by the operation of the Holy
Ghost. Having by this means gained an entrance into our
limited world of time and space, yet He still transcended
these limitations as the Divine Logos, and submitted to some
form of *Kenosis*. How exactly He managed to do this is a
mystery, but does not destroy the fact that He did so. We
do not understand how it could have been done, but the
Gospels tell us the fact that it was done. He did really lead
a human life, and this was not by dwelling in somebody
else's life, but by living His own personal life from the
cradle to the grave. Then He rose again after death, and
took the manhood He had assumed with Him where it still
abides. All He left behind Him were the grave clothes.
His glorified Manhood now abides in the Heavenly Places,
and He pleads His sacrifice once offered for the sins of all
those He came to redeem.

The possession of Two Natures, intellectually considered,
does make Him the possessor of a composite personality but
this is only an abstract conception (*Composita hypostasis*) μία
ὑπόστασις σύνθετος ἐκ δύο φύσεων. The Chalcedonian
Definition distinguishes between the two natures and the
one person of Christ. The two natures can be separated in

thought, but not in fact. They are eternally united in His One Person.

In some sense if the Logos is the One Person in the Two Natures, then the Manhood is *impersonal*, having had no existence before it was assumed by the Logos, and, as Ottley points out, it was created in the act by which it was assumed. In this sense it is an accident or instrument of the Godhead. So Athanasius in his Orations against the Arians (ii, 45) speaks of συμβεβηκός, ὄργανον. The human nature became personal (ἐνυπόστατος) only by being incorporated with, assumed by, the person of the Logos. Thus the manhood is described sometimes as ἑτεροϋπόστατος or συνυπόστατος i.e. ἐν αὐτῇ τῇ τοῦ θεοῦ Λόγου ὑποστάσει ὑποστᾶσα. In later theology it is insisted that the personality of the human nature was extinguished or absorbed by the person of the Word. (See Ottley, *op. cit.* pp. 480, 481.)

Adoptionism on the positive side is a protest against any dissipation of the human nature. Alcuin holds a kind of transubstantiation theory of Christ's Person, as against Adoptionism: *In assumptione carnis a Deo, persona perit hominis, non natura.* And this theory of the extinction of the human personality was apparently for a time the received doctrine of the Western Church. (See passages in Dorner, *loc. cit.*)

It is very significant as appearing to allow that personality is a necessary element in the perfection of a human nature. It is also a tacit recognition of the danger to which the received theology was exposed: the danger of reducing Christ's humanity to a mere appendage of His person, the mere organ for a theophany, and against this the whole Antiochene school is opposed. Thus in Alcuin's treatment of the personality of Christ we see the lingering trace of a monophysitic mode of thought.

Clearly a careful study of Monophysitism *after the Council of Chalcedon* shows that hardly any of the questions we are now facing afresh in the Christological Problem were not debated and canvassed by the ancient, especially Eastern, speculative thinkers. There was then a strong feeling that the Council of Chalcedon had gone too far in the direction of the Antiochene approach, and needed therefore fresh consideration as against the possibility of Nestorianism being reintroduced. The Monophysites feared this, and so went to the other extreme, in spite of all that Leontius of Byzantium did to avoid the errors both of Nestorius and of Eutyches.

The question then is what constitutes Human Personality, and was the Manhood which the Logos assumed really fully human in the sense that it was a fully constituted Human Personality ? How could it have been, if it was *impersonal* ? Leontius maintained that it received *its* personality from the Logos when He assumed it. Were there then in the One Christ two personalities, and, if so, how do we avoid the Nestorian error ? Leontius tries to solve the problem by maintaining that the greater Personality of the Logos contained the lesser personality necessary to complete the full humanity by giving to it, its personality.

Thus the Nicene insistence upon the One Person of the Logos incarnate and the insistence by the Second General Council that Christ was completely human as against Apollinarianism seem to contradict each other. If ’Aληθῶς Θεός, how can He be Τελέως ”Ανθρωπος ? What does τελέως really amount to ? If the Godhead is substantive, the Manhood must be adjectival, and *vice versa*. Can the *whole* of Human Nature be assumed without human personality ?

If we reject the solution offered by Leontius, and we make the Manhood substantive, we inevitably make the Godhead adjectival, and, if so, does not this make the *homoousion* really homo*i*ousion ? If the Logos becomes a human being, and lives as an individual man amongst men, must He not inevitably develop a human personality and grow from a baby in arms to the full stature of a man by contact with His fellow beings ?

If from start to finish of His incarnate life on earth He still possesses a full Divine and perfected Personality, how can He grow in wisdom and stature as a human individual developing a human personality, as we do, through fellowship?

If we say He possessed Two Wills and Two Consciousnesses, does not this mean that He was Two Persons, the One Divine, the other Human?

If we say He was One Person in Two Natures, which Nature lacked its completion in personality? If we say 'The Manhood', does not this necessarily make it incomplete? How then can we call Him Τελέως Ἄνθρωπος? If we say 'The Godhead', does not this necessarily make the Godhead less than Ἀληθῶς Θεός? This would mean only as much of the 'Godhead' as could be contained in the fulness of the Godhead 'bodily', i.e. less than GOD as He is in Himself, but only so much of Him as could be revealed in an *Incarnate* Life on earth. If then we go on to ask 'What is GOD like?' and answer 'Look at Christ Jesus', we must add that what is there revealed is not the whole of GOD, but only so much as could be revealed in a GOD become Man. GOD in Man made manifest is not all that GOD is in Himself.

So we are driven back to the Trinitarian Problem in any attempt to do justice to the Nicene Credal Symbol 'being of *one substance* with the Father as touching His Godhead': μία οὐσία ἐν τρισὶν ὑποστάσεσιν. In GOD there is one substance but three Persons or Hypostases; three modes of subsistence of the one undivided Divine essence. And in relation to the Godhead, the term 'person' means, as Ottley points out, something between (*a*) mere manifestation or personation and (*b*) the independent, exclusive individuality of a human being. The 'Persons' are mutually inclusive, i.e. in one another by mutual indwelling or, as Chrysostom puts it, 'Where one hypostasis of the Trinity is present; the whole Trinity is present; for it is inseparably united, and conjoined together with the utmost exactness' (Chrysostom, *Hom. in Ep. ad Rom.*, viii, 10). In later theology the term applied to this absolute intercommunion is περιχώρησις (*Circuminsessio*) coinherence: *Una substantia, tres personae.*

As regards the Impassibility, Ottley suggests that when we say GOD *suffered*, we do not mean that Deity is passible, but that He who was personally GOD suffered. The *Communicatio Idiomatum* does not involve more than this? (See Ottley, *op. cit.* pp. 592-3.) Are we sure of this?

If the essence of the being of GOD as revealed by Christ is eternal Love, then our sins must hurt Him, and He will continue to suffer so long as we go on sinning against Him. The Cross is the revelation in this world of a fact in the eternal world. It is sacramental, an outward visible sign of an inward and spiritual reality, and it shows the passibility of the Personal GOD as against the abstract conception of the impassability of Deity as a metaphysical idea.

Ottley points out that the περιχώρησις is usually held to be possible only for the higher nature which controls, dominates and pervades the lower, but, as he says, the ἀντίδοσις is surely not entirely one-sided. We may dare to think that in some sense the 'measures of humanity' were suffered to 'prevail' over the Deity, in such degree and sense that the Divine attributes themselves became modified or coloured by the unity of the manhood with the Godhead.

Applying this thought to the problem of the Impassibility of the Suffering GOD, may we not say that if we lift the conception of Deity to the ethical and spiritual level of Eternal Love, then we have a *Personal* GOD who is full of compassion and mercy, long-suffering and of great kindness towards us sinners? We are dealing not with an abstract concept of impassible Deity, but with a Personal GOD on a mission of redemption, and the cost to Him is indicated by the human life which culminated in the Calvary Sacrifice. And the repercussions of this human life so lived 'prevailed' over the Deity. In this sense a suffering GOD is a fact revealed by the Incarnate Christ, and the measure of His suffering is the measure of His Love and infinite patience and forbearance with us His sinful creatures.

Calvary reveals a fact which continues to be a fact long after the wooden cross has disappeared. And that fact is that GOD still continues to suffer, and will continue to do so, *until we cease to sin.* That such suffering should be transmuted into joy in the redeeming act was, and still is, revealed in the One who for the joy that was set before Him endured the Cross and is now set down at the right hand of GOD. Anthropomorphism, if we use such language, it certainly is, but none the less containing a profound truth, however inadequately expressed the phraseology may be.

As regards Nestorianism, if we reject the doctrine of the Enhypostasia of Leontius of Byzantium as we have tried to express it in terms of modern thought, what is the alternative ? How can we still do justice to the Antiochene school of thought ?

We shall need, as Dr. Vine has suggested, some effort to formulate a doctrine of the *Enhypostasia in reverse*.[1] This would mean making the Manhood of Christ substantive, and the Godhead adjectival.

Could this be done by a reformulation of the idea of Nestorius, in the Bazaar of Heracleides, of a *prosôpon* of union? Here is the chance for a younger student to try a further step forward in the never-ending quest after a solution of the Christological problem.

[1] Article in *Expository Times*, November, 1955, and his book, *An Approach to Christology* (1948), which has not received the attention it deserves by students of the subject. It is a masterly analysis of the metaphysic of Nestorius and his Christology.

CHAPTER 5

A STUDY IN SACRAMENTALISM

(*a*) THE CHURCH

The Incarnation the master key to an understanding
of the nature and function both of the Church and
Sacraments in the world and human life.
A practical step in the movement towards Reunion

CHRISTIANITY is of supernatural origin, though rooted in
history. So is the Church. Our view of its nature and
function will be governed throughout by our verdict concerning its origin. Either it is a man-made invention or a
God-given gift; an accident of history or part of a Divine
plan. Any discussion concerning the Church must be preceded by certain definite decisions as to what we believe
concerning Christianity itself, and the central truths of our
Christian Faith. The order of the Creed itself suggests this,
and our belief in the Holy Catholic Church, or the One
Holy Catholic and Apostolic Church, is part and parcel of
a larger faith in the Christian conception of God, and of His
saving purpose through Jesus Christ our Lord. We do not
begin to express our belief in the Church until we have made
certain affirmations of a far-reaching and vital character
concerning the Trinity, the Incarnation, the Work of Christ
and its issue in the Pentecostal outpouring of the Holy
Spirit. We believe in the Church, and derive our conception
of its nature and function in the world and human life,
because we have reached certain conclusions concerning
God, Man, Sin and Grace, which are distinctive of the
Christian revelation. If Christianity be other than a
religion of revelation and redemption such as is suggested
by those summaries of its essence which we possess in our
historic Creeds, a discussion of the nature and function of
the Church is idle and profitless. What was our Lord's

purpose in coming into the world? If we accept the reading of His mission as that of a prophet, and regard Christianity in its essence as the religion of Jesus the worshipper, and rule out the deeper conception of His work as Priest and King; if we regard the religion that worships Jesus as a later and mistaken excrescence upon a supposed more primitive and purer form of Christianity, or if, again, we accept the more thoroughgoing eschatological reading of our Lord's life and ministry, and the view which would regard His Passion and Death as due to a mistaken conception on His part of the true significance of His Messianic rôle, we must rule out at once any possibility of arriving at the Catholic conception of the Incarnation and its corollary: Church and Sacraments, as in some real sense organic to Christianity.

We begin, then, with certain assumptions from which we shall deduce the nature and function of the Church.

We assume in the first place the reality of a Divine revelation, mediated to the world pre-eminently and specifically through God's Chosen People, the Jews. The whole line of argument suggested, for example, by Hamilton in his work on *The People of God* is a necessary presupposition of any attempt to understand the Church as in a real sense the Divinely ordained continuation of the Israel of God. Christianity did not come into the world as a bolt from the blue, or as Athena, full-grown from the head of Zeus. On the contrary, it arises from the womb of Judaism, and has, as its presupposition, Hebrew ethical monotheism. It is in this sense the culmination of a progressive revelation which finds its climax in the Incarnation of the Second Person of the Blessed Trinity. The expectation of a fuller revelation of God in connection with the Jewish religion found its fulfilment in Christ Jesus. The Jewish religion in His hands was reorganised; the ancient Church-Nation was expanded into a potential universal brotherhood. The New Covenant superseding the Old carries with it by implication the abolition of the restrictions contained in Jewish nationalistic particularism. The new Church of Christ is the old Church of God's Chosen People launched upon a world-wide missionary campaign: reorganised: reconstituted and freshly equipped for its task by its Divine Head. This Church did not spring into being for the first time at Pentecost, nor was it an after-thought of the Apostolic band following a period of disillusionment and the fading-out of the hope of the immediate Parousia of the Risen Master. On the contrary, the New Israel has its roots in the Old, and is the successor to all the privileges and blessings of the People of God.

If we believe in the principle of Election; if we discern any Providential plan behind and through and in the history of the Jews as God's Chosen People; if we accept the belief that to them, constituted as a Church in a special covenant relation with Yahweh, was vouchsafed a Divine self-revelation and a supernatural authority, then to the Church of Christ, as the continuation of the Covenanted People, belongs everything in the nature of supernatural origin, supernatural revelation, and authority, which can rightly be claimed for the Old. The work of Christ, in one of its aspects, was the institution of a New Covenant, the effect of which was a complete transformation of the ancient Jewish religion and the making it into what we call 'Christianity'.[1] The Christian Church is part and parcel of this transforming process, and for the origin of the Church, and for a true appreciation of its nature and function, we must look to this source, namely the work of Christ.

The Training of the Twelve

That Jesus did indeed choose Twelve men to form an inner circle marked by a closer attachment to Himself, and that, as time went on, He withdrew more and more from public teaching and concentrated His attention upon them, admits of no dispute. The Twelve plainly occupied an important place in His thoughts and plans.

What place? 'To them was entrusted the stewardship of the Messianic salvation; they know the mind and the plans of the Messiah; they understand the mystery of His

[1] Cf. Hamilton, *People of God*, vol. i, p. 261.

death; it is for them to proclaim it to others and to assure them of it.'[1]

Moreover, the Messiah had authority over the whole national religious life, i.e. He could and did institute a New Covenant. The Apostolic band was 'the authoritative centre or nucleus of the New Israel around which believers should gather'. They are, again, 'The trustees of a rite which brings into a single focus the religious life of all believers, and in which is outwardly expressed and inwardly realised the unity and communion of all individuals with each other in GOD the Father and in His Son Jesus the Messiah'.

'Accordingly, it seems only just to say that the compact company of Twelve was selected to form the nucleus and centre of the common life of the Church, the New People of GOD. As the old Israel began with the Twelve tribes, so the new Israel begins with the Twelve Apostles, one for each tribe. Where the Apostles are, there is the Church; their communion and fellowship is the communion and fellowship of the true People of GOD. Any beginning which is not from them, or is in opposition to them, if such a thing is conceivable, is not the true Israel of God.'[2]

'It is not that they were a privileged class within the Church; they were the whole Church; and others, who were "added unto them", shared at once in all the fullness of the Messianic blessings. . . . They constituted the point of contact between the Israel of old and the great society which called itself the New Israel . . . the Church derived its consciousness of itself as the true Israel, the People of God, through the Apostles; for they were the representatives of the Messiah, to whom He had revealed His will and whom He had commissioned to carry out His work and to proclaim the new Covenant.'[3]

As regards their authority, it necessarily was not clearly defined at first, least of all in terms of constitutional government.

---

[1] Hamilton, *op. cit.* p. 64.   [2] *Op. cit.* p. 65.   [3] *Op. cit.* p. 66.

'They were undoubtedly the trustees of the teaching of Jesus, the recipients of the Holy Ghost, and the fountain-source from which the brethren had received the Gospel': 'collectively they form the centre of gravity in the Church': 'in them resided the capacity for representing the Church and for deciding and acting with the consent of the brethren in her name'.

The Incarnation was decisive in the history of God's Chosen People. The acceptance or rejection of His Messiahship determined the membership of the new Covenant. The new and the true Israel came into being by means of this test. Hamilton sums up the position in a few pregnant sentences:

'That which had constituted the old Israel was a common devotion to one God. The same tie now bound the believers in Jesus into one; they and they alone were the servants of the true God.

'All that belonged to the Israel of old now belonged to the new; what was true of the pre-Messianic Israel was true of the post-Messianic Israel; the Messiah did not diminish but increased the privileges and the blessings of the People of God. As the old Israel had been a definite and visible religious society, one among many others, so also the Apostolic band necessarily became a definite and visible society. They could no more think of themselves as an invisible body, but as a society whose real limits were known to God alone, than they could think of the nation of Israel as being without clearly defined marks and limits to distinguish it from all other religious organisations.'[1]

And again:

'Israel after the flesh had cut itself off by its unbelief; hence the Apostolic Company remains the one People of the Living God, the sole possessor of all religious privileges which are worth having. . . . Time was needed to show that the Messiah would not return at once, and that in

[1] *Op. cit.* ii, p. 28.

consequence the new Israel would enjoy a continued period of existence under the present conditions of earthly life. Time, again, was needed to show that the bulk of the nation would not accept God's Messiah, and that in consequence the new Israel would be deprived of its natural home and centre in Jerusalem and forced out to take up a position of its own independent of, and in a sense in opposition to, the national life of the Jews. But that they became, before many years had passed, fully conscious of themselves as the true Israel is clearly shown by the New Testament itself. This is visible in every passage in which an Old Testament saying, originally spoken to or of the Israelite nation, is applied to the Christian community.' [1]

Harnack [2] admirably sums up the relevant points:

'Convinced that Jesus, the teacher and the prophet, was also the Messiah who was to return ere long to finish off His work, people passed from the consciousness of being His *Disciples* into that of being His *People*, the people of God (1 Peter ii, 9); and in so far as they felt themselves to be a *People*, Christians knew they were the *true Israel*, at once the *new* people and the *old*. This conviction that they were a *people* — i.e. the transference of all the prerogatives and claims of the Jewish people to the new community viewed as a new creation which exhibited and put into force whatever was old and original in religion — that at once furnished adherents of the new faith with a *political* and *historical* self-consciousness. Nothing more comprehensive or complete or impressive than this consciousness can be conceived. Could there be any higher or more comprehensive conception than that of the complex of momenta afforded by the Christians' estimate of themselves as "the true Israel", the "new people", "the original people", and "the people of the future", i.e. of

---

[1] *Op. cit.* p. 29.
[2] *Expansion of Christianity*, i, pp. 300 f.; *Mission and Expansion*, i, pp. 240 f.; cf. also *Hist. of Dogma*, i, pp. 43 f., 88 f., and *Constitution and Law of the Church*, pp. 221, 224 n.

eternity? This estimate of themselves rendered the Christians impregnable against all attacks and movements of polemical criticism, while it further enabled them to advance in every direction for a war of conquest. Was the cry raised, "You are renegade Jews"—the answer came, "We are the community of the Messiah, and therefore the true Israelites". If people said, "You are simply Jews", the reply was, "We are a new creation and a new People". If, again, they were taxed with their recent origin and told that they were but of yesterday, they retorted, "We only seem to be the younger People; from the beginning we have been latent, ever in existence to any other people; we are the original People of God".

'*We are the community of the Messiah and therefore the true Israelites.*' In this one sentence, says Hamilton, is summed up the whole philosophy of the foundation of the Church.

'The Messiah could not found a new and independent religious society to rival the old Israel; but it was inevitable that all who accepted the Messiah should consider themselves as the true Israelites, as comprising a society which was rightful heir and successor to all the prerogatives and claims of the Jewish people. To this society the name 'Church' was afterwards given. Hence we do not need any special passages to prove that Jesus intended to found a religious society. It was implicit in his claim to be the Messiah.' [1]

Hamilton further points out that the New Israel not only inherited all the exclusive privileges of the old; it also had received yet greater blessings through the Messiah. The chief of these were: (*a*) the forgiveness of sins through the sacrificial offering on the cross; and (*b*) the assurance of salvation through the consciousness of fellowship with GOD in the Holy Spirit.

Now these new privileges given through the Messiah

[1] Hamilton, *op. cit.* p. 31.

involved nothing less than a transformation, a complete reorganisation of the old religion. . . .

An entirely new set of relations between God and His people were set up. Hence a new Covenant.

The effect of all this was one of those implications of the Gospel which were not perceived all at once . . . the New Covenant had been inaugurated with a rite based upon a sacrifice . . . given by the Messiah Himself.

'Here was a rite given them by the Messiah Himself, and one which at once commemorated the central fact of the New Covenant, the self-oblation of the Messiah on the cross, and also brought each individual soul into close personal union with Him.

'This rite, then, must come to play a prominent part in the common life of the new Israel. And it was a rite out of which a ministry must inevitably spring; for that of which all are to partake is the fragments of the one bread which is broken and the contents of one cup which is blessed in memory of Jesus; but if there is to be one bread broken and one cup blessed, it is clear that there must be one person to preside on each occasion and to minister to the others; hence there arises at once the need of a distinctly Messianic Ministry, to minister this distinctively Messianic rite.' [1]

Moreover, in the new Israel the barriers of Jewish Nationalism are broken down and the Gentiles stand on the same footing as the Jews. This meant a complete reorganisation of the Jewish religion.

This whole line of thought necessarily raises many questions concerning the precise nature and function of the Church in the Divine purpose of redemption; the relation, for example, of the Kingdom of God with the visible Church. If Christ really refounded the visible Church, the New Israel of God, did He mean to make discipleship to Himself coincident with membership in His Society? Did He in fact mean to found a Church, and if so does not the Church,

[1] *Op. cit.* p. 33.

considered as a visible society, involve some centre of unity such as the Divinely authorised ministry and sacraments we have come to know in history as part and parcel of the One Holy Catholic and Apostolic Church?

Here, of course, we stumble upon whole areas of controversial discussions upon which no large measure of agreement has yet been reached either with the Nonconformists or with the Roman Catholics. The Church of England has its own peculiar and particular place in Christendom, endeavouring to hold a position between the extremes of Rome and Geneva and striving to justify such an attitude by reference to history and a direct reference to the Bible and the story of the rise of Christianity from the womb of Judaism.

The essential point to establish for the moment is this question of our Lord's purpose in coming into the world. Did He intend to found a visible Church, and, if so, is the story of its rise and extension, as we find it recorded in the New Testament, in accord with the mind of the Master? Here we cannot do better than follow the late Canon Scott Holland in his admirable handling of the subject: [1]

'Belief in a Church affects our belief in Christ Jesus; it involves, that is, a particular reading of His Life-work, a particular conception of His purpose, of His Mind, of His desires, of His plan while He was here with us on earth. If we include the Church in the Creed, we must mean that the story of our Lord's life includes and involves the story of the Church, and that we could not read the Gospels themselves without seeing there the origin and the necessity of Christ's Church.'

Now do the Gospels, as we ordinarily read them, convey that to us?

1st impression. He went about doing good. 'The sower scatters the seed, and is careless where it falls.'

2nd impression. (*a*) He sets himself to throw off the

---

[1] *Creed and Character*, Sermons III-IX, ' The Church in the Gospels '.

crowds which dog His footsteps and to concentrate upon a small selected inner circle of chosen Disciples.

(*b*) His purpose is not to teach but to go up to Jerusalem, i.e. to do something: to be baptised with a Baptism — His meat is to do the Father's will.

(*c*) He has work to do, urgent, vast and awful, before the night draws on.

> 'Why is He here? He is come, not to heal a few sick folk only, but in the mind of those eternal counsels which reach from the beginning to the end, He is come to cast the stone from Heaven which shall break all the Kingdoms of the earth and grind them to powder. . . . He is here to beget the new race of men; He is here to build the new House of God, the Temple of His Body. To build! How can He build on that loose and shifting rubble, on that blind movement of the crowd, so vague and so undetermined. To build on this is to build on the sand; and He is to build for eternity, and in the face of Hell. . . . He must have rock. . . . He finds it in the living faith of Simon, Bar-Jonas. Upon confession of His Name: belief in Himself as Saviour — upon such a solid foundation — upon Jesus Christ and Him crucified — is the Church built.'

Was He content to throw the truth down upon the open area of the world and to leave it to make its own way, to shape its own course among the listening crowds, undirected and unorganised?

Some seed he flung but His full significance He did not reveal to the Crowd, even though they cried out, 'Tell us plainly, art thou the Christ?'

> 'The Gospel story is the record of the pains and anxiety with which the Lord sifted, selected, prepared those few to whom this, His vital and essential message, should be committed. . . . Very slowly they are made ready, chastened, purged; until that last awful hour was reached when, with feet washed clean, and with hearts made pure by the word implanted — alone with Him in

the upper chamber, apart, hidden from the world, they
receive the uttermost secret, no longer in parable, but in
plain speech; and share in the New Covenant, and take
of His Body, and drink of His Blood. That is the story.
. . . How is it, then, that we allow people still to assert
and believe that our Lord cast His word loose among
mankind — that His message was independent of all embodiment, of all organisation? Yet the exact contrary
holds. His message, His secret of Redemption, is never
given except in an organised form. He occupies Himself
with little else but the framing and perfecting of its
Tabernacle. This Sower is very far from being careless
where His seed falls. There is a seed He keeps in hand
until He is quite sure of the ground; only to a certain
plot will He commit it — a plot deliberately selected,
painfully prepared, by shrewd and wise husbandry, dug,
weeded, harrowed, watered. His spiritual force has to
be held back, until it can effect a lodgment, until it can
secure for itself an organised home, until it can house
itself within a body. And that body, that home, can only
be built of living men, who can apprehend His true Name.
To discover such men, to choose, call, stablish them, this
is the life-task of Jesus Christ, as recorded in the Gospels.

'Give Him but twelve men, so found, chosen, and
secured, and He is ready to go up to Jerusalem, and die,
and be seen no more. Give Him but these, who are to
Him not as servants but as friends, who can understand
Him, feel with Him; live and die in Him, and His
Church is based on a rock . . . there it is! There is the
rock on which all is built . . . a knot of men, selected,
set apart, elect, precious, on whom alone the final attention of the Lord is concentrated, to whom alone His inner
heart commits its secret, — here is the seed plot of the
living Word. Here is the issue of the Gospel story, the
fruit of the Lord's earthly mission. This is what he left
behind Him on earth when He died. . . .'[1]

'Christ's Church exists in order to make possible, to

[1] *Op. cit.* p. 58.

make known, to make active, the work which Christ, by His Incarnation, Death, and Resurrection, achieved once for all. It was done, it was finished, the task given Him to do. But only through man could it be laid open to man. He needs men to be His instruments, His organ, by which His own activity, supreme and unique, may find channels of entry — may be solicited, evoked, distributed. In securing men who know his true Name, He is securing a seat, a home, into which He can throw His own spiritual forces. They become, through so believing, the means by which His special and personal powers can liberate and discharge themselves. As He is the Light of the world, so they become, in Him, the eye through which the light illuminates the body: "Ye are the light of the world". . . . What He Himself has been in the world that is what they will now become. They are His organ of communication with the world, the material of His manifestation.' [1]

Hence the Church as the Extension of the Incarnation. [2]

'He needs a body through which He may make Himself intelligible to men, and even to unbelieving men, make Himself felt, certified, effective, enduring. This body He must have and that body He has with pain secured Himself. And now into that prepared body His spirit issues from Him, to gather it up into organised life, to inhabit it, to unify its capacities, to regulate its aims, to quicken its impulses, to fix its offices, to direct its gifts, to correlate its functions, to shape and distribute its parts, to feed and govern its entire frame.

'A Spirit-bearing body — that is the agency which the ascended Lord has organised for His Spirit's service on earth, and its office, therefore, is clearly determined for it by the conditions of its existence, and that office is summed up in one word, "witness". . . . And in accomplishing the conversion of the world, the Church has two points to prove and testify: (*a*) that Christ is alive and at

[1] *Op. cit.* pp. 64-5.   [2] Cf. p. 88.

work now to-day on earth, and that He can be found of them that believe, and manifest Himself to those that love Him; and (*b*) that He is so by virtue of the deed done once for all at Calvary — by which the Prince of this world was judged and the world was overcome and man given access to GOD.' [1]

What proof can the Church offer for these two points? It has three proofs to give:

1. Its own actual life: 'I live, yet not I, but Christ liveth in me'.
2. The Gospel Book, the Apostolic witness — this book the body of Christ carries ever before it, declaring to all, 'This record is true'.
3. The Apostolic *Rite* as well as the Apostolic record, the seal and pledge of our redemption 'till He come'.[2]

So far Canon Scott Holland, and we know no better summary of the Gospel evidence for our Lord's intention to leave behind Him a Body so constituted, so trained, so organised as to be capable of continuing His Work after His Ascension and in the power of His Life-giving Spirit. In this sense the Church is, and is meant to be, the Extension of the Incarnation.

Such was the Catholic Church, in origin Divine, and launched out upon its task of subduing the Kingdoms of this world to the Kingdom of God and of His Christ. It is no product of earth but comes from above. It is no man-made invention or the creation of any State or States. It is in the world and yet not of it. It has distinctive marks by which it can be readily distinguished from other religions and other religious bodies. It is One, Holy, Catholic and Apostolic. Through all its chequered history it has partaken however imperfectly of this character, and the Church of England is a part of it, Catholic though Reformed, claiming continuity with the historic past with an historic episcopate, valid sacraments, the open Bible, an episcopally ordained

[1] *Op. cit.* pp. 88-9.   [2] *Op. cit.* p. 90.

ministry and a Faith intellectually formulated in the Creeds and Ecumenical documents of the Faith.

The appeal of the Church of England is back behind the mediaeval period to an earlier and, as we believe, more truly Catholic and uncorrupted Church of the New Testament. The Church in the New Testament is not primarily a theological or ecclesiastical club, a society where people meet together to discuss genially or otherwise doctrines, theories, politics or ritual. Nor is it a social institution for Pleasant Sunday Afternoons. Nor is it a philanthropic and charitable institution designed to further the interests of democracy and to break down social distinctions. The Church is not a democracy nor was it ever meant to be governed either by the ballot-box or by Acts of Parliament. It is from first to last a theocracy and its form of government is a Divine autocracy. The whole principle of the ministerial priesthood stands or falls with this fundamental conception of Divine authority and power from above conferred through chosen and ordained channels upon a Society which itself is of Divine workmanship and consists of those who are regenerate as the result of a miracle of Divine Grace in Baptismal regeneration. Its franchise is therefore Christian Baptism, and its membership governed by that initiation. It is a Body of men and women who have been born anew of water and the Holy Ghost; who are banded together in a spiritual fellowship as the outcome of a vital union with the Head — Christ Jesus — a Christocracy governed by Him and called into being to realise His life and to manifest Him to an unbelieving world.

To such a Body He gave the Power of the Keys and thus founded His Church upon the foundation of the Apostles and Prophets, Himself being the head corner-stone.

The modern attempt to drive a wedge between Christ and His Church is thus fundamentally subversive of the whole Catholic conception of its true nature and function.

This is a point to which the late Bishop Neville Talbot directed special attention.

A great many minds, he told us, are swayed by a deep-seated tendency to make a divorce between Christ and the whole sphere of organised Christianity. He is to be relieved of any responsibility for institutional religion. The Church is to be treated as a matter of human convenience and is not to be supposed to have any organic connection with Him. If we magnify the Church, we give a diminished place or value to Jesus Christ; so would some people argue.

Protestantism, he asserted, as its name implies, has a native aversion to and suspicion of the Church; and at the same time it has an evangelical passion for the Person of Christ. Its tendency since the Reformation has been to drive wedges in between both Christ and the Church, and between the Gospel and the Church. It has gloried in the belief that personal devotion to Jesus and an acceptance of the Gospel are essentially independent of the Church. For it, individual conversion and discipleship have been the primary thing and Church membership only a subsidiary consequence. It has tended to look upon the individual as prior to the Church, and upon the Church as constituted by the aggregation of converted individuals for purposes of fellowship and organisations.[1] Hence the disparagement of Church and Sacraments, the depreciation of institutional religion; the steady drive towards an exaggerated individualism; the breaking away of individuals and the formation of sectional groups and schisms without any sense of loss, from the fellowship of the One Body of Christ. The fundamental cleavage between this conception of the nature and function of the Church and that which we believe to be the true one is illustrated by a significant passage in the late Archbishop F. Temple's sermon at the consecration of Truro Cathedral:

'Men speak as if Christians came first, and the Church afterwards; as if the origin of the Church was in the wills of the individual Christians who composed it. But, on the contrary, throughout the teaching of the Apostles, we see that it is the Church which comes first, and the members

[1] Vide *Before we Meet* (at the Lambeth Conference), pp. 3 and 10, *passim*.

196

of it afterwards. Men were not brought to Christ, and then determined that they would live in a community. Men were not brought to believe in Christ and in the Cross, and then decided that it would be a great help to their religion that they should join one another in the worship of the Father through His Name. In the New Testament, on the contrary, the Kingdom of Heaven is already in existence, and men are invited into it. . . . The Church takes its origin not in the will of man but in the will of the Lord Jesus Christ. . . . Everywhere men are called in; they do not come in, and make the Church by coming. They are called in to that which already exists; they are recognised as members when they are within; but their membership depends upon their admission; and not upon their constituting themselves a body in the sight of the Lord. In the New Testament, the Church flows out from the Lord, not flows into Him. In the New Testament, the ministers are sent forth to gather the children of men within the fold, and are not simply selected by the members of the Church to help them in their spiritual life.' [1]

We have dwelt at this length upon the nature and function of the Church because we believe that in this conception of it lies the key to the true understanding of its whole history, not least since the Reformation in relation both to the 'Free Churches' outside its borders, to the varied schools of thought within its membership, and to the State whose national organ it still is. We shall not understand in the least degree the significance of its claim to spiritual freedom unless we have first firmly grasped the true nature and function of the Church as we have outlined it.

And it is in this setting and context alone that we can profitably contemplate the possibility of reunion either with Rome or with the Nonconformists. All discussions ultimately run back to the nature and function of the Church in the Divine economy.

[1] Archbishop F. Temple, when Bishop of London, in *Twelve Sermons preached at the Consecration of Truro Cathedral* (Heard & Sons, Truro, 1888).

We will content ourselves by drawing attention to one amongst many recent books dealing with this acute problem of the divisions of Christendom and the possibility of reunion.

The Church of England and Reunion (S.P.C.K.) was a notable contribution to the debate on the reunion of Christendom by the late Dr. H. L. Goudge. Three convictions govern what the late Regius Professor of Divinity in the University of Oxford has to tell us on this vital issue. First and obviously that the reunion of Christendom is not only desirable but absolutely necessary, if the work of God is to be rightly done. Few would be likely to question this. The second is that the Church of England, which by its position should make a great contribution to Reunion, is not playing the part which it ought to play. Those in the Anglican Church who are at all familiar with the facts will be the first to admit the justice of this criticism. The third is that little further progress will be made without far more vigorous discussion of our differences. Dr. Goudge's work ought to prove a definite stimulus in this last direction. Many would go further and stress the need for deeds, not words. A study of Dr. Goudge's book shows how difficult even at this eleventh hour deeds are, in spite of the growing conviction that the issue confronting Christians is now not so much the survival of any one section of the Church or the likelihood of the Protestant religious denominations returning to the Mother Church of England or of Canterbury submitting to Rome, but of the survival of Christianity itself in the face of a menacing and increasing secularism. Yet Professor Goudge would bid us hope rather than despair. He felt that in important respects Catholics and Protestants are nearer together than they used to be and so the future holds within it the promise of better things to come. But even at the Edinburgh Conference we were more successful in understanding one another, and registering our agreements and disagreements, than in getting rid of the disagreements. This fact points the way to the next steps. We need to define our position beyond the possibility of misunderstanding. We need to bring out clearly the fundamental presuppositions of a Church Catholic, though Reformed. We must reveal to those who still remain in separation from us, why it is that our place in Christendom as the 'Bridge Church' forbids any solution of the reunion problem short of a full acceptance of the Church, and its corollary in our view, as against the Protestant view, of the Ministry and the Sacraments. More and more is it coming to be realised that behind our differences lie two totally diverse conceptions of the nature and function of the Church and the Ministry. Not the least valuable feature in Dr. Goudge's contribution is his clear recognition of this fact and his insistence that nothing is to be gained by minimising differences or attempting in the interests of Christian charity to slur over or attempt to explain away what we believe to be the truth. He divided his work into three parts — the first, Critical; the second, Constructive; the third, Practical. Of these Part II will, we think, prove of most value, especially as it is the ripe fruit of years of study and research work by a trained theologian. His chapters on the meaning and purpose of the Church; the Word of God; the Church and the Ministry in the New Testament; and the place and value of Apostolical Succession — to name but a few of the themes he handles — are models of exact scholarship and challenge refutation. To this constructive part we may with confidence bid our separated brethren to address themselves. The issues are there defined in clear and unambiguous form. We should ourselves define them even more acutely in an Either-Or. *Either* the Church is supernatural in origin, though rooted in History, *or* it is a man-made institution, the result of an afterthought. If the latter, then questions of its necessity or relevance are a matter for human judgment and turn upon human convenience in any given age or situation. If, on the other hand, it be part and parcel of a Divine Revelation and an essential element in a Divine plan of salvation for the whole world, its nature and function are Divinely determined and 'given'. It is not within the power of men to frustrate the Divine intention or alter the Divine plan to suit their own convenience, or to minister to their own personal prejudices or preferences. Again, as regards the Ministry and the Sacraments, *either* we must accept the principle of Devolution from above *or* that of evolution from below. Either the ministry is from God, through Christ, and from Christ through the Apostles, and the Apostolical Succession in consequence is of the *esse* of the Church; or the ministry is a matter of human election and decision on the part of individuals or congregations, and Episcopacy at best is a matter of the survival of the fittest and to be preferred, if at all, as the best form of Church government yet tried, though there is no reason why in the future a better form might not be evolved. *Esse* or *bene esse*, or even *plene*, is still the issue, and nothing is to be gained by concealing or evading that fact as regards Apostolical Succession and Episcopacy. Again, attention needs to be paid to the function and status of the prophets, both under the Old and the New Testament dispensations. More and more, we believe, will it come to be recognised that priest and prophet are not necessarily exclusive terms. We can wholeheartedly recognise in non-Episcopal ministries the prophetic office, so far as these bear upon them the undoubted signs of a Divine inspiration. Yet for the work of a priest in the Church of God even the most inspired of the prophets must be ordained.

A reading of Part III of Dr. Goudge's book, dealing as it does with the practical side and facing the present situation, leads us again to emphasise a suggestion we made some years ago as to a possible practical step which could be taken in our own day and generation and which in our considered judgment would be an immense help towards the solution of the whole problem. And it is this. A frank recognition of the fact that the Church is founded upon the Apostles *and Prophets*, Jesus Christ Himself being the head corner-stone, should lead us to a clearer appreciation of the *twofold* character of the ministry of the Word and Sacraments, and of the *twofold* function of the prophet and the priest in the ministerial priesthood inherent in the whole Church, which includes both the lay and the clerical elements. Why then cannot we recognise without any reservations all that is implied and involved in the Nonconformist ministerial work, whilst at the same time asking them to recognise the need for a further ordination for a wider ministry in the Anglican Church, covering a ministry both of the Word and of the Sacraments? Ordination to the priesthood implies no disparagement of a prophet's previous work in the Lord's vineyard. It is a call to wider service and enlarged ministerial functions as prophet and priest. Now not all non-episcopal ministers can with fullest confidence, perhaps, claim that they are prophets, and certainly not all priests feel no further need of inspiration in the ministry of the Word. We need priest-prophets and prophet-priests. If by episcopal ordination we can confer the priesthood upon our Nonconformist ministers, and in all humility be ourselves willing to receive from them such prophetic gifts as the Holy Spirit may confer upon us by the laying-on of their hands, why should we or they hesitate to solve our problem and heal our divisions by mutual ordination? If from them we ask a conditional ordination for a wider ministry amongst us — which was not contemplated by them when they received authority from their own people to minister to their own religious community — and they on their part were to demand that we receive from them such authority as they are able to confer upon us for our ministry to their people, such a mutual conferring of gifts would find us, prophet-priests and priest-prophets, ordained for a united ministry of the Word and Sacraments amongst a united people of God. Such a service of ordination in which Bishops and Presbyters had each their respective parts is well within the sphere of practical ecclesiastical politics, and would at once enable us without any violation of Catholic principle to co-ordinate our work; to learn in mutual service a deeper trust in one another, and in the issue, as friends to serve God in sincerity and truth. What prevents it? Human pride. If this is, as we believe, the real stumbling-block, must we wait indefinitely and acquiesce in the rent robe of Christ whilst the world moves further back towards paganism? Must we wait indefinitely, or why not now let Christ have His way with us ? Whenever we pass from words and debate to a suggestion of definite action, the cry is raised for caution lest over-hasty steps prove in the end to have done more harm than good. None the less, a study of the immense progress made in mutual understanding as between ourselves and Nonconformists in recent years does seem to point to the fact that deeds and not words should now be the order of the day. The strategic advantages of such a practical step as mutual ordination along the lines we have indicated are fairly obvious. Many are convinced that the only way to reach reunion is to practise it; to throw down barriers and to exchange pulpits and admit to our altars those who desire to make use of them, no matter what their religious denomination may be, and to invite our people to receive sacramental grace through non-episcopal ministries. Catholics shrink from any such 'short-cuts' as a betrayal of principles. Once, however, by mutual ordination, the validity of non-episcopal ministries were put beyond question, and at the same time our own wholehearted desire for a full recognition of the value and need of the ministry of the Word and the prophetic office were manifested by our acceptance of an ordination through non-episcopal channels as supplementing our own, we could go forward without any further hesitation in experiments in every direction to close the divisions at present existing and to clear up the differences between ourselves and the Nonconformists in this country. We should not achieve reunion at once but we should have removed the outstanding obstacle to any fruitful experiments of a practical kind which at present prevent our passing from words to deeds. If it be urged that such a mutual ordination would be at worst hypocritical and at best artificial, we can only reply that the whole value of such a step would obviously be governed by the spirit in which those concerned entered upon it. Their sincerity in giving and receiving for the definite purpose of mending the rent robe of Christ and by so doing fulfilling His known will for the unity of His Church, could scarcely be questioned if the fruits of it were before their eyes in vision as they bowed their heads to receive through the laying-on of hands a commission to a wider ministry and a consecration to a more sacred task, the reunion of Christendom. Artificial in one sense it might be as all outward acts must seem, but charged with a spiritual content and meaning as identified with the will and work of the Master Himself. The danger of hypocrisy is there, true, but the value of the experiment is worth the risk. We have reached a stage in the problem of the reunion of Christendom when further progress involves a willingness to take risks. Mutual ordination is not a safety-first experiment but a risky venture of faith. It could but fail and little harm would have been done. It might succeed !

We outlined this practical step in the movement towards Reunion in an article in *The Church of England Newspaper* (18th June 1937), and more fully as far back as 1939 when reviewing Dr. Goudge's book in *The Church Quarterly Review*.

Since then we have had a stimulating work on *Revelation and Reunion* by Dr. G. W. Broomfield, which he wrote as a 'Response to Tambaram'. It was hailed as a very remarkable book, not only in the circumstances of its composition, dedicated as it was to 'The Younger Churches', and prompted by the appeal made by some of their representatives at the Tambaram Conference, but also in the solid worth and definiteness of its contribution to our knowledge of the New Testament.

That was in 1942. Dr. Broomfield went a step further in 1944 in a pamphlet on *Anglican and Free Church Ministries* in which he advocated unification through reciprocal supplementary Ordination. The late Archbishop Temple wrote a foreword and welcomed it as a fresh contribution to the solution of this obstinate problem. Dr. Temple pointed out that if we are to enter on the way of advance towards reunion, it must be in a spirit completely detached from claims and counter-claims. We see, as he said, that GOD's work is hindered by our divisions; we know much of what He has given to us through the tradition we have ourselves received; we see something of what He has given through the tradition which others have received. In complete humility we agree to receive from one another whatever may be GOD's gift bestowed through the tradition which is not ours, not feeling bound to define beforehand with precision what that is, but ready to learn by experience the value of each tradition, and the new power which unity itself enables us to receive.

Since then we have had Dr. Fisher's Cambridge sermon (3rd November 1946, published under the title *Church Relations in England*), and an exchange of views is now going on between us and the Free Church representatives on the basis of the proposed line of approach which our present Archbishop put forward in his University sermon.

Dr. Fisher called the Church of England 'the nodal point' of the world-wide Anglican Communion, and frankly admitted the tensions within it which were not yet resolved. None the less within its comprehensive borders, Catholic, Evangelical and Liberal are learning to live together as brethren. If, the Archbishop suggested, the non-Episcopal Churches now recognise the principle that episcopacy must exist along with other elements in a reunited Church, why not 'try out' episcopacy on their own ground, by taking it into their own system, and in this way begin to grow through inter-communion and fellowship towards full communion? If agreement on this as a venture were reached, he would thankfully receive at the hands of others their commission in their accustomed form, and in the same way confer our own. That is the mutual exchange of love and enrichment to which Lambeth 1920 called us.

It is too early yet to speak of any practical outcome of these fresh proposals but the strength of the plea for a unified ministerial system should be obvious, especially to all those of us who are suspicious and profoundly uneasy regarding the South India scheme. What we want to do is to go back to the Lambeth proposals of 1920, advocating 'supplementary ordination'. The whole of Dr. Broomfield's pamphlet was a commentary on that, and a strong plea for 'supplementary ordination' as a necessity, if there is ever to be visible union of Churches previously separated in their corporate life. Such acceptance of it need imply no repudiation or depreciation of a previous ministry or call from GOD. The episcopal ordination of Free Church ministers, as part of an act of union, would bring them, and their Churches, into 'visible' integration with a ministry and corporate church life which have retained their identity unbroken since the time of the Apostles. The acceptance by Anglican clergy, also as part of an act of union, or ordination at the hands of the Free Churches would add to the inheritance of themselves and their Church everything which GOD has granted to the Free Churches.

Such a scheme avoids what some of us feel is a fundamental weakness in the reunion movement in South India. There eventually it is hoped that all the ministers of the united body will have received episcopal ordination, but over a lapse of years there will be ministers of the non-episcopal bodies who are not being required to accept such ordination, yet are allowed to minister as if they were priests.

This leads us to put in again a word of caution, and to repeat what we said as far back as 1930, before this South India scheme had reached anything like the stage of practical experimentation. We repeat the warning, because we feel strongly that any attempt to ignore the difference between 'prophet' and 'priest' in the Church, and any failure to face the issue of the status of the prophetic office relative to the priesthood, can lead to no lasting results. It will only land us in confusion worse confounded in our efforts towards a corporate union. We see no use in asking 'prophets' to accept ordination as 'priests' unless they whole-heartedly believe in the priesthood in the visible Church of Jesus Christ our Lord, wherein hitherto they have laboured as prophets.

In one of the most penetrating of our modern commentaries on the Epistle to the Hebrews (Dr. Nairne's *The Epistle of Priesthood*), attention is drawn to two clearly marked methods of dealing with the sin problem: (*a*) by way of repentance, and (*b*) by way of cleansing. The first is essentially the method of the prophet; the second the method of the priest. The one reflects the action of man relative to God: the other mediates the action of God upon man. The prophet reveals God's attitude towards sin and exhorts men, either by fear of a judgment to come or by the appeal of the Divine love, to turn and repent, and thus by a change of heart to secure the Divine forgiveness.

There are, however, many souls who feel that their deepest need is not so much deliverance from the bondage of sin and freedom from its chains, as cleansing from its pollution and washing from its stains. Such cleansing lies not within the power of the human soul itself to accomplish. Hence the realisation of the need of the Divine action.

'Thou must cleanse and Thou alone.'

Here lies the true significance of the sacrificial system in religion. Whether we trace it in a study of comparative religions, or in the developed Levitical sacrificial system of Judaism, the essence of it is a desperate attempt to find a way of cleansing from sin's defilement. God's chosen people were convinced that the way of sacrifice was an ordained way due to a Divine revelation and a Divine command. It found its acutest expression in the horrible shambles at the Jewish altars with their consequent sickening realisation (*a*) that without the shedding of blood there is no remission, and (*b*) that the blood of bulls and goats and the ashes of a heifer, sprinkling the unclean cannot take away sin.

Nevertheless, the whole system was prophetic of One whose act could and would do so. Dr. Nairne has suggested that if the prophetic method of dealing with the sin problem by way of repentance finds its culmination in the parable of the Prodigal Son, the priestly method of dealing with the same problem by way of Divine cleansing finds its culmination in an Apocalyptic enthusiasm with which Jesus flung Himself upon a Cross. Thus, in His own Person and work, He fulfilled the functions of both Prophet and Priest and by this means was able, as King, to inaugurate a Kingdom in which His prophetic and priestly work might be perpetuated and consummated. Clearly, then, if we to-day would keep the proportion of faith, we must not lose sight of any of those essential parts of our Lord's work which are suggested by these three titles: Prophet, Priest and King.

Many of our theological controversies and unhappy divisions may be traced to our failure to give due weight and relative emphasis to this threefold significance of our Lord's work. Our whole view of our Lord's Person and work and of the nature and function of the Church in the world and human life will be found to be governed by our appreciation of the true significance and relative value of His work as Prophet, Priest and King.

If the essence of His work is to be sought not so much in what He said but in what He did for us men and for our salvation, and if, moreover, the work He did was one mighty act of sacrifice for the sin of the world, clearly the Person who alone could accomplish so momentous a change in the relationship between God and man, with all its universal consequences and implications, cannot have been less than the God-Man in the act. Hence the richness of content which the Church has attached to the saving work of Christ on Calvary drives us back upon a belief in His Person which cannot stop short of the category of Incarnation. If the essence of His work lies not so much in revelation but in redemption, if He is not only the Light of the World but its sole and only Saviour, then the content of the 'Good News' is to be sought not so much in what He said as in what He did and He transcends the category of prophet in the doing of it.

Again, our whole conception of the Church and Sacraments will turn upon our belief in the Incarnation. If the Incarnate Son of God came from Heaven to teach and to preach and to give His life a ransom for many, and if, moreover, He left a Divinely constituted extension of Himself to perpetuate and accomplish His saving work on earth, then the Church and Sacraments are vital. If the Church and Sacraments are in a real sense the extension of the Incarnation, then we have in the world no man-made institution but a Divinely constituted and supernaturally derived Body of Christ, through which will be continued not only the Lord's prophetic ministry of preaching the Word, but also, and centrally, the conveyance to sin-stained souls of the cleansing efficacy of His Sacrifice once offered. The work of the Church will thus be more than prophetic and will point beyond the pulpit to the altar and be in essence priestly even as was the work of its Lord and Master.

The ministerial priesthood of the clergy is the direct outcome of the priestly character of the whole Body of Christ (1 Peter ii, 5), and the priestly character of the Church is itself in its turn derived from the Head of the Church, our great High Priest. Moreover, the Sacraments are not only revelational of eternal truths, but also ordained instruments for the achievement of spiritual acts and effects in things pertaining to God, through a ministerial priesthood.

In such a Church, while there is ample room for the exercise of the prophetic office, there must also be a central place for the extension of the sacrificial and mediatorial work of the Master. As the Word was made flesh, so the Word to-day is to be made flesh and dwell among us. As He was Incarnate, so is He still to make Himself known to us in the Breaking of the Bread. As He healed and cleansed as well as taught, so is He, through His Church to-day, to heal and cleanse as well as to teach.

Again, the Kingship of Jesus is fundamental. It is at once a reality and an ideal. It is real in the Kingdom of the redeemed and an ideal for the kingdoms of this world. The Church exists in the world as a supernatural creation for the extension of Christ's Lordship over the hearts of men. It is in the world and yet not of it. As such its relations and functions need to be clearly defined, if it is to do its work in the world at all effectively.

The fellowship of the Church is to be the great experimental exhibition to the world of what the world, by its wisdom, has so far failed to realise. Such a fellowship cannot come about in the ordinary course of world development or be a product of evolutionary processes. It is essentially supernaturally born and nourished from above. Here lies the secret of our failure to impose the idealism of the Christian ethic upon human society. We cannot have the Christian codes divorced from their supernatural setting. We cannot expect the precepts of the Sermon on the Mount to be followed by unregenerate human nature. The life of man needs to be humanised by Christ before we can hope to expel the demon of secularism from the body-politic. At present we are trying to apply Christian principles for the solution of our social, industrial, national and international problems over vast stretches where the Kingship of Jesus is either unknown or studiously ignored.

If the Church is to plunge into the world of affairs and to overcome the spirit of the world, it is surely advisable to pause first and to get some large measure of agreement among its own members (*a*) as to precisely what is its main objective, and (*b*) how it proposes to set about the task. A Church divided against itself or torn between two minds can scarcely hope to achieve much.

If the Church in the world is a moving stream of spiritual energy and power, as indeed historically it has proved itself to be in the past, then indeed we need to study it afresh in the story of its conquest of the pagan world-State of ancient Rome.

So to-day we need to recover our balance and to concentrate afresh upon spiritual renewal as the condition of world conquest. The Church will become again a great spiritual power-station or a moving stream of spiritual energy for the healing of the nations if and so far as we work with God in Christ for the conversion of souls and the transformation of sinners into saints. We must wait upon the Lord to renew our strength. We must submit to His ministrations as Priest before we can go forth as His prophets to proclaim His Kingship and subdue the world to His obedience.

The controversy between Prophet and Priest is a perennial theme of religious history. It finds expression throughout the Old Testament and in post-canonical Jewish literature. It reveals itself all through the history of the Christian Church. We find it in an acute form as the result of the

Reformation upheaval, and we experience it in the relations existing between the Church of England, Catholic though Reformed, and those English varieties of Continental Protestantism which we in this country have come to know under the heading of the 'Free Churches'. All questions of reunion with those religious bodies lead us sooner or later to face the issue of the status of the prophetic office relative to the priesthood, and involve us in considerations of Church Order; the sacred ministry of the Church; and the principle of the historic episcopate.

The problem confronting us to-day is to find a method of achieving an ultimate organic unity between our branch of the Church, Catholic though Reformed, and therefore committed by its whole history and traditions to the idea and doctrine of the Apostolic succession through the episcopate, with a variety of religious bodies whose very existence is an emphatic repudiation of the whole underlying implications of a ministerial priesthood. Can it possibly be done by an attempt to place side by side for a period of years prophets and priests in the hope that their mutual appreciation of one another's status and standing, function and place in the Church, will in due course change a prophet into a priest or enable a prophet to perform priestly functions without the necessity of episcopal ordination? The question at issue is not any failure on the part of the Church to appreciate the value of a prophet's work or to recognise the fruits of the Spirit's working through men inspired of God and called by God to preach the Word. We can outvie one another as Churchmen in a Christian charitable recognition of all that God has undoubtedly accomplished through the prophetic ministry of Nonconformist religious communities. We are unfaithful witnesses to the truth, however, if such charitable recognition leads us to call a prophet something which he has never believed himself to be, never has been and never can be except by Ordination, namely a priest. Apart from any question of conflicting historical data, or even of theories concerning the origin and development of the historic episcopate, the practically universal system of Church govern-

ment has been that laid down in our English Ordinal, where
we are reminded in the Preface that—

'It is evident unto all men diligently reading Holy
Scripture and Ancient Authors, that from the Apostles'
time there have been these Orders of Ministers in Christ's
Church: Bishops, Priests, and Deacons. . . . And therefore, to the intent that these Orders may be continued, and
reverently used and esteemed, in the Church of *England* ;
no man shall be accounted or taken to be a lawful Bishop,
Priest, or Deacon in the Church of *England*, or suffered to
execute any of the said Functions, except he be called, tried,
examined, and admitted thereunto, according to the Form
hereafter following, or hath had formerly Episcopal Consecration, or Ordination.'

The Formularies of the Church of England may legitimately, perhaps, in some respects be accused of ambiguity
in the interests of a charitable comprehensiveness. Its position, however, on this question of the priesthood and episcopal
Ordination could not be clearer and cannot be misinterpreted.
A layman may preach, teach, read and expound the Word;
he may lead a congregation in prayer and praise. What he
cannot do in any conceivable circumstances is to consecrate
a valid Eucharist. He may be God's revealer and the mess-
enger sent before His Face to proclaim the good news and
make clear the way of repentance for the solution of the sin-
problem. He may, under God's hand, be wonderfully
instrumental in the conversion of souls. When it comes,
however, to the deeper question of cleansing; to the more
awful mystery of the Word made Flesh; and the instrumental channels ordained for the conveyance of Angel's
Food to cleanse and to nourish sin-stained souls; the priestly
office comes into play as a Divinely instituted ministry, not
only of the spoken Word but also of the Sacraments as means
of grace. Here no man can or dare take upon himself such
an Office or presume to exercise it except he be called and
duly ordained and consecrated for such specific purposes,

by those who alone have the power and authority to commission him. Hence, far from insistence upon Ordination being any disparagement of a previously exercised prophetic ministry, it is, on the contrary, the natural and inevitable condition for the exercise of a more glorious and richer rôle of usefulness in the most sacred of all callings. Messengers we may have been, and gloriously used as such in the spread of the Kingdom. But now, as ordained priests, we are more. We are stewards of the mysteries of God; ministers of the Word and Sacraments; Divinely ordained and chosen men to exercise the office of the priesthood in the Household of God.

A summons to new functions carries with it necessarily a conferring of authority for their exercise from those who alone are in a position to give it. Ordination is no disparagement of the prophetic office but a conferment of authority to exercise the functions of the priesthood. We gain nothing by attempting 'short cuts' as the outcome of a muddle-headed inability to think clearly or an unwillingness to adhere in loyalty to the principles of the Catholic Church, of which we are members. A reunion falsely based upon artificial compromises must issue sooner or later in a wider disunion.

We dare not impair the great heritage of our priesthood in the Church of God in our eagerness to welcome back into the Church those who, in the past, have carried on a relentless warfare against that whole side of the Catholic truth which is represented by the great conception of the ministerial priesthood. If we deplore the spectacle of so many prophets carrying on a guerrilla warfare of their own and cut off from co-operation with us, the remedy is to reason together and discuss our differences in the atmosphere of prayer and upon the basis of sound learning to which the Church of England can fearlessly appeal. We do not solve our problem by calling prophets priests. This can only issue in making confusion worse confounded. We can, however, thank God for the blessing which has rested upon non-episcopal prophetic ministries and, while fully recog-

nising it, insist upon Ordination for those who are desirous
of exercising priestly functions in the things pertaining to
God, and believe themselves to be truly called of God to do
so. The Church already contains prophets who are also
ordained priests. We may seek to add to their number by
ordaining those who are at present only prophets, and so
making them priests also.

Let us, in conclusion, for a moment think of the individual
soul. Are you really happy? Or do you feel not only the
chains of sin but also its stains? It may be that you have
heard far too many prophets and listened to numerous sermons, attended services of prayer and praise, while all the
time your real need was not so much the ministrations of
the prophetic but of the priestly order. If so, the remedy is
simple. *Go, show yourself unto the priest.* There is, in the
Church of God, a ministry of cleansing which is unknown or
repudiated by the Nonconformist prophetic ministry. Our
Lord has left power to His Church to absolve all sinners who
truly repent and believe in Him. The sacrament of penance
in the Church provides for your need. The ministerial
priesthood in the Church exists for that purpose. The power
of Absolution awaits the penitent soul. Will you make use
of it? Not that we make our confession to a priest, but
through a priest; not that a priest forgives, but God forgives
through him. He is the ordained channel for the conveyance
of the cleansing Blood of the Lamb to your soul and mine,
and he has received God's commission and authority through
the Church to do it.

As you kneel at the feet of Jesus and sob out your confession, casting yourself upon His mercy and trusting in His
redeeming Blood, you will hear a voice out of the thick
darkness — a human voice, but speaking and conveying to
your soul God's Word of Absolution.

'After which confession,' says our 1662 Prayer Book,
'the Priest shall absolve him (if he humbly and heartily
desire it) after this sort: "Our Lord Jesus Christ, who
hath left power to His church to absolve all sinners who

truly repent and believe in Him, of His great mercy forgive thee thine offences: And by His authority committed to me, I absolve thee from all thy sins, in the Name of the Father, and of the Son, and of the Holy Ghost. Amen.'''

One such personal experience of the healing touch of the Crucified is for the sin-stained soul worth a thousand sermons or eloquent exhortations. The soul will feel in itself, like the poor woman who drew near and touched the hem of His garment, that it has been healed and cleansed. After that the man or woman will not have much difficulty in distinguishing between the prophetic and the priestly methods of dealing with the sin-problem. We shall also appreciate, perhaps, more fully why in His love the Lord provided both ministries and gave some to be Apostles, and some prophets.

Before, however, we invite Nonconformists to return to the Mother Church and make with us a concerted effort to heal the divisions still separating us from English varieties of Continental Protestantism, it is above all essential that we make a similar concerted effort to reach a larger measure of agreement amongst ourselves. We still have within the large comprehensiveness of our Church, Catholic though Reformed, three schools of thought, and it is most desirable that these should be drawn much closer together than they are at present in the effort to minister to the needs of the nation at large.

The existence of these party differences calls for an Anglican Armistice and we renew a plea made a quarter of a century ago to close our ranks.

What is our place in Christendom?

We have to remind ourselves at the outset that our Church could not expect to go through the upheaval of a Reformation without making enemies. And we made foes in two quarters: Rome and Geneva. From that day to this Roman aggression and Continental Protestantism have done their best to destroy us. Yet we still survive and continue to thrive. We have always to remember the peculiar difficulties

which confront a Church aiming at the avoidance of the
extremes of Roman Papalism on the one side and Continental
Protestantism on the other. We have to recognise clearly
that our Church at the Reformation definitely repudiated
both these extremes. In doing so it necessarily found room
for the vast body of Central Churchmen, and at the same
time embraced, in a large inclusivenes, men biased in one
or other direction; men inclined by temperament and upbringing either towards Rome or towards Geneva. The
history of our Church since those days has been a history in
which this double strain within the ranks of Churchmen,
stimulated by both Rome and Nonconformity without, has
been more or less acutely felt. Hitherto, in spite of it, the
Church has flourished and has been held steady on its *via
media* by the influence and work of the vast majority of sane
Catholic Evangelicals in its fold. The present situation
simply means a somewhat more acute sense of strain within
the Church, due to many causes. We need not be unduly
alarmed at this in the light of history.

The Prayer Book controversy was the crystallisation of a
growing feeling of alarm as to the direction in which the
English Church is moving. Many, quite honestly, have convinced themselves that what is known as 'Anglo-Catholicism'
really means sooner or later 'Romanism'. They see in
the activities of Anglo-Catholics, both in teaching and in
ceremonial, plain indications of an attempt to go behind the
Reformation. Hence an attempt is made to raise an alarmist
cry and to suggest that, unless Churchmen halt and pull
themselves together, they will be driven by the extremists
within the Church into the arms of Rome.

Within Evangelicalism itself, however, there have been
for some time past promising signs of a new life associated
more particularly with those who have been engaged in an
effort to reinterpret Evangelical ideals in terms of modern
thought. 'Liberal Evangelicalism' has much in common with
true Churchmanship. It is wide awake to the need of
adapting the expression of the Church's belief to a world of
advancing knowledge. It is 'modern' but not necessarily

'modernist'. It has a firm grasp upon some of the great fundamental beliefs of the Church's Creed, and it is stung to the quick by the attempts of 'modernists' to undermine, by explaining in a way that really explains away, much in the Gospel truths of the Incarnation, the Atonement, the Resurrection which the Evangelical holds dear and feels to be vital to a true Christianity.

There are, moreover, signs of appreciation among Evangelicals of the essence of Catholic worship, and, as they come to understand more and more of Catholic ceremonial, they will enter more fully into its spirit and value its benefits. The long debates in the Church Assembly and the discussions in the country arising from these have proved to be an immense education in the meaning and value of Catholic thought and practice. Evangelicalism has profited consciously or unconsciously by this education, and has had its attention focused upon the Prayer Book as a Catholic document in a way that has startled many into a fresh discovery of its value. So much so, that there are large numbers in the Church who would be quite content to go back to the Prayer Book of 1549 as containing all that is essential for the expression of a sane Catholicism, adequate to meet the needs of many congregations which have benefited from the Catholic revival and are advancing slowly but surely to a higher level of teaching and ceremonial.

The very fact that so many would be content with a return to an earlier edition (1549) of the old Prayer Book is in itself, first, a vindication of the essential catholicity of the English Prayer Book, and, secondly, a hopeful sign of the large measure of agreement, in spite of differences, existing between Evangelicals and Catholics in the English Church at the present day.

But such slow and steady movements towards a closer *rapprochement* will not be helped but only hindered by rash action. If Anglo-Catholics are 'suspect' as regards Rome, militant Protestants are more suspect as regards Nonconformity. If we are to be summoned to a campaign against the extremists on one side, why should we not also demand action against those who, whilst in the Church, conduct its services in a way hard to recognise as consistent with Prayer Book teaching and Catholic custom?

It is well for us who love our English Church to rally round it in these days and to strive to draw closer together in a summons not *anti* this or that but *pro Ecclesia Anglicana*. If we remember what our nation owes to the Church of England, we may well pause to consider what the severance of the Church from the State would mean in our English life. If we consider for a moment the possibility of the disappearance of the Church of England in the future, and the substitution in its place of either a heterogeneous collection of warring sects or the dominance of Rome, we may well pause before so gloomy a prospect, and ask ourselves whether the time is opportune for the accentuation of internal strife when the enemy of secularism is at the gates, and when, if we quit the field, the alternatives are either the dreary negations of Protestantism or the arrogance of an aggressive Romanism. Above all, in an endeavour to grasp the true significance of English Catholicism, we have to remember that we are living in a world of advancing knowledge and consequent changing outlook in every department of thought and life.

In the sphere of politics this is clearly enough manifested. We have the strange spectacle of a Conservative Party embarking upon a political programme which would have been denounced a half or even a quarter of a century ago as radical and revolutionary. Conservative politicians who undertake to condemn Anglo-Catholics as revolutionaries may well be reminded to look to their own spheres of public activity and to justify themselves first against an equally false and misleading accusation. They would plead, no doubt, that Conservatism must move with the times.[1] We agree. But we draw an obvious conclusion in applying the

---

[1] *The Times* comment (Tuesday, 18th September 1951) is significant in this context: 'The Conservatives have hitherto been as much tied by the ideas and jargon of the thirties as the Labour party. The proposal now is that they should speak instead in the language of 1951. It can at least be said that is the language which the voters of 1951 will understand.'

same principle to other departments of thought and activity. Are we to acquiesce in change in every other department, and condemn the Church to a static stagnation? Is the Church alone to be condemned to a world-view peculiar to the sixteenth or any other century, whilst the State is free to adapt itself to modern conditions?

We are living in the twentieth century, and the Church is faced with the problem of presenting its message in terms of modern thought and adapting its services to the needs of modern men. The demand for Prayer Book Revision was a legitimate demand, and any revision undertaken must still do justice to that vastly keener appreciation of the essentially Catholic character of the English Church which has come about as the result of the Oxford Movement and the new wealth of spiritual experience which has followed from it.

We have to remember that in our own day loyal Churchmen in vastly greater numbers have learned to centre their religious lives in the altar. They have consequently come to appreciate the ordained means of grace so clearly taught in our Prayer Book, and, above all, they have been brought into intimate and vital contact with our Saviour, and have come to know the meaning of His Real Presence in that Sacrament which He Himself ordained for that very purpose and explicitly commanded His followers to use.

All this, it may be said, is true, but the complaint centres upon new forms of ceremonial, new rites and customs, many of which are at present without Episcopal authority, and some of which, at any rate, are suggestive of what is distinctly Roman and not English Catholicism.

This raises large issues upon which we will say this much at least.

(1) What is distinctively and exclusively Roman? Before we rashly condemn outright in our ignorance something as being 'Roman', let us make quite sure by careful liturgical study that what we are condemning is distinctively Roman and not part of the common heritage of the Catholic Church both Roman and English. We as members of the Catholic Church of England have much which we share in common

with our brethren of the Roman Communion. What is common to us both is ours as much as theirs, and its presence therefore in our services and ceremonies is no more 'Roman' than a hundred other things which we possess in our English Church and for which the Nonconformists refuse to join us.

(2) Our Church is quite within its legitimate right in adopting, under due authority, new forms of ceremonial, no matter where they came from originally. The crucial question is not their origin, but their usefulness for the purpose of helping religious devotion and worship. Origins are secondary to ends. The question is not whence came they, but of what real use are they.

(3) The problem we have to face is this: in a period of transition, when men's hold upon the Unseen is so precarious, when the things of sense and a rampant materialism tend to cut us off hopelessly from any sense of the spiritual world, are we to forbid any means by which souls may be helped to break through and pierce into the Unseen and touch Reality at a sensitive point? We would plead in this matter for a large measure of toleration. To legislate rigidly in a period of transition and to evoke the aid of external authority for the suppression of varied ways by which some are seeking to retain and to deepen their hold upon the Unseen, is a wrong policy. In a period of unrest and unsettlement we need to legislate (if legislate we must) on large inclusive and not exclusive lines, so as to embrace as wide a difference of opinion and practice as is consistent with the Catholic Faith in a world of advancing knowledge, experiment and fresh discovery.

It is no sign of decadence or retrogression if we find religious formulae breaking down under the strain of new experience. We need not despair if we are acutely conscious that the old order is changing, yielding place to new. The stirring of the waters witnesses to movement, life — not stagnation and death. It is the breath of the Spirit; the movement of that Divine Spirit of Promise, who should lead His Church into all Truth.

(4) This brings me to what we believe to be the crucial

issue and the most urgent need at the present time — viz. the necessity for English Catholics to define their attitude towards Rome and to say quite definitely where the line is to be drawn between English and Roman Catholicism. It is because this line has never been closely defined that there exists in so many quarters widespread suspicion as to the direction in which English Catholics are tending. It is because people suspect Roman tendencies and because they believe that some are definitely working to undermine the position of the English Church with a view to surrender later on when the time is ripe to throw off all disguises. It is for this reason that any change in ceremonials or Catholic customs excites suspicion and leads at once to alarmist cries. There is a widespread failure to distinguish between what is common to English and Roman Catholicism and what is peculiar to each. Where is the line to be drawn? If the vast majority of English Churchmen were assured in their minds that Anglo-Catholics as a whole were loyal and had no intention in the last issue to submit to Papal aggression, they would, we think, be prepared to tolerate much in Anglo-Catholic thought and practice which did not commend itself to them, but which none the less they could countenance as finding a legitimate place within the wide bounds of a distinctly English Catholicism. If, however, the line of demarcation remains undrawn, they have no guarantee whatsoever that concessions here and there to new forms of worship, new practices and the introduction of a more 'advanced' form of service to meet the needs of a new generation are not really an abandonment of the defences against Rome, an undermining of the whole Reformation and the selling of the pass to the enemy.

Were such a line drawn, all such suspicions would be groundless, and, except for extremists and irreconcilables, the way would be open to a much fuller and franker exchange of views and efforts at mutual understanding between those who at present find themselves reluctantly ranked in opposition and driven by the present position to mutual suspicion and recrimination.

Can such a line be drawn and are Catholics willing to draw it?

Clearly the line must be drawn at a point where the question between Canterbury and Rome is acute. Where is that point? We suggest that it is not to be found primarily or essentially in the sphere of Catholic worship or Catholic ceremonial at all. We have to look for it where the Reformation found it in the first instance — viz. in the question of Papalism and the whole claim to temporal power which Rome has not yet withdrawn and still dreams of possessing. The issue at stake is English liberty still, and if the Catholic party in the English Church were to state explicitly that there was the line upon which it would fight till it dropped and beyond that line no English Catholic would move an inch Romewards, then we believe that it would only be a question of time before the vast majority of English Churchmen would find themselves in large measure in agreement within the wide bounds of a sane English Catholicism such as could and would, under God, win England. The line of demarcation, we suggest, lies in the sphere of jurisdiction.

We defined this issue more fully in a lecture delivered at the time of the Prayer Book revision controversy in 1927 (*vide* 'The New Prayer Book') and more recently in a letter to *The Times* in the discussion which arose from an article, 'Catholicism Today', published in October 1949, and subsequently reprinted as a pamphlet. This pamphlet brings together in a more compact and permanent form the original special article, the letters (with a few minor exceptions) which were published, and the final article. It will repay careful study as showing present-day trends both in Roman and in Anglican Church circles.

In our letter we made it abundantly clear that we still repudiate Papalism and the ultra-montane claims. We refuse to accept the findings of the Vatican Decree. We are prepared, as we said, to concede in the light of history a primacy of honour or of order by human right and historic sanction, but never a primacy of Divine right such as Rome still claims.

The Vatican Decree is fatal to our English position, as fatal to Anglicanism as it is to Eastern Orthodoxy. We believe in constitutional episcopal government, and not in a primacy as pertaining *Divina Providentia* to the Holy See.

The line of demarcation lies there. It is for Rome to move across it towards us, if she can, and in moving make possible in the twentieth century a reunion impossible in past history. Will she do it? If she does not, we must acquiesce in a divided Christendom rather than betray a sacred trust and yield our liberty under pressure from an ecclesiastical totalitarian Roman supremacy.

Where is the leader amongst English Catholics who will summon the rank and file in these critical days to come to some such definite decision? If we are wrong in our diagnosis as to where the line is to be drawn, we have no objection personally to its being drawn at another point. What we are absolutely convinced of is this: that the time has come to draw the line, and if it is not drawn there will be nothing but confusion worse confounded, chaos and internecine strife, ending finally, as some hope, in disruption and disappearance of the Church of England.

It has been aptly and, we think, not unfairly said of this age that its coat of arms is 'an interrogation-point rampant, above three Bishops dormant, with the motto "Query" '.

If the mark of our times is a question-mark and a query, surely this is not a call to quarrelsome interference with one another's right to a place in the sun. The Catholic Church of England is still wide enough to embrace our differences, and Mother enough to reconcile us one to another, bidding us compose our family differences in a united effort to present a bold front to the common enemy.

The recent Anglo-Presbyterian correspondence in *The Times* introduced by the Archbishop's letter, which seemed to take away with one hand what was given by the other, serves only to remind us that we have it on the authority of Capablanca that bishops are doomed by nature to move diagonally. We should have thought that since the publication of Dr. Goudge's book, the two books on *Episcopacy Ancient and Modern* (S.P.C.K., 1930) and *The Apostolic Ministry* (Hodder & Stoughton, 1946) were almost definitive on the fundamental issue of the Episcopate as of the *esse* of any branch of the Church, Catholic though Reformed, and that this is the rock upon which all schemes of reunion which seek to avoid this vital element in Anglicanism must prove ineffective, and only lead to further schism. Even if Churches have continued to exist for centuries without it, the invalidity of their Orders is not, and cannot ever be, validated with the passage of time.

On the eve of the recent Lambeth Conference (12th July 1958) *The Times* published our letter on Anglican unity in which we said:

'The prominence given to the Lambeth Conference in the public Press should lead thoughtful people to assess afresh the vocation of the English Church. What precisely is our place in Christendom, and what should be our special contribution towards a solution of the vexed problem of a reunited Christian Church? The answer surely lies in the study of the history of the *Ecclesia Anglicana*. Our position has arisen historically out of the situation caused by the divisions of Christendom, and our contribution is in the nature of an experiment to heal those divisions. We are in this sense a bridge-church. Rightly or wrongly we believe that we have been able providentially to preserve intact all those essentials of Christian Faith and Apostolic Order which mark us as a true part of the visible One Holy Catholic and Apostolic Church founded by Christ Himself upon the foundation of the apostles and prophets. We claim an unbroken historic episcopate, as witnessed, for example, by the impressive Holy Communion Celebration, in which bishops from all over the world participated, and this in spite of the fact that they were of divers languages, and representing high, low and broad churchmanship. They are one in their adherence to the Apostles' Creed and the Sacraments ordained by Christ Himself, and in believing in the Holy Scriptures as containing all things necessary to salvation, and as being the rule and ultimate standard of faith.

'This means, in short, that we are a Church of England, catholic though reformed. As such we are experimenting in the search for a blending of all three elements, catholic, evangelical and liberal, with a view to the production of some such synthesis as a catholic evangelical with broad Church sympathies. Such a harmony alone can meet the needs in matters spiritual, of our modern Christendom, and we are trying to show the world how it can be done on a small scale.

'As a bridge-church we have something worth preserving for the benefit of the whole Church in the future. Our contribution is thus not to part with anything vital in our inheritance, but to deepen that none too strong "unity in diversity" among ourselves, which points the way towards an ultimate reunited Church.

'We think of the British Commonwealth of Nations as a sketch in miniature of the federation of the nations of the world, and we like to feel that ours is an experiment in showing the world how it can be done, and the way to do it. So also with the Anglican Communion, which has expanded like the Empire, and now embraces a fellowship of Churches historically associated with the British Isles. These, while preserving Apostolic Faith and Order, are independent in their self-government, growing freely in their own soils, and, in their diverse environmental settings, handing on a great Christian heritage and tradition, a federation of free, self-governing communities, like the British Commonwealth, linked to Canterbury by no compulsive order save a loyal adherence, and yet with all the call of family origin and affection.

'Such is our heritage. Such our vocation. In a land of free institutions, let us still, as the Anglican Church, prove all things, and try to hold fast that which is good.'

So the debate continues to drag its slow length along, but the case for Episcopacy, Ancient and Modern, remains unshaken.

(b) THE INCARNATION AND ITS EXTENSION IN CHURCH AND SACRAMENTS

A suggested Formula of Concord in the Church of England, Catholic though Reformed

Discussion on Sacramental doctrine in connection with the New Prayer Book served a useful purpose in focusing the attention of a wide audience upon the whole subject of the Incarnation and its Extension in Church and Sacraments. Many have been, however reluctantly, compelled to examine the grounds of their belief in Sacramental Grace and its media of communication, whilst the charge of 'magic' brought against some of the most sacred intimacies of the religious life has forced thoughtful people to question afresh the ultimate validity of their religious experience of the real Presence of Christ in the Church's sacrament of the Lord's Supper. The fact of communion of the Christian with GOD is not questioned, nor is the experience of the presence of Christ in Holy Communion open to doubt. What is at issue is the question as to the exact nature and mode of that Presence through Sacramental channels. What is the exact relation of the Living Lord to the Sacraments He is believed to have ordained? In the light of errors in Sacramental doctrine, and the past history of controversy in this respect, the time seems ripe for a fresh survey of the whole question in full view of our modern knowledge both of the uniformities and the varieties of religious experience; their psychological conditions; and their ultimate pre-suppositions; the postulates of faith involved in them; and the findings of reason relative to them.

We propose to outline a theory of the Incarnation and its Extension in the Church and Sacraments; to survey recent contributions from various quarters so far as they bear upon this theory, and to suggest in conclusion some tentative results, which we venture to hope may be in the nature of a contribution towards that final synthesis in sacramental doctrine of which the Church in the modern world stands so much in need, and the lack of which is, perhaps, one of the chief stumbling-blocks in the way of Christian Union, to say nothing of Christian charity.

If Christology is an attempt to explain in terms of personality the relation between GOD and the world, it is clear that a metaphysical problem lies behind the Christological construction of ancient times and the attempted, but so far unsuccessful, reconstruction of modern times.

According to Dr. Luce, the Nestorian, Monophysite and Catholic Christological systems are really three phases of the cosmic problem — the attempt to conceive and find expression for the relation between GOD and the world.

Dualism postulates the co-existence of GOD and the world. GOD is and the world is; the relation between them is expressed by an 'and'. GOD *and* the world. The counterpart of dualism and Deism is Nestorianism. The dualist, content to couple GOD and the world by an 'and', so couples the Logos and Jesus in his Christological theory.

Monism postulates the identity of GOD and the world. GOD *is* the world and the world *is* GOD. The counterpart of this Monism and Pantheism in terms of personality, Dr. Luce suggests, is Monophysitism — the assertion of the absolute numerical unity of the Person of Christ.

Theism would take as its starting-point neither GOD nor the world, nor the two as co-existing, but the relation between the two. Not 'GOD and the world' in an irreconcilable dualism nor 'the world and GOD' as ultimately identical in any pantheistic sense, but 'GOD of the world' in a relationship. The relationship must be such that the terms related are preserved in the relation. Neither identity nor difference is the full truth, but identity in and through difference. The cosmic relation is then expressed not by an 'and' nor by an 'is' but by an 'of'.

So in Christology. We have in the Person of Christ not

'GOD and man' co-existing side by side in an unreconciled dualism, nor have we any pantheistic identification of Deity and humanity such as Monophysitism suggests. On the contrary, we have, in Catholic Christology, the Two-Natured Christ Jesus. In His Person the difference between the human and the Divine is preserved in their union, inasmuch as the 'Two Natures' or 'Substances' are not confounded nor merely juxtaposed, but rather there is One Person in Two Natures. The relationship between the human and the Divine in His Person is of such a character as to conserve the truth of an affinity between the two, whilst the preservation of that relation between the two in their difference the one from the other, precludes any thought of an ultimate identification such as would confound the Creator with the creature, Deity with humanity, GOD with man. The very fact that Divinity is not humanity, whilst at the same time it is, none the less, akin to it, makes such a relationship possible, whilst avoiding the pitfalls of pantheism.

The Chalcedonian Christology which makes Jesus Christ consubstantial with GOD and Man, and thus reveals Him as the Mediator between the Two — the GOD-MAN — is a Christology which has as its background such a solution of the cosmic problem as excludes a Monism of identity and a Dualism of difference; a Christology, moreover, which steers a midway course between Monophysitism and Nestorianism whilst conserving the truth in both, refusing to confound the substances or divide the persons; rejecting alike any confusion between the human and the Divine, and repudiating the idea of the Incarnation as the climax of the Divine Immanence in a human person called Jesus.

The Church rejects the idea of the Incarnation as a theophany GOD in the semblance of a man called Jesus. The Church equally repudiates the idea of a man called Jesus who in some sense can also be called GOD; a Divine Being because and only because He was a perfect Man.

The Church has rejected both Docetism and Adoptionism in all their varied forms, whether ancient or modern. The

Church steadfastly adheres to the thought of the Incarnation as the condescension of the Second Person of the Blessed Trinity. The Church steadfastly holds our attention to the thought of one who was GOD and became Man, of One who though He was rich yet for our sakes became poor, that we through His poverty might be made rich.

The relation between the cosmic problem and Christology and the careful distinctions to be observed in dealing with both, to which Dr. Luce draws our attention in his able monograph on Monophysitism, are vital for our enquiry. The Church owes Dr. Luce a debt for one of the most illuminating and clear contributions to Christological discussion in recent times.

Our thesis is that where these distinctions are either ignored or forgotten or blurred over in the efforts of our finite minds to grapple with the mystery of the Word made flesh or indirectly with an ultimate problem in philosophical speculation — the cosmic problem — there we inevitably fall into error when we come to apply the conception of the Incarnation to its extension in Church and Sacraments. Errors in speculative thought on the cosmic problem are reproduced in Christology. Errors in Christology are reproduced in sacramental doctrine. Only so far as we adhere in philosophy to a *via media* between Monism and Dualism, in Christology to a *via media* between Monophysitism and Nestorianism, shall we in sacramental doctrine find a *via media* between conflicting theories relative to the mode and manner of Christ's Presence in the Church and in the Sacraments. 'The Fathers,' says Bishop Jeremy Taylor, 'by an elegant expression, called the Blessed Sacrament the extension of the Incarnation.' [1]

We must be careful, however, to remember all through that this restricted application of the thought to the sacrament of Holy Communion owes its justification only to the validity of a wider reference. The 'extension' applies primarily and essentially, if at all, to the Church as the Body of Christ, and rests upon the Pauline concept as worked

[1] We owe the reference to Dr. Morgan Dix, *The Sacramental System.*

out, e.g. in such passages as Colossians ii, 19 and Ephesians iv, 16. We find it as early as Clement of Rome in a reference which we borrow from Dr. McNeile's work on *An Introduction to the Study of the New Testament* (p. 331). 'The Apostles', writes Clement (ch. 42), 'received the Gospel for us from the Lord Jesus Christ; Jesus the Christ was sent forth from GOD. The Christ, then, (is) from GOD, and the Apostles from Christ.'

This passage McNeile rightly interprets to mean that the Apostles *are* Christ as manifested in the succession from Him; the Church is the extension of the Incarnation, and the Apostles are the first stage in the extension.

We move a stage further when we contemplate the Living Lord as functioning through certain chosen channels in His Body; through all believers as 'living Epistles'; through chosen vessels as ordained for special work; through chosen *media* as vehicles for the conveyance of His gifts. It is thus only through the Church that we come finally to the thought of the Sacraments as in some sense an 'extension' of the Incarnation.

Here we avail ourselves of a distinction suggested by Canon Quick who asks us to differentiate between what he calls 'natural' sacraments and 'official' or 'ritual' sacraments. This distinction takes us back ultimately to the question whether *the* Incarnation is to be regarded as the climax of the Divine Immanence, or whether we must draw a clear line of demarcation between Incarnation and Immanence. We have already decided in favour of this latter alternative. Holding firmly to this, we may now proceed to a study of Canon Quick's brilliant exposition of the Christian Sacraments.

He suggests that the term Incarnation may properly be used in two senses: first, of the historical life of Jesus Christ; secondly, of the created universe as perfectly expressing or embodying the nature of Him through whom the worlds were made. The link between the historical and the universal Incarnation of the Divine Logos, so far as our earthly experience is concerned, is the life of the Church Militant.

It is the Mission of the Church to represent GOD to the world, both as the expression of His incarnate being and as the instrument of His atoning work (p. 126). It is when we come to the thought of the Church 'not only as the trustee or steward of certain sacraments but also as having herself on earth a sacramental being of which the external marks have been definite and manifest from the beginning' (p. 127), that the true significance of the difference between a 'natural' and an 'official' sacrament appears.

We do not hesitate to say that by far the most weighty and illuminating contribution to recent discussion on the sacraments is to be found in the late Canon Quick's two works, *Catholic and Protestant Elements in Christianity* and *The Christian Sacraments*.

In his earlier work he directed our attention to the kind of relation which is thought of as connecting the outward and the inward element in sacraments. In his later work he has embodied this distinction in what we may describe as a philosophy of sacraments. For our immediate purpose we must concentrate upon what he named the 'declaratory' and 'effective' value of sacramental signs.

The declaratory or symbolic relation is that in which the outward is the expression of a spiritual reality or situation already existing. The effective or instrumental relation is that in which the outward is used to bring about a spiritual reality or situation which comes into existence only through the outward means. The typical and quite general case of the declaratory is the relation of words to their meaning in intelligible propositions. The typical and general case of the effective or instrumental is the relation of acts to purpose.

Whilst differentiating sharply between these two for purposes of exposition and clarification of the issues involved in the distinction, Canon Quick was careful to show that these two ways of conceiving of the kind of relation between outward and inward elements in the sacraments were not necessarily mutually exclusive, since no symbol is ever a mere symbol and no instrument is an instrument and nothing more. So in all the Church's sacraments the declaratory and effective aspects, though distinct, tend to pass into each other. The distinction thus indicated runs back ultimately through theology to philosophy, and involves us in a consideration of the relation of time to eternity. It reveals itself again in what some would have us believe is a radical difference between Greek and Hebrew conceptions of history. The Hebrew thought which is taken up by St. Paul and worked out into something in the nature of a 'philosophy of history' conceives of GOD essentially as the Living One engaged in the working out of an Eternal Purpose in the world for man.

Applying this for a moment to the Incarnation, if we ask the question; Is the character of that Life in relation both to its source in GOD and to its outgoing towards man, primarily declaratory or effective? Is it revelational or the great *act* of GOD? Ought we to say first and chiefly that the life of Jesus Christ is, as it were, the great word or symbol of GOD, declaring, signifying, expressing a universally and identically active Godhead, and displaying a final pattern of human goodness? Or is this same life, as it were, the great act of GOD, doing what GOD had never done before, bringing in a new creation which had never existed before, reconciling and exalting a humanity previously exiled and degraded, vanquishing powers of death and sin before insuperable?

Here Canon Quick contended that we touch the fundamental difference between Catholic and Liberal Protestant Christology. We pass over the question whether the difference is so acute and so fundamental, but in any case it does clearly mark a vast difference whether we conceive of God's manifestation of Himself in Christ to men merely as revelational and not as something infinitely more, viz. redemptive — i.e. whether we think of GOD in Christ as still active, purposive, engaged in Christ Incarnate and ever since in the Church, His Body and in the Sacraments. His channels or media or instruments, in *acts* for redemptive ends. It is, in short, this insistence upon the Sacraments as essentially purposive, instrumental, effective which governs the whole

Catholic approach to the subject and which determines our doctrinal position relative to them.

We pass, then, from the Incarnation to its Extension in the Church and through the Church to the Sacraments of the Church.

> The Word was made flesh : the Word is made flesh
> We beheld His Glory : we behold His Glory

Here in a sentence we have the connection between the Incarnation and the Eucharist.

Elsewhere we have drawn a clear distinction between the Catholic conception of the Incarnation and Adoptional Christology both ancient and modern.[1] It is the difference between the thought of GOD THE SON living a *personal life* and GOD manifesting Himself in *a person's* life. The one is a real Incarnation of a pre-existing Divine Person, the Second Person of the Blessed Trinity, who was GOD from all eternity and became Man: the other is the climax of the Divine Immanence in a human person, GOD in a man made manifest. Between these two conceptions there is a great gulf fixed. What the Catholic Church taught and still teaches in its Creed concerning our Lord's Person is thus poles asunder from much 'modern' thought on the subject.

In all our efforts, then, to study the extension of the Incarnation we have to bear in mind exactly what the Church conceives that Incarnation to have been. The principle of the Incarnation is for Deity to express itself in terms of human life. It is from beginning to end the story of a Divine condescension. That condescension did not cease with the close of our Lord's earthly life. It has continued since the Ascension. Its sphere of manifestation has been and continues to be the Church, which is His Body.

The extension of the Incarnation is thus primarily and essentially in and through the Church. The mystical union which is betwixt Christ and His Church is the ground of this possibility. In and through the organs and instrumental channels of the Church — the means of Grace — and

---

[1] *The Catholic Conception of the Incarnation* (S.P.C.K.).

pre-eminently through the two great Sacraments of the Gospel — Baptism and the Eucharist — the Ascended Lord continues to become Incarnate. As in days of old the Word was made flesh and, in His body, tabernacled amongst men, so to-day, through another Body fashioned for Him by the Holy Ghost, does He continue to dwell amongst us, so that we also may behold His Glory, the Glory as of the Only Begotten of the Father, full of Grace and Truth. The Extension of the Incarnation is the Church. In and through it He is still incarnate.

'He wears a bodily presentment upon earth, which expresses Him and is identified with Him. Clothed in it, He acts and speaks among men still. It is a true body, with a clear and visible and well-defined outline, as well as with a strong differentiation of its parts, and an organic bond between them. That body is His Church.' [1]

The Church is thus not the delegate of an absent Lord, but the visible representative of an invisibly present Saviour. His Body is Divinely alive with His Presence and in it, to its members, and through it to the hungry world outside, the Ascended Lord continues to pour out His gifts and to bestow His Blessings upon the sons of men.

Bishop Wilberforce was never tired of impressing upon us that the blessed Presence of Christ is not so much an individual as a collective privilege, belonging not so properly to separate Christians as to the Church; adhering not so peculiarly to persons as to communities; a Presence promised not to single hearts, or isolated acts of worship, but to exercises of joint prayer; to duly gathered congregations, to offices of communion and united devotion.

And amongst these, His Blessed Presence is most pre-eminently and peculiarly related to the Holy Communion of the Body and Blood of Christ. In no other ordinance is the blessed Presence so nigh, so assured, so awful.

Here is the extension of the Incarnation in the Eucharist. We must here resist the temptation to turn aside and use

[1] Mason, *The Faith of the Gospel*, p. 232.

the language of devotion in a vain effort to describe the indescribable — the Real Presence of our Lord as He tabernacles amongst us and makes Himself known to us in the Breaking of the Bread.

> Oh could I tell, ye surely would believe it!
>   Oh could I only say what I have seen!
> How shall I tell or how can ye receive it,
>   How, till He bringeth you where I have been?
>
> Therefore, O Lord, I will not fail nor falter,
>   Nay but I ask it, nay but I desire,
> Lay on my lips thine embers of the altar
>   Seal with the sting and furnish with the fire.
>
> Quick in a moment, infinite for ever,
>   Send an arousal better than I pray,
> Give me a grace upon the faint endeavour,
>   Souls for my hire and Pentecost today!

In that spirit of devotion, let us address ourselves to an intellectual grappling with this mystery.

No more masterly summary of the doctrine of the Incarnation can be found in English than that given by Hooker in Book V of *The Ecclesiastical Polity*. Let us follow closely his summary and try to show that errors in Christology are reproduced in the doctrine of the Eucharist regarded as an extension of the Incarnation. This whole line of thought was admirably worked out by Dr. Morgan Dix in his Bishop Paddock Lectures on *The Sacramental System*, and we reproduce it here as by far the most suggestive line of approach to a philosophy of sacramentalism.

There are, says Hooker, four things which concur to make complete the whole state of our Lord Jesus Christ:

(1) His Deity;
(2) His manhood;
(3) the conjunction of both;
(4) the distinction of the one from the other
      being joined in one.

Now let us consider in this context our Prayer Book teaching concerning the Blessed Sacrament:

There is the sign, the Thing signified; the conjunction of both and the distinction of the one from the other being joined in one.

As in Christology, so in Sacramental doctrine, errors have arisen through a failure to do justice to one or other of these four essential features.

Four principal heresies are discernible in Christology and a corresponding four in the doctrine of the Eucharist.

In Christology we have:

1. Arians bending themselves against the Deity of Christ.
2. Apollinarians maiming and misinterpreting that which belongeth to His human nature.
3. Nestorians rending Christ asunder, and dividing Him into two persons.
4. The followers of Eutyches confounding in His person those natures which they should distinguish.

In the doctrine of the Eucharist, corresponding to Arianism, Apollinarianism, Nestorianism and Eutychianism, we have:

1. Those who deny the Real objective Presence of Christ in the Sacrament. *Zwinglianism.*
2. Those who deny the permanence of the outward sign in the Sacrament. *Transubstantiation.*
3. Those who rend the sign from the Thing signified, and divide the two, failing to secure any real unity between them. *Virtualism.*
4. Those who confound in the Sacrament sign and Thing signified, which they should distinguish. *Consubstantiation.*

As against all these four errors in Christology and the corresponding errors in the doctrine of the Eucharist we have the Catholic conception of the Incarnation and the doctrine of the Real Presence in the Eucharist.

In four words, says Hooker, ἀληθῶς, τελέως, ἀδιαρέτως, ἀσυγχύτως, truly, perfectly, indivisibly, distinctly; the first applied to His being GOD, and the second to His being Man, the third to His being of both One, and the fourth to His still continuing in that one Both; we may fully, by way of abridgement, comprise whatsoever antiquity hath at large handled either in declaration of Christian belief, or in refutation of the aforesaid heresies.

Dr. Morgan Dix, whose treatment of this subject we have followed closely throughout, shows that it is possible to sum up errors in Sacramental doctrine exactly along the lines of Hooker's survey. We can paraphrase Hooker's summary in these words:

'There are four things which concur to make the sacrament complete in itself: the Sign, the Thing signified, the conjunction of both, and their Distinction.

'Four principal errors have withstood or obscured the truth: that of Transubstantiation, which denies the permanence of the sign; that of Zwinglianism, which denies the presence of the thing signified; that of Virtualism, which separates the sign and the thing signified, so that the thing is really absent, and only present in virtue and effects; that of Consubstantiation, which so confounds the two that neither retains its reality.

'And to all these errors we oppose the truth, which accords with the words of Holy Scripture and the statements of the Old Catholic fathers; which retains the sign in its substantial integrity while admitting in it a mystical and spiritual change on consecration; which declares the real, true, objective presence of the body and blood of Christ under the forms of bread and wine; which makes the *virtus*, the benefits of the sacrament, a result of its worthy reception, and thus confers on man the fullness of the blessing while withholding him from the presumptuous claim "that it is his faith rather than GOD's act which brings to him his Saviour".'

The parallelism, then, between the Incarnation and errors in Christology on the one side and the Eucharist regarded as an extension of the Incarnation and errors in sacramental doctrine on the other, is complete.

We have:

Zwinglianism	corresponding to Arianism.
Transubstantiation	corresponding to Apollinarianism.
Virtualism	corresponding to Nestorianism.
Consubstantiation	corresponding to Eutychianism.

Let us now consider the Catholic doctrine of the Real Presence in the light of these four errors. The best analogy we can produce in the effort to understand the relation of the Two Natures in our Lord's Person is (as we have pointed out elsewhere) that of ourselves as human persons possessing body and soul or spirit. In Catholic Christology the unity is secured in the Person of Christ, and in that unity the difference between manhood and Godhood is seen in the Two Natures, which, again, in that unity are never separated and never confused.

Let us consider the body-mind relationship as an analogy.

We are conscious of ourselves as a unity, and yet in that unity we know of the difference between our bodies and our minds. Ultimately we are not in any monistic sense identical either with our minds or materialistically identical with our bodies. We rule out Epiphenomenalism and psycho-physical parallelism. We know ourselves to be a unity in diversity. So in the Incarnation we have the unity of the Divine and the human Natures in the One Person of Christ.

Now apply this to the problem of the manner of the Presence of Christ in the Sacrament.

Is there a real objective Presence in the Sacrament? We rule out at once the conception of that Presence as being a purely subjective creation of our own imagination or of the activity of faith. Faith cannot create, but does perceive a Presence which is real first. The Catholic is convinced of the real objective Presence of our Lord's glorified Humanity in the consecrated elements before reception by the faithful.

There is thus secured a true connection: a true union between the sign and the thing signified.

But now note our phraseology: the Presence *in* the consecrated elements *before* reception.

We have struck the notes of *place* and *time*. We have used spatial and temporal phraseology. Is it legitimate?

The answer is 'Yes and No'. We must press our analogy of body-mind relationship in an effort to overcome the plain objections which confront us.

What is the relationship between the Body and the Mind? Can the Mind in any sense be said to be *in* the Body, and if so, in what sense? Do we mean spatially?

Here again, just as in the case of the Incarnation, we had to avoid any pantheistic confusion between the human and the Divine, so in the case of the Body and the Mind we must avoid a crude materialism, and in the case of the sign and the Thing signified in the Blessed Sacrament we must avoid a materialisation of the spiritual.

Mind is not a by-product of the Body or a 'foam' thrown up by brain activity. We reject Epiphenomenalism. We refuse to regard 'thought' as a by-product of chemical or mechanical changes in the brain. We refuse equally to regard the Thing signified in the Sacrament as a result of some chemical or mechanical change in the elements.

Equally we repudiate a thoroughgoing Idealism which fails to do justice to the reality of the material and regards the all-pervading Mind as in some sense creating the brain or reorientating the accidents of matter around a new centre of activity. This would be a kind of spiritual Epiphenomenalism equally unsatisfactory, since it fails to do justice to the material as in some sense retaining its relative independence, and continuing to exist in its own right apart from the relation in which it stands to Mind. We have, in all this, to steer some midway course between Idealism and Realism as philosophical systems in their bearing upon the Body-Mind relationship. The corresponding cosmic problem is seen in the consideration of both Material and Spiritual Monism as solutions of the relation of GOD to the world and Eutychianism in Christology.

We come next to Psycho-physical parallelism in the Body Mind relationship: corresponding to Dualism in the solution of the cosmic problem and Nestorianism in Christology. Here no real union between Body and Mind is secured, any more than in Dualism GOD and the world are really united or in Nestorianism a real union between the human and the Divine natures results in the Person of the One Christ.

In the Body-Mind relationship we have (1) the Body, (2) the Mind, (3) the union of the two in one Person, (4) the permanence of the distinction between the two in that union.

We have errors arising from a materialistic identity of Body with Mind or a spiritualisation of body by Mind; a theory of psycho-physical parallelism which never unites the two in any real union and a confusion between the two in the union by which it is imagined that the one is the aspect of the other or the other is an aspect of the one.

What is the truth? In experience we know ourselves to be a unity in difference. We know that Mind and Body whilst existing in that unity are never confused though intimately related. We cannot conceive of the one as producing the other. We know Body as Extension in time: we know Mind as boundless and eternal. The Mind cannot be conceived of as spatially located in any particular part of the body and yet in some sense where the body is, there am I.

You could not have a more interesting and fascinating analogy than that between the Body-Mind relationship and the relationship between the sign and the Thing signified in the Blessed Sacrament.

To the extent to which any one of us is prepared to swear that he is in his body to that extent Christ's Presence is in the Sacrament.

Locally present? No more or less than we are said to be locally present where our bodies are in space. If we say that we are not in space, whilst occupying bodies which are in space, so we may say that Christ's presence is not in space, whilst He occupies the species of bread and wine which are in space.

We as spiritual beings are not locally present in our bodies: i.e. we could not be detected as being present by any quantitative analysis: a microscopic search through every particle of our bodies would not yield the discovery of the presence of our souls or spirits. A chemical analysis would not reveal us nor would any X-ray photograph show the inner Ego. Yet we are present. And we are entitled to claim the same reality of Presence for Christ in the Sacrament of His Presence. The proper sphere of the Divine Indwelling is the sphere of the spiritual. That is what we mean when we say that Christ is spiritually present in the Sacrament. The spiritual pervades the material through and through, is to be found in any and every section and fragment of it, and yet is never by any process of materialisation to be confounded with it, so that spiritual and material should be identified.

There is an immanence of the Divine in the human which, though it escapes analysis, is not identification. There is a Presence of the Christ in the Sacrament which, though it escapes analysis, is not material. The spiritual is in the material, yet not of it: vitally united to it, yet not to be confused with it. It is not a natural Presence which would be spatial, but a supernatural Presence which transcends space.

'The Body of Christ', says Aquinas, 'is not locally (*localiter*) in the Sacrament of the Altar.'

Is not this the solution of our differences? Are we not here in the face of a baffling mystery as remote from solution as is the problem of the Body-Mind relationship, and yet so simple in the terrific reality of its truth? May we not go on our way quietly repeating to ourselves the simple formula, 'To the extent to which it is true to say that I, a spiritual being, dwell in my body yet not locally, to that extent Christ dwells in the Sacrament of the Altar, yet not locally'?

He is a real Presence: a spiritual Presence in matter, just as I am a real Presence: a spiritual Presence in my body.

May we draw a distinction, then, between a 'local' presence, materialistically conceived, and a spiritual Presence, sacramentally conceived?

May we say that we are in our bodies sacramentally and He is in the species of bread and wine sacramentally?

In this way we repudiate the charge of materialism whilst conceiving the great truth of the Real Presence.

We must in contemplating the Incarnation always consider the two Natures only as they are united in the One Person. So in the Eucharist there is a real danger of our becoming too occupied with the sign and forgetting that it has no significance in itself, nor is it to be regarded except in its union with the Thing signified. Moreover, we must not attach undue importance to the Thing signified in itself apart from both the sign and the union.

What is the sign? Bread and Wine.

What is the Thing signified? The Body and Blood of Christ, i.e. His Glorified Humanity.

Yet that Humanity in itself is of no worth to us except it be quickened by the union of it with the Divine Nature. We do not worship the Humanity of Christ apart from His Divinity. We do not worship, we mean, one Nature only, and that Human. The worship of the Sacred Heart is a perversion of the truth, a Eutychian deification of a particular part of Christ's sacred Humanity. We must not allow our minds to be drawn away from the worship of His Divine Person by any temptation to fix our gaze upon the Body and Blood of Christ or upon the material elements which clothe them. His Body and Blood have no meaning except they be the Body and Blood of Him whose they are. Dr. Mason has warned us of the danger of an unwise adoration of our Lord's humanity:

'That the humanity of Christ is indeed a fitting object of adoration is recognised by all Catholics, but not His humanity by itself.

'The Eutychian tendency, which draws the mind's eye away from the Divine Person, to fix it upon the human nature, or even upon the material elements, which that Divine Person has assumed, and worships what it thus contemplates, ends in an idolatry, or creature-worship.

Unguarded modes of adoring the Blessed Sacrament of the Altar; the cultus — not harmless because symbolical — of a special portion or aspect of the creaturely nature, like the Sacred Heart, are an outcome of this wrong deification of our Lord's humanity.' [1]

Christ's human nature did not become deified by its union with the Divine nature in His One Person, any more than our bodies by union with our spirits become spirit — they become spiritual bodies. The Bread and Wine of the Eucharist do not become deified by transubstantiation so as in any sense to cease to be what they were. Whilst still remaining what they were, they become other than they were. They become related to, intimately associated with, used by the Unseen Celebrant as vehicles for the transmission of His Life to the kneeling worshipper, verily and indeed taken and received by the faithful in the Lord's Supper.

We may now take two incidents from the Gospel narratives which in our opinion do help to illustrate the kind of attitude it is possible to adopt towards this difficult problem of the nature of the Real Presence of Christ. We are aware of formidable objections which can quite legitimately be urged against them and of criticisms which will at once suggest themselves against our use of them. None the less we put them forward as at least a stimulus to thought upon the subject. The first is suggested by a passage in the published volume of the Farnham Conference on Reservation and it embodies an idea of Canon Streeter, who always impressed us as a stimulating thinker even when, as in Christology, we find him singularly unconvincing and inadequate in his handling of the subject. We must try, he says,

'to get back into our ritual and, therefore, first of all into our thoughts, the atmosphere of the Emmaus story — the first Eucharist, be it noted, after our Lord had risen from the dead. Here, surely, we have a glimpse of what a Communion service should be. They talk together of the things that had happened, their thoughts are full of

[1] *Faith of the Gospel*, p. 142.

Jesus of Nazareth, his might in work and deed, how he was crucified, and how it had been told them that he was now alive. So natural, so human, is their intercourse with one another and the unseen stranger — then suddenly, at the simple friendly meal, their eyes are opened, and they know that what they have been doing is to hold converse with their Lord.'

We will not turn aside to discuss the adequacy or inadequacy of this description as covering the full content of the experience of the Disciples in this incident. We will, however, note at least these points: (1) Remembrance, commemoration of the Wonderful Person and His Work, followed by (2) a sudden full realisation of a Presence which none the less *had been there all the time*, (3) that consciousness of the reality of the Presence synchronises with a particular act at a particular moment of time: He makes Himself known to them in the Breaking of the Bread, and finally, (4) He vanished from their sight.

They would have loved to have retained Him, or if we prefer so to express it — to have retained the vivid consciousness of His Presence but (5) work remains for them to do as the result of the experience. They must forthwith go and tell the good News to others. (6) The Presence is vouchsafed in this context, i.e. it is an experience intimately bound up with Commemoration of Himself and His Passion. Moreover, (7) He Himself is the Unseen Celebrant and it is His act which brings about, or is instrumental in effecting so blessed, a realisation in them of His Presence.

Our second illustration is taken from the Appearance to the assembled company in the Upper Room.

The doors being shut . . . Jesus came and stood in the midst and saith unto them — Peace be unto you. And when He had said this, He showeth unto them his hands and his side.

Here, again, we have the marks of time and place intimately associated with the appearance of the Risen Lord or the realisation in the experience of His followers of the

Real Presence of the Risen Lord. There is a moment or interval of time when in some sense He is not *in* the room followed by another moment when He is. And presumably the interval between these two moments in time is covered in some sense by His passage through space. He is not in the room to all appearance. The doors are shut. There is a passage *through matter* without any visible disturbance or alteration of its particles and then He is in the midst of them making visible the marks of His Passion. Let us note again the whole context culminating in this reiterated reference to Calvary.

May we now in the light of these two illustrations consider, if only in passing, the vexed and thorny questions of (*a*) the Sacrament Reserved and (*b*) the extra-liturgical cultus of the Blessed Sacrament.

Reservation for the sick and whole needs no justification in the light of the practice of the Primitive Church, and the admitted needs of our Church members under modern conditions. Given the Church's belief in a real presence of Christ in the Sacrament and of the fellowship of the gathered communicants with their Risen Lord and one with another in that Service, it would follow inevitably that those present at the Service would desire to extend to absent ones the benefits of the Eucharist. Again, since the Church is the only society which refuses to part with its members at death and declines to believe that the links which bind living and departed members of the one Body of Christ are severed but, on the contrary, are preserved and strengthened in the Communion of Saints, the logic of these convictions was shown in the annual commemorations of the 'birth-days' of the confessors and martyrs and the anniversaries of the departed were accompanied by celebrations of the Eucharist in the cemeteries. There were other ways also by which the Church sought to relate the Eucharist to the daily lives of the members of the Church and so to emphasise the sense of fellowship and membership in the One Body of Christ.

That abuses were likely to arise and in fact did arise in connection with a permission to carry the Sacrament away from the Church and to reserve it for reception in another place than that in which it had been consecrated, pointed obviously to the necessity of rules and regulations which should govern the use to which the Sacrament Reserved might be put. Quite clearly the primary and essential purpose of Reservation was governed by the purposes for which the Eucharist itself was celebrated, viz. (*a*) Commemoration, (*b*) Offering and (*c*) Communion. That worship and adoration should be an underlying and expressed accompaniment of all these purposes need not be stressed. The point to note is that what is called an extra-liturgical cultus formed no part of the practice of the Primitive Church nor could it be justified by the purposes for which the Primitive Church was led to introduce and to sanction the custom of Reservation.

Given that there is a real and actual Presence of Christ Himself in the Eucharistic elements after the act of consecration, that Presence and the benefits conveyed are clearly dependent upon the purpose of the whole Eucharistic Service. Any effort to extend the Service so as to embrace absent members, whether whole or sick, can only be justified if the desire behind the effort is to embrace a larger company within the field of operation of the Service enacted and the benefits resulting therefrom.

It is quite another matter to use the fact of the Sacrament Reserved for this purpose as an opportunity of commencing *another Service* of a relatively different character and purpose from that original Service which resulted in securing the Sacrament Reserved. Put more briefly, the point is whether Reservation for one purpose can legitimately be made use of to render possible Reservation for another purpose.

The theological implications of the Extra-Liturgical cultus of the Blessed Sacrament were very carefully canvassed at the Farnham Conference on Reservation, and we may refer to that for a study of the case as it presents itself to-day to theologians. We are not concerned to examine it on these lines, still less to register our opinion or a verdict for or against it. If both Exposition and Benediction have become regular features of the devotional life of the Western Church and if members of the Anglican Church, Catholic though Reformed, assure us of its undoubted devotional value and plead for its practice, at least let us be quite clear (i) that upon whatever other grounds such a cultus may be defended, we must lay down as beyond dispute the fact that the Presence of Christ in the Sacrament is essentially a Presence as our sacrificial Food, and (ii) that we cannot claim either primitive practice or the theology of the Primitive Church as sanctioning a belief that the Presence in the Eucharistic Bread and Wine was and is a Presence vouchsafed for any purpose other than that we have indicated. It may be so, but we cannot claim that it is so on any of the above grounds. It was clearly pointed out at the Farnham Conference that the cult cannot be based on the Institution of our Lord nor on Apostolic teaching and practice nor on primitive custom nor on Catholic usage. This is not to condemn it outright but certainly to indicate the precarious foundations upon which it rests and to justify the Anglican bishops in their refusal to authorise it in the efforts at revision of the Prayer Book in the additions and deviations proposed in 1928.

If now we go back to our illustrations we can perhaps perceive a reason why perpetual Adoration is not possible this side of the grave. How the two on the road to Emmaus would have loved to have retained Him! Yet He vanishes in the Breaking of the Bread and leaves them free in the glory of that experience, not like Mary, to sit for ever at His Feet in worship, but like Martha, to be up and doing in the strength of that Meat.

The whole impetus behind the movement in favour of a wide extension of the extra-liturgical cultus, we may well believe, is devotional and arises from a more intense desire in the heart of the faithful communicant to be ever with the Lord. We must remember, however, that a devotional experience which does not find expression in active service and self-sacrifice may easily degenerate into a morbid and unhealthy mysticism. If the devotional use of the Blessed

Sacrament, outside its immediate purpose, is a good and desirable form of prayer, like, for example, the 'Three Hours' Devotion on Good Friday, or *Tenebrae* or the Evangelical Prayer Meeting, we must above all things else be careful lest the strong current of sacramentalism, at present making itself felt both inside and outside our Church life and worship, should carry us off our feet and land us in religious excesses ultimately harmful to the best interests of the devotional life of the people. If the permanent results of 'revivalism' are seriously in question, we do well to view with suspicion something of the same kind in what some would ask us to believe is the 'Catholic' equivalent of it.

Moreover, a use of the Reserved sacrament such as we find in Exposition or Benediction does tend to suggest, if not to teach, a localisation or materialisation of the Presence in the elements.

We are prepared, in the light of the foregoing examination of the doctrine of the Real Presence, to accept fully and frankly the proposition that there is a Real Objective Presence of Christ in the Sacrament. When we have said this, we must go on to safeguard ourselves by adding: (*a*) that such a Presence is not 'material' nor (*b*) is it 'local'. Our proposition is best perhaps expressed in this way: *There is a Real Objective Presence of Christ in the Sacrament, which, though it eludes definition and escapes analysis, is not material.*

If this be accepted as a sound Sacramental principle, we are bound to safeguard ourselves from any dangers of superstition or any tendency towards magical conceptions of the Sacrament which must result if we forget our saving clause '*not* material'. We must remember Canon Quick's warning against the danger of confusing 'objectivity' with 'externality', as spatially conceived. We must reject Transubstantiation to the extent to which it involves us in a belief in a physical change in the elements and a *localised* Presence. With Aquinas we must agree that 'the Body of Christ is not locally (*localiter*) in the Sacrament of the Altar', and with Newman when he reminds us that 'we do not know *how*. We can only say that He is present, not according to the natural manner of bodies, but sacramentally.' Canon Quick gives us these two references and adds a third from the Council of Trent to the effect that 'Christ the Lord is not in this sacrament as in a place'. He sums up his penetrating examination of this point in words which we shall cordially endorse. If by 'local presence' (he says) you mean that our Lord is present in the consecrated sacrament in a distinctive way, then the phrase is true: but if by local presence you mean the natural presence of a body in dimensions of space, then the phrase is untrue.

May we take now our second illustration so far as we can conceive it to have any bearing upon our immediate problem?

'The doors being shut . . . Jesus appears in their midst.' There is a passage of His Person *through* matter. If, however, He is to be conceived of as locally present *in* it, then in some sense He is caught by and fixed in the material particles of the door. Hence if He is to move towards the disciples in the room, the door must move with Him. He is a prisoner in the tabernacle! His movements are in some sense confined and circumscribed by the material substance of the door through which He had to pass in order to reveal His Presence to those in the room. Dare we compare such a passage to the passage of the Host from the Side Altar to the High Altar? At once the crudity of the thought is apparent. The thought of God being carried about, lifted up, conveyed from one place to another and of a worshipping company watching His progress as He is removed in the Tabernacle from one place in a Church to another before being 'exposed' to view is, of course, only possible for the ignorant and foolish. Yet if we are to insist upon a localised Presence or a material accompaniment of that Presence as in some sense indissolubly one with that of which it is the accompaniment, we are really only expressing in another way the idea of the Risen Lord in His passage through the material door of the Upper Room being in some sense so incapable of wholly dissociating Himself from that through which He passed as to be caught or entangled in it. And this is not what we mean or the way in which we try to conceive of the nature either of His Presence in the Upper Room or of His Presence in the Sacrament Reserved.

Might we agree finally to abandon once and for all the word Transubstantiation? The thought of the Risen Lord passing *through* matter in order to reach His assembled Disciples does suggest another word which is at least well worth our careful and sympathetic consideration, viz. the word *Trans-elementation*.

Attention has more than once in recent times been drawn to Gregory of Nyssa's Catechetical Oration on the Incarnation and its extension in the Eucharist. There is a resemblance, of course, between Gregory's thought of trans-elementation and the later doctrine of Transubstantiation. There are, however, clear differences, not the least of which is an escape from the doctrine of substance and accidents to the Aristotelian distinction of elements (στοιχεῖα) and form (εἶδος). 'Transelementation', if used, for example, in the way we have suggested in the light of the illustration of our Lord's Presence in the Upper Room, might well enable us to preserve our belief in the reality of that Presence in the Eucharist and in some definite sense associated with the material elements, and yet quite clearly not permanently caught or located in the material vehicles of which He makes use in passing through them to reach us.

This brings us to elaborate the Sacramental theory suggested by Gregory of Nyssa and to put forward as an alternative to the doctrine of Transubstantiation, a doctrine of Transelementation.

CHAPTER 6

THE DYNAMIC SACRAMENTALISM
OF ST. GREGORY OF NYSSA

TRANSELEMENTATION *versus* TRANSUBSTANTIATION

The Sacramental Principle and its Philosophical
presuppositions, in the light of the New Physics

Gregory of Nyssa's Catechetical Oration

IN speaking of the Supper he raises the point as to whether
we really eat the Lord's Body and drink His Blood. He
points out how during the earthly life of Christ the bread
and wine were changed in the natural processes of digestion
into body and blood, and he says that in the Invocation a
similar change takes place in the elements, though the form
is unchanged.

This view resembles the later doctrine of Transubstantiation but there are two differences:

(i) The change takes place at the Invocation;

(ii) Instead of the later philosophy of substance and accidents, we have the Aristotelian distinction of elements
(στοιχεῖα) and form (εἶδος).

Not transubstantiation but transelementation, i.e. a true
doctrine of Metabolism.[1]

The passage from Gregory runs as follows:

'If the existence of the whole body depends on
nourishment while this consists of food and drink; if,
further, bread serves for food, and water mixed with
wine, for drink, and if the Logos of GOD . . . is united
(συνανεκράθη) in his character as GOD and Logos with
human nature, and, having entered our body, produced
no different or new constitution for human nature, but

[1] See E. Lampert, *The Divine Realm*, Part III, pp. 125 ff., on Metabolism.

rather sustained his body by the usual and fitting means and supported life by food and drink, the food being bread; then, just as in our case, he who sees the bread to some extent perceives the human body therein, because when the bread enters the latter it becomes part of it, so in that case the body which conceals GOD within it, and which received the bread is to a certain extent identical with the bread . . . for what is characteristic of all was also admitted regarding the flesh of Christ, namely, that it was also supported by bread, but the body was by the residence in it of the Divine Logos transformed ($\mu\epsilon\tau\epsilon$-$\pi o\iota\acute{\eta}\theta\eta$) to a divine sublimity and dignity. We accordingly are now also justified in believing that the bread consecrated by the word of GOD is transformed into the body of the GOD-Logos. For that body was also virtually bread, but was consecrated by the residence in it of the Logos, who dwelt in the flesh. Accordingly, as the bread transformed in that body was invested with divine energy we have the same thing happening here. For in the former case the grace of the Word sanctified the body which owed its existence to, and to a certain extent was, bread, and similarly, in the present instance, the bread, as the Apostle says, is made holy by GOD's Word (Logos) and command; not that it is first changed into ($\epsilon\dot{\upsilon}\theta\grave{\upsilon}s$ $\mu\epsilon\tau a$-$\pi o\iota o\acute{\upsilon}\mu\epsilon\nu os$) the body of the Logos by being eaten, but that it is at once transformed into his body by the Logos (by its consecration) in accordance with the saying of the Logos, "This is my body".'

Gregory argues similarly as regards the wine and blood, and then continues:

'Seeing too that all flesh is nourished by what is moist . . . just as we support by food which is firm and solid the solid part of our body, in like manner we supplement the moist part from the kindred element; and this, when within us, by its faculty of being transmuted, is changed to blood, and especially if through the wine it receives the faculty of being transmuted into heat.

'Since, then, that God-containing flesh partook for its substance and support of this particular nourishment also, and since the GOD who was manifested infused Himself into perishable humanity for this purpose, viz. that by this communion with Deity mankind might at the same time be deified, for this end it is that, by dispensation of His grace, He disseminates Himself in every believer through that flesh, whose substance comes from bread and wine, blending Himself with the bodies of believers, to secure that, by this union with the immortal, man, too, may be a sharer in incorruption.

'He gives these gifts by virtue of the benediction through which He transelements the natural quality of these visible things to that immortal thing.' [1]

Gregory's belief is that, just as the Word, when Christ was here in the flesh, rendered holy His body that assimilated bread, which still in a manner remained bread, so now the bread is sanctified by the Word of GOD and prayer. 'The idea of the repetition of the consecration of the Logos had taken hold of his mind.' [2]

Gregory wished for a spiritual and corporal 'communion and mixing' (μετουσία καὶ ἀνάκρασις) with the Redeemer.

The only help against the poison which has crept into our body is the antidote of the body of Him who was stronger than death. This antidote must be introduced into the body. It accordingly transforms and alters our body (μετα-ποιεῖν καὶ μετατιθέναι; μετάστασις, μεταστοιχείωσις, ἀλλοίω-σις). The actual body of Christ as immortal is thus the

---

[1] *The Great Catechism*, ch. xxxvii; cf. Gavin in *Liturgy and Worship*, p. 116 — 'The Eucharist in East and West'. St. Gregory of Nyssa (d. 394) 'is outspokenly a realist and metabolist'. 'The bread sanctified by the Word of GOD we believed to be transmuted (or transmade, μεταποιεῖσθαι) into the Body of GOD the Word.'
'So man by a sort of union with that which is of immortality becomes a sharer in incorruption. These things are achieved by the power of the Blessing to that end, transelementing the nature of the things which appear.' (*Oratio Catechetica*, 37.)
Pp. 116-17: The bread and wine are conceived by Gregory to be transformed, transelemental, transmuted, into the Body and Blood of Christ through the prayer of the priest.
[2] Neander.

remedy against death; it must, therefore, like (all) other sorts of good, be partaken of *bodily*. This partaking takes place in the Supper; for through the act of consecration the bread and wine are changed into the flesh and blood of the Lord (μεταποίησις) in order that through partaking of them our body may be transformed into the body of Christ (μετα-στοιχείωσις).

Gregory clearly connects the Eucharist with the Incarnation. He thinks of the transformation of the consecrated elements into the Body and Blood of Christ as a continuation of the process of the Incarnation. When on earth Christ lived as we live by partaking of earthly food, bread and wine, and the food thus taken was, as Gregory puts it, changed into the nature of His body. The same process takes place in the Eucharist. The difference is that whereas in the case of the assimilation of earthly food, the process is slow and the transformation one through a period of time, in the case of the Eucharist, the transformation is instantaneous (εὐθύς).

This, of course, suggests the idea of transubstantiation. There are, however, significant differences, and it is to these we wish to direct particular attention.

Note carefully that his theory is one of transformation. It is in line with the realistic and mystic view represented, as Schaff reminds us, by several Patristic Fathers and Liturgies. They see in the mystical union of the Body and Blood of Christ with the sensible elements a sort of repetition of the incarnation of the Logos. Schaff sums up their line of thought and cites passages in support of it. With the act of consecration a change takes place in the elements, whereby they become vehicles and organs of the life of Christ, although by no means necessarily changed into another substance. To denote this change very strong expressions are used, like μεταβολή, μεταβάλλειν, μεταβάλλεσθαι, μεταστοιχειοῦσθαι, μετα-ποιεῖσθαι, *mutatio, translatio, transfiguratio, transformatio*, illustrated by the miraculous transformation of water into wine, the assimilation of food, and the pervasive power of leaven.

But closely as these and similar expressions verge upon

the later Roman doctrine of transubstantiation, they seem as Schaff points out, to contain at most a *dynamic*, not a *substantial*, change of the elements into the Body and Blood of Christ.[1]

Gregory speaks of the form (εἶδος) of the elements, not the οὐσία of the bread and wine, as being changed. Tixeront [2] notes that Gregory does not express himself as completely as theologians were to do later. He claims, however, that the Father explicitly directed Christian thought towards the idea of transubstantiation. On the contrary, we should contend that this is precisely the direction towards which the Father was not pointing. He speaks of the change not of the οὐσία of the bread and wine, but of their φύσις and of that of their στοιχεῖα; and when he comes to mention the change of the food into the body, he says simply that this food is changed into the form (εἶδος) and nature (φύσις) of the body. In other words, this is not the Aristotelian distinction of substance and accidents, but that of elements (στοιχεῖα) and form (εἶδος). It is not a transubstantiation but a transformation, and there is a world of difference between the two conceptions. The one is a *substantial*, the other a *dynamic* change.

Why stress this difference? It is precisely the issue between transubstantiation and transelementation. The latter is in the main line of thought of the Eastern rather than that of the later Western theological tradition, and accords with the classical doctrine of the Lord's Supper in the Greek Church up to the present day, so we gather from E. Lampert's recent work to which we have referred, viz. the doctrine of Metabolism.

By the Holy Ghost bread and wine are received into the body of Christ. The eucharistic body is that which is born of the Virgin, not, however, by a transubstantiation, as if the body of Christ descended suddenly from Heaven and took the place of the elements, but as Lampert reminds us, by a transformation and assumption, just as in the Incarnation.

---

[1] *Vide* Schaff, *History of the Christian Church*, i, pp. 493-5.
[2] *History of Dogmas*, ii, p. 181.

The bread-body is received, he says, into the real body and is thus identical with it. That is the last word of the Greek Church on the subject.

This concept of metabolism will well repay our careful scrutiny, and Lampert draws our attention to the fact that, as he says, the 'change' does not consist in the substitution of one element for another within the realm of the physical world. The miracle of metabolism, sacramental metabolism, lies in that something is that which it is not, and is not what it is.

Metabolism does not imply any physical change such as takes place, for instance, in the conversion of matter.

Meta — *trans* in meta-bolism; *trans*-elementation, or *trans*-lation denotes not the change from one thing into another within the physical world, but the union of two worlds, of two distinct spheres of being — a metaphysical *transcensus*. . . .

There is no question of a substance believed to have changed and accidents which have not changed remaining as they are. The whole discussion of the theory of transubstantiation is ultimately concerned with the transformation of one element into another within the limits of this world. No such transformation takes place at all, because transformation is, strictly speaking, only possible between different things of one and the same world, and not between things belonging to two distinct spheres of being, like bread and wine and the transfigured body of our Lord. These can only be translated and consequently preserve their identity and their own reality. The elements of bread and wine, then, as such, directly, without any transformation become the body of Christ. They are the body and blood of Christ but also: the body and blood of Christ in the Sacrament are bread and wine. [1]

May we then plead for a rejection of the word 'transubstantiation' and a substituting of the word 'transelementation' in its place? Our Anglican Article condemns the word transubstantiation, because it 'overthroweth the nature of

[1] Lampert, *op. cit.* pp. 125-7.

a Sacrament'. Canon Mason puts in a succinct form the objections to the whole scholastic dogma of transubstantiation, and we may well bear all this in mind as we seek to find some better way of expressing our belief in the reality and objective Presence of Christ in the Eucharist.

'The bread and wine, according to this theory,' says Canon Mason, 'at the touch of that more glorious Substance which takes possession of them, pass out of existence and are lost, leaving behind nothing but shadowy appearances of themselves which serve to indicate the Presence of something else instead. Such a doctrine is, as he says, capable of being stated in ravishing terms, and it was indeed first formulated with the best intention. It appeared to guard the true honour of the Sacrament of the Altar, to afford a clear position on which the intellect could repose, and to bring the Presence of Christ into the midst of His people in an indisputable way.'

But, nevertheless, as he goes on to point out, it loses, like Eutychianism, some rich elements of truth, and so imperils the rest.

The first objection to the dogma, as Mason says, is that it is based upon a discarded philosophy. It is questionable whether any well-instructed thinker of the present day holds the metaphysical theory of substance and accidents which it perpetuates. That theory is not itself *de fide*, even in the Roman communion, apart from the doctrine of the Eucharist. Possibly some assembly of competent scholars from that communion might be given liberty to revise the terms in which their doctrine of the Eucharist is couched, and, while preserving the essential thought which the Councils of Lateran and Trent aimed at expressing, to clothe it in formulae less crude, and therefore with spiritual insight.

Meanwhile, even if the philosophy of Transubstantiation were tenable, the miracle which would be involved in it would be unique among Divine actions. GOD does not usually deceive our senses; nor is it His method to annihilate what He has made, in the way that — according to the

Roman doctrine — the substance of the bread is annihilated. He treasures every atom of His universe.

If indeed there were no other way of obtaining as rich and full a meaning from our Lord's words about the Sacrament, such an objection might be soon disposed of; but if the same meaning can be retained by some other 'method of interpretation, we shall give the greater glory to GOD by not discrediting our divinely given senses, and by setting a more reverent value even upon the material creation, with which GOD has so closely associated us'.[1]

Is there an alternative way of expressing our belief in the Sacramental Presence without accepting the later mediaeval explanation or evasion of the mystery?

There have been attempts from time to time to suggest alternative terms. The late Dr. Temple favoured the term 'Transvaluation' or 'Convaluation', and in *Essays Catholic and Critical* Dr. W. Spens gave his approval to 'Transvaluation' as the best philosophical expression of the Sacramental doctrine for us to-day. Dr. Temple felt that if 'transubstantiation' means 'transvaluation', the objections to it partly disappear. Luther's consubstantiation has the right devotional value, the Archbishop felt, but unfortunately it is nonsense. If, however, as he said,

'Substance is understood to mean Value, the objections to consubstantiation also disappear. Convaluation is, in fact, just what is wanted. The Bread still has the value of bread, and it has also the value of the Body of Christ.'

This attempt, however, to avoid a philosophy of substance and accidents only lands us in what for the moment is a more fashionable philosophy of values, and we would prefer to line up more closely with our Eastern Orthodox brethren and think in terms of 'transmutation', 'transformation', 'transfiguration', 'transenergisation' or, best of all, Gregory's term 'transelementation'.

Canon Mason held that the Eastern Church might be able to mediate between the Anglican and the Roman views

---

[1] *The Faith of the Gospel*, pp. 290-2; cf. to the same effect Moberly, *The Law of the Love of God*, p. 129.

on this subject. We think he is right and we may still look hopefully to the Eastern theologians of our day to aid us and Rome in this point of separation and bar to reunion. Certainly in their doctrine of Metabolism there does seem to be a possible way of escape from a scholastic metaphysics, and, as we think, a mode of thought more in accord with our modern conceptions of matter and its relation to mind and spirit.

In commending the concept of transelementation as more closely in line with our modern ideas concerning matter, we should naturally turn to the revolutionary ideas suggested by the New Physics.

Sir Cyril Hinshelwood addressing the British Association drew attention to some of the profound changes in thought and intellectual attitude which had in the past few generations come over science as a whole. Mind and matter in philosophy at large, individual ultimate particles in physics and chemistry, so far from being immutable essences, have become fictions providing illusory answers to improper questions. Sir Cyril went on to suggest that if our present notions of particles and forces have involved us in difficulties and contradictions, then the plain inference is that we must go on thinking. All attempts to say something helpful about the relation of mind to matter, or matter to mind, the relation of what he called these two interpenetrating but apparently immiscible worlds, had so far led to contradictions, frustrations and absurdities. Clearly there was a mind-matter problem and thoughtful people would go on wrestling with the question.

This suggests the question: After Materialism — what? And the late Sir Richard Clifford Tute, in a book under this title, did his best to enlarge our minds on the implications of the new conceptions of matter suggested by the research work of modern physicists. Gone is the excessively naïve and crudely mechanical conception of the early atomic theory, and nineteenth-century materialism is bankrupt. What in the twentieth century is to take its place, and is there in our more modern view of the nature of matter any room for the sacramental principle in its widest reference? We think there is, and this gives to our suggested new terminology an added strength by way of commendation.

A glance at the line of thought suggested by Sir Richard Tute's book is a healthy reminder that, as he says, Physics has come to the stage at which it does not know what a physical frame is.

When we come to the ultimate particles of Nature — the electrons, protons and photons — he reminds us, we are at a loss to say in what manner they exist.

The photon is a pocket of action and is accepted to be four-dimensional. The only continuum in which such an entity can exist is space-time. Whether an ether, a curvature, a mighty atom or what not, it is filled with life. He suggests that if the ultimate particles of Nature — the electrons, protons and photons — are alive, then the four-dimensional continuum is a plenum of life.

Moreover, our three-dimensional world must be related to the four-dimensional as the shadow is related to the substance.

Hence motion may be the shadow, the projection, of the interaction of these lives on our world.

All modern physicists, to whatever camp they belong, are conscious of an obligation to search for some reality behind physical phenomena, and they agree to admitting that such reality must exist.

The relativists find the fundamental frame of reference in a cosmic curvature; the rigid physicists in other ways. Sir Richard Tute suggests it may be found in life which he equates with space-time regarded as a *plenum* of the life or lives behind all physical and natural entities.

James MacKaye pictures an absolute which is composed of points of tremendous radical energy distributed throughout the universe. This he suggests as a substitute for the ether.

The Michelson-Morley experiment showed that light has the same velocity for all observers, whether they are in motion relative to it or not. It follows that time and space must be regarded as arbitrary divisions of a more fundamental continuum which merges them both in space-time.

Space and Time must be forms of thought and not forms of things.

Our minds produce 'space' and 'time' by some alchemy out of an underlying mystery called Space-Time, in which they are both merged.

The external world therefore has no form which can be attributed to it.

Indeed the form turns out to be a mode of existence which is a fiction of our minds. What the reality behind the fiction may be is unutterably mysterious.

If, then, Science is now pointing us to a space-time continuum behind, beneath, the shadow world of space and time, what is this but the verdict reached through all the varieties of religious experience by the mystics and the religiously minded seekers after ultimate reality? We are greater than we know, and in moments of cosmic consciousness we touch at a sensitive point what in the language of religion we mean by GOD, and what in the Sacrament of the Altar we know as the Real Presence of Him who was dead and is alive again for evermore, and hath the keys of death and of Hades.

In other words, Science has deduced what Religion has intuited, viz. the existence of another world interpenetrating this world through and through. The Sacramental principle finds its vindication in the possibility of us humans, whilst still in the body pent, living a life in intimate union and communion with the Unseen but life-giving Celebrant on His mission to give the Bread of Life to believing souls.

> Two worlds are ours; 'tis only sin
> Forbids us to descry
> The mystic heaven and earth within
> Plain as the sea and sky.
>
> Thou who has given me eyes to see
> And love this sight so fair,
> Give me a heart to find out Thee
> And read Thee everywhere.

There is little hope of winning any wide acceptance of this Sacramental principle, unless we convince people that its intensification within the sphere of the Church and the means of grace within the Church, are, in their turn, part of a larger medium through which the all-pervading Presence makes itself known and energises within the sphere of the world and human life.

If Physics is now dissolving matter into energy, and we are now seriously considering the possibility of harnessing cosmic rays, the concept of transelementation should commend itself readily to our imagination, as the normal action of spirit functioning in a space-time continuum. Who would now deny the possibility of our world being subjected to bombardment by forces on even higher levels of vibration? Why should we hesitate to think of spiritual forces set free by prayer to minister to the bodily, mental and spiritual needs of mankind? With our new understanding of the universe in which our lot is cast, Science and Religion may now join hands in the recital of that article in our Creed which registers our belief in the Holy Ghost, the Lord and Giver of Life.

Our children's children may yet learn to tap these potent spiritual energies — planetary, solar and even cosmic — of which we are dimly aware in moments of cosmic consciousness, and experiences baffling analysis. They may take as normal what to us at present are abnormal irruptions in our all too mundane and grossly material life. The East, perhaps, is more alert than the West to the possibilities of the triumph of mind over matter, and the subjection of the flesh to the spirit.

The science of prayer and meditation may yet gain added reinforcement from the New Physics and find an intellectual justification for a way of living not after the flesh but after the spirit.

We may therefore venture to repeat here what we wrote in working out the theological and philosophical implications of the sacramental principle.[1]

---

[1] *Confirmation*, i, pp. 322 ff.

(a) *In Nature*

All nature is a sacrament of His Presence. He lives and breathes in the material universe. He is found speaking to us in the beauty of a landscape or in the magnificent grandeur of the mountain scenery. He has a message for us in the flowers, if only our eyes were open to see His glory in and through them. William Blake, poet and artist, was once asked what he could see in the sun; whether, when it rose, it was not simply in appearance a round disc of fire somewhat like a sovereign. 'Oh no, no!' he cried, 'I see an innumerable company of the heavenly host, crying, Holy, holy, holy is the Lord God Almighty.' And who shall say that, in and through that mystic vision, the poet's soul was not nourished and something of God's life-giving grace conveyed to it?

All the world is full of voices, and in a thousand ways God is speaking to us, if only we have the attentive ear, the heart receptive. Through Nature He speaks: through the material He functions: through varied channels He keeps open His living contact with the souls of men, and conveys to them His life.

> If any flower shall breathe for thee
> A fragrant message from its pencilled urn;
> If spring airs glad thee; if the sunset bring
> Into thine eyes the tears of solemn joy;
> If any radiant passion come to make
> Existence beautiful and pure to thee;
> If something deepest in thee wakes
> To a dim sentiment of mystery —
> Ponder such ministrations, and be sure
> Thou hast been touched by GOD,
>   O human heart!

Thus does the all-pervading Presence of the Almighty Spirit of God live and breathe through all creation and make Himself known to men. This is the sacramental principle in its broadest and widest sense. This also is the principle of the Incarnation; the Divine, because of its kinship with the human, able to express itself in terms of human life; able to take a Body, and, dwelling in it, to redeem it from corruption and to lift it up to the level of the spiritual, using it as a means in and through which it may function in time and space.

(b) *In the Church System*

If we are ever to convince people of the normal character of the sacraments of the Church as ordained channels of Divine grace, we must lay the foundation for them in the Incarnation itself, and exhibit them as an extension within the Church of the Incarnation. And more than this, we must show that they are but the highest revelation of a great sacramental principle which runs through all creation and is the method whereby the Spirit of God reveals Himself through the material to the spirit of man.

Two books may be mentioned in this connection: the one by Dr. Morgan Dix, *The Sacramental System*; the other by Paul B. Bull, *The Sacramental Principle*. Both writers have set forth in a convincing manner the way in which the system of grace, through sacramental channels, may be thought of as based upon the nature of God, the constitution of man, and God's relationship to His creation. Nature, to some, may appear in the guise of a godless phenomenon, the outcome of a blind movement directed by no intelligent ruler; to others it is the creation of God, and thus all creation is the veil of His Presence, all His works a mirror into which we may gaze and see His face. So St. Paul would teach us that 'the invisible things of God may be understood by the things that are made, even His eternal power and Godhead', i.e. creation reveals the Creator and is a sacrament of His Presence. 'Whenever visible things reach out into the eternal and carry us with them to God, there is a sacrament', the basis of such a belief being in the Apostle's words the fact that 'of Him and through Him and unto Him are all things'. Thus the whole universe is full of sacraments; 'the heavens declare the glory of God, and the firmament showeth His handiwork'. So man, made after His image, in virtue of his constitution as material and spiritual, in touch with the material through his senses, and with the spiritual through spiritual faculties, is able to find the living God.

(c) *In Human Life*

Thus, in the sacramental system, Dr. Morgan Dix would teach us that throughout God's universe is effected an alliance between man and God. Why, then, should not the same Hand which beckons to us through the veil of Nature be laid upon us as we kneel in adoration before His Altar? Why should He not use material means for bringing about spiritual effects? He is Lord over the material, and in the days of His flesh He made it subserve His spiritual purposes. Nature offers medicine to heal our bodies, vegetable and mineral helps, tonics, anodynes. Why, then, should not the Holy Ghost, through natural elements exalted to a supernatural efficacy, minister to the diseases of the soul? The element of water, of which the human body is to some extent composed, why should it not be sanctified to the mystical washing away of sin? The corn, the staple food of man; the grape, the wine, the common drink amongst Eastern people: why should not these be instrumental means of sanctification, holy gifts to purify, feed and hallow human life? If God is present in Nature, why not in one of Nature's products? So argues Dr. Morgan Dix; and it is surely a reasonable contention. He which hath said of the one sacrament (Baptism), 'Wash and be clean', hath said concerning the other likewise, 'Eat and live'. We need more than ever to-day to grasp the fact that Christ Himself is the crowning illustration of the sacramental principle; that He was made man in order that man might know God, and that God in Christ is the Sacrament of sacraments. We need to realise afresh to-day that, as Paul Bull puts it, 'from the cold, passionless message of the stars to the burning brain of man, the spirit of God is using matter as the medium through which He communicates Himself to man'. Thus by this sacramental interpretation of the universe we are enabled 'to realise the interpenetration of what seems to be material by what seems to be spiritual. This interpenetration preserves for us the real mystery, the spirituality of the universe, the mentality of the body. And this living mystery is preserved in all its rich vitality in the sacramental system of the Church, in which we at all times see the material used as the vehicle and the instrument of the Spirit — in Holy Baptism the water interpenetrated by the Spirit, Holy Communion the bread and wine caught up into living union with the risen and ascended humanity of Christ and becoming His most holy Body and His most precious Blood — in fact, see the whole universe, not as a dead machine, but in St. Athanasius's phrase, as "the Body of God".'

(d) *The Real Presence*

This broader conception enables us to see that whilst the two sacraments are God's ordained channels in a special sense and for a special purpose, yet they are not the only means of grace. It will enable us to understand how it is that many who neglect, and in some cases definitely repudiate, the sacraments, are yet in vital and spiritual relationship with God outside the covenanted mercies of His Church. If it be urged that the Real Presence of Christ in the Eucharist is only another manifestation of His Presence which can be known and experienced at other times, in other ways, through other means; if men assure us, as they do, that they find Him in the fields and lanes; in the privacy of their own prayer-life, in times of meditation and feeding upon His written Word, the Bible; in public worship, at morning and evening prayer, and so on, we gladly accept their assurance, and know the truth of it in our own religious experience.

(e) *The Conception of Purpose*

But there is a difference, if not in kind yet in degree, between the Real Presence at the Altar and in other ways. Dr. Walpole has suggested in what precisely this difference consists. It is that the Presence admits of modes and degrees. He suggests that the Reality of the Presence may be dominated by *purpose*. Hence it is the purpose of the Eucharist that determines the power of the Presence.

> 'Our association with our High Priest in His dread offering of His Blood is the highest privilege we can enjoy. . . . We have, wonderful to relate, boldness to enter into the holy place here, and be as near our Lord in this great rite, as though we were with Him in the Upper Room on the night that He suffered. This is, then, the peculiar glory of the Eucharist, and we can easily see why it deserves the unique position that it holds in the Church.'

So in the Eucharist He is not more really present than in any other service, nor less really present at any one point than at any other in His own service. But at the moment of Consecration there is a manifestation of His Presence in a special way and for a special purpose.

> 'The great High Priest', says Dr. Walpole, 'has been present from the beginning, as the Head of the Body, and is not more really present after the consecration than before. And yet there takes place now a new manifestation of His Presence. He desires that the whole body of the worshippers shall be one with Him, not only in will and intention, but in substantial unity. He seeks to incorporate them into Himself, so that they may be actually one with Him in His great presentation. . . . This communication of Himself to us is, of course, to teach one who is spiritually fitted to receive Him a new manifestation of His Presence. We are nearer then to the moment when the veil will be lifted, and we see Him face to face, than at any other time, for He is imparting to us Himself. And the fact that He is communicating others besides ourselves gives a new expression to His Divine Presence. We rightly kneel to receive His Body and Blood into ourselves, because He is turning to us now and communicating His whole life into our starved lives. And it is natural that the elements, being what they are, should, as it were, focus that Divine

Presence which fills the Church. They make the point at which we touch Christ and receive Him into our being. They are to us the meeting-place where He comes to us and we come to Him. We, to use the words of the Catechism, take as well as receive the Body and Blood of Christ. It is true that we are one with Him before we receive, being members of His Body; but we now receive a fresh draught of His Life into ourselves.'

Now such a line of thought as is suggested in these words of Dr. Walpole enables us to see how unique is the place of the Lord's own Service in any consideration of the various means of grace through which the soul is brought into contact with God and God is given to the soul. The fact that it is still a living reality in the Catholic Church, and that, humanly speaking, it will continue to be celebrated 'till He come', suggests that Christian experience has decided conclusively in its favour. Those who in every age have been obedient to His Command have received His blessing and have been vouchsafed His Presence in so real and unmistakable a manner that they have guarded this means of grace at all costs, and handed it down from generation to generation as the most sacred privilege in the Christian Church.

Conclusion

In these chapters we have travelled over well-worn ground and glanced again at controversial issues which still divide the Church acutely. Our attention has been focused necessarily upon the position of our own Church of England, Catholic though Reformed, and if we have any fresh contribution to make to the discussion we should make a strong plea for what we called an Anglican Armistice. Our position as a bridge-church in Christendom means that within our own borders we are working towards some reconciliation between three contending schools of thought, Catholic, Evangelical and Liberal, or what in an older terminology were named 'High', 'Low' and 'Broad' Church views. In a larger context the time is over-ripe for a more precise defining of our position relative both to Rome and to Geneva. We cannot but feel that unless and until we can register a larger measure of agreement amongst ourselves concerning the nature and function of the Church in the world and human life, we cannot hope with any success to mediate between the rival claims of the Papacy on the one side, and those English varieties of Continental Protestantism which we know here in this country as 'the Free Churches'. We must close our own ranks before attempting to play any decisive part in the larger movement towards Reunion.

There do seem to be more hopeful signs of a way towards concord in this matter of Eucharistic doctrine, and in many quarters a wholehearted acceptance of the great truth of the Real Presence of the Risen Lord in the Sacrament of the Altar. The point of divergence is still on the problem of the *mode* of that Presence, and here we have ventured to suggest a new terminology more in accord with our modern knowledge, and much more likely of acceptance in the light of the findings of the New Physics and our revolutionary conceptions of the nature of the material universe and its relation to a larger space-time continuum beyond our ken. If we are right in thinking that Science and Religion are nearer to one another in this larger reference to two worlds, the visible and the invisible, the temporal and the eternal, the relative and the absolute, then there does seem to be a much better chance for the acceptance of the Sacramental principle in our day than was the case when an all-dominant materialism seemed to shut out the possibility of any commerce with the world invisible.

Hence our plea now for a reassessment of the whole problem in terms of the New Physics; and a reconsideration of the concept of transelementation rather than transubstantiation as a way towards a better intellectual presentation of the mystery of the Word made Flesh. Not that such a conception of the relation between mind and matter, Creator and creatures, solves the problem. It is an experience which ultimately baffles analysis and eludes definition. What we can claim is, first, that experience convinces us beyond all shadow of doubt that the Lord is verily and indeed with us. Secondly, that, if in adoring gratitude for His gifts thus bestowed, we seek to understand more fully the How and manner of His bestowal, we can bring to our aid our modern knowledge of the material universe and the interaction between spirit and matter such as suggests the Sacramental principle in its largest and widest reference. There is an immanence of the Divine in the human, as there is an immanence of the Divine in the whole universe, of which the human is a part. The analogy of the body-mind relationship suggests a corresponding intimate interpenetration of the human by the Divine indwelling of One who is closer than breathing and nearer than hands and feet.

Finally, we would draw our discussion to an end in a very practical conclusion as is done by Lampert in his thought-provoking volume to which we have so often referred. In his treatment of the Divine-human relatedness of the creature to the Creator and to Divine GOD-manhood and GOD's sacramental action in man and in the cosmos, he would claim, and we think rightly, that Nature is holy and theandric. The sanctity of Nature is the absolute condition established by GOD's own transcendent creative power, who both reveals Himself in her and in her realises the sacrament. This sanctity constitutes, as he says, a correlation of every living atom of Nature with the sanctifying and consecrating action of the Holy Spirit. This is the Sacramental principle in its widest and deepest significance. Sacraments in the Church are but its application to the members of the Body.

A very practical consideration results. We can, in the light of this, plead for the abolition of the false distinction between the secular and the sacred. As Lampert puts it, the sacrament never becomes a thing existing beside other things as something extrinsic and fixed in its extrinsicality, but, on the contrary, is ontologically representative of them all.

In other words, the elements of Nature which enter into the sacrament (e.g. water, bread and wine) are not something sacred existing side by side with other things non-sacred or profane, but symbolise and signify the transcendent meaning inherent in all of them. They anticipate that in which all things participate. It is just this universal, integrating nature of the sacrament which makes it a truly decisive factor in the Christian destiny of man, and indeed is the destiny of all mankind.

What is the practical lesson to be learned from all this? A clarion call to all of us to retrace our steps, and to help the whole world towards a recovery of a true sacramental consciousness. It is the loss of this which accounts for so much of our secularity and materialism. Lampert does not, we think, put it too strongly when he says that the modern world stands on the edge of an abyss as a result of the dissolution of true sacramental consciousness: it is overcome by the sin of secularisation, of profanation, of the disintegration and evacuation of life. Hence the plea for a return to sacramental consciousness, and the Church is powerful only in the living awareness of her sacramental life. As such she has a message for the whole of mankind and of the universe.[1] Hence the message the Church can still deliver: the reminder to one and all that the real presence of Christ in the Church and in the world, still stricken by sin, is mediated through sacramental channels, and is available for those wise enough to make use of the means of grace, and conscious of a sickness which the Divine Physician of souls alone can cure. Cross and Altar are thus intimately linked and related to the needs of men. Evangelical and Catholic might well unite in a more wholehearted appreciation of the truth conveyed in both Cross and Altar, and link their forces together in the great work of spreading the Good News of Salvation to a desperately sick modern world.

[1] Lampert, *op. cit.* p. 122.

THE END

PRINTED BY R. & R. CLARK, LTD., EDINBURGH